URBAN LIFE IN THE MIDDLE A
1000–1450

EUROPEAN CULTURE AND SOCIETY
General Editor: Jeremy Black

Published

Lesley Hall   *Sex, Gender & Social Change in Britain since 1880*
Keith D. Lilley   *Urban Life in the Middle Ages: 1000–1450*
Neil MacMaster   *Racism in Europe, 1870–2000*
W. M. Spellman   *European Political Thought 1600–1700*

European Culture and Society Series
Series Standing Order
ISBN 0–333–74440–3
(outside North America only)

You can receive future titles in this series as they are published by placing a standing order. Please contact your bookseller or, in case of difficulty, write to us at the address below with your name and address, the title of the series and the ISBN quoted above.

Customer Services Department, Macmillan Distribution Ltd
Houndmills, Basingstoke, Hampshire RG21 6XS, England

Urban Life
in the Middle Ages
1000–1450

Keith D. Lilley

palgrave

First published 2002 by
PALGRAVE
Houndmills, Basingstoke, Hampshire RG21 6XS and
175 Fifth Avenue, New York, N.Y. 10010
Companies and representatives throughout the world

PALGRAVE is the new global academic imprint of
St. Martin's Press LLC Scholarly and Reference Division and
Palgrave Publishers Ltd (formerly Macmillan Press Ltd).

ISBN 0–333–71248–X hardback
ISBN 13: 978-0-333-71249-8 ISBN 10: 0-333-71249-8

This book is printed on paper suitable for recycling and made from fully managed and sustained forest sources.

A catalogue record to this book is available from the British Library.

Library of Congress Cataloging-in-Publication Data
Lilley, Keith D.
    Urban life in the Middle Ages, 1000–1450 / Keith D. Lilley.
        p. cm.—(European culture and society)
    Includes bibliographical references and index.
    ISBN 0-333-71248-X (cloth)—ISBN 0-333-71249-8 (pbk.)
    1. Cities and towns, Medieval. 2. Civilization, Medieval. I. Title II. Series.

HT115 .L55 2001
307.76'094'0902—dc21   2001045148

10 9 8 7 6 5 4 3 2 1
11 10 09 08 07 06 05 04 03 02

For Catherine

CONTENTS

LIST OF TABLES, FIGURES AND PLATES

Tables

Figures

Plates

ACKNOWLEDGEMENTS

The author and publishers would like to thank the following for permission to reproduce copyright material:

Bibliotèque Municipale de Valenciennes for Plate 1.1, *The Heavenly Jerusalem*
Bristol City Museum and Art Gallery for Figure. 7.1 from R. H. Jones, Excavations in Redcliffe 1983–5, Figure 3.3;
Cambridge University Collection for Plate 5.1, *Aerial View of Chipping Campden*
Centro Italiano di Studi Sull'alto Medioevo for Figure 3.5 from D. Jacoby, *Crusader Acre in the Thirteenth Century: Urban Layout and Topography, Studi Medievali*, 20, Figure 4;
James Clarke & Co. Ltd for Figure 4.1 from M. W. Beresford, *New Towns of the Middle Ages*, Lutterworth (1967), Figure 57;
École Française de Rome for Figures 6.3 and 6.4 from J-M. Vigueur (ed.), *D'une ville à l'autre, Collection de l'École Française de Rome*, 122 (1989), pp. 596, 208;
Osterreichische National Bibliothek for Plate 5.2, Codex 2554 *God as artifex principalis, 'supreme architect'*
Princetown University Press for Figure 6.1 form C. Lansing, *The Florentine Magnates: Lineage and Faction in a Medieval Commune*, Figure 5.3. Copyright © 1991 by Princetown University Press;
Wissenschaftliche Buchgesellschaft for Figure 3.2 from Gunter P. Fehring, *Einführung in die Archäologie des Mittelalters*, 3rd edn, p. 197. Copyright © 2000 by Wissenschaftliche Buchgesellschaft, Darmstadt.

Every effort has been made to trace all the copyright holders, but if any have been inadvertently overlooked the publishers will be pleased to make the necessary arrangement at the first opportunity.

PREFACE

Thinking about Europe in the Middle Ages today conjures up images of a landscape of dramatic castles, splendid cathedrals, majestic abbeys; a landscape of peasants working in fields, of lords feasting in halls and hunting in forests, of knights jousting in meadows, and bishops, priests, monks and nuns all singing the Lord's praise in countless churches and cathedrals. Whatever ways we encounter the Middle Ages, whether it is in movies, books or television series, or on vacation visits to castles or 'medieval' theme parks, there is little doubt that this historical period continues to exert a very powerful presence on the modern imagination. This book is about the towns and cities that thrived in Europe during the Middle Ages, about urban life as it was between the eleventh and fifteenth centuries.

Europe was a highly urbanised continent in the Middle Ages. There were towns and cities everywhere, some very large and ancient, some very small and recent. While these towns and cities were centres of trade and production, and learning and authority, they were, above all, centres of population. It is difficult to know how many urban dwellers there were in medieval Europe, for not only were towns and cities places where people would come and go, but in the Middle Ages there were no records made of exactly who was living in a town at any one time. Rough estimates of medieval urban population are possible, however. The largest urban centres, such as Paris, Bruges and Venice, had populations of at least 100 000 by the fourteenth century, while below them, lower down the urban hierarchy, there was a long tail of middling and smaller urban centres, some of which might only have as few as 300 inhabitants.[1]

Across the period, from the turn of the last millennium until the middle of the fourteenth century, population levels in medieval

Europe were rising. This was a period of great urban expansion, with old, established towns growing larger as more and more people came to live in them, while 'new towns' filled the surrounding countryside and channelled rural produce towards the larger urban centres. The towns and cities, whether new or old, were the centres of medieval authority – the seats of kings, bishops and lords – places where the elite of society exercised their control over their lands and people. They were also the places where this authority was contested, where political power was brokered and principles of democratic government forged, particularly in the latter years of the Middle Ages, in the fourteenth and fifteenth centuries. The late-medieval period saw the population of Europe under stress, with plague and famine all taking their toll on the inhabitants of town and countryside alike. For some urban dwellers, however, this was a period that created new opportunities, and even prosperity, as people found themselves in a stronger position and able to capture political and economic control, and mould it to their own advantage.

This book aims to look at how Europe came to be so thoroughly urbanised in the Middle Ages, and explores how people at a variety of social levels engaged with urban life. The period covered in this book represents, in my view, a crucial time in the history of European urbanism. I decided on the dates 1000 and 1450 as chronological parameters because they mark significant changes in the history of European urbanism – the start of a pan-European boom in urbanisation during the eleventh century, and the diverse cultural transitions and transformation associated with the Renaissance during the fifteenth. There are many aspects that make the later Middle Ages a distinct historical period, not least the fact that it put into place a new urban order in Europe which has lasted for centuries, but I am wary of creating simplistic distinctions between the 'early' and 'later' Middle Ages, and most of all, cautious about drawing a line between 'medieval' and 'modern'. As will become clear from this book, there are many aspects of urban life in the Middle Ages that still have a familiarity even today. I realise that one has to recognise not only those things that do change, but also those things that do not – the continuities in history, as well as the changes.

Any periodisation will present problems, so I have endeavoured to treat my 'start' and 'end' dates with some degree of flexibility. I have also tried to balance chronological breadth with depth, covering some issues in chronologically broad terms, while focusing on others by looking in detail at particular periods within the Middle Ages. As well as treating my chronological parameters with some flexibility, I have done likewise with the book's geographical coverage. Some readers may be surprised with my rather broad view of medieval 'Europe'. but in my mind it would have been a nonsense to ignore, for example, the Crusader cities of the Levant when they were such an important part of the medieval conception of, not Europe as such, but the unifying force that was at its core – Latin Christendom.

My reason for writing this book was to provide an informative, accessible and challenging account of urban life in the Middle Ages. While there are a number of books about urban life in the Middle Ages, they are often presented in a chronological format, charting the economic, social and political development of European towns and cities historically. There are some excellent studies of this sort, notably the two-volume encyclopaedic study by Nicholas.[2] However, unless one is familiar with a variety of European languages, particularly Italian, French and German, many important and influential works on European medieval urban history are in effect 'inaccessible'. Some 'classic' texts have been translated, of course, notably Pirenne's *Medieval Cities*, Rörig's *The Medieval Town*, and Ennen's book, also called *The Medieval Town*.[3] But we still await (with anticipation) English translations of important works by, among others, Braunfels and Guidoni.[4] One of the most valuable contributions to the study of European medieval urbanism is the collection of essays edited by Clarke and Simms under the title, *A Comparative History of Urban Origins in Non-Roman Europe*.[5] The rider is significant though, for it means that the towns and cities of southern Europe are not included. While we might bemoan the relative paucity of anglophone books about European medieval towns, it has to be said that in contrast there is an abundance of books written in English about urbanism in medieval Britain and Ireland. Two which have appeared recently are particularly worth looking at, one by Swanson and the other by Schofield and Vince.[6]

My aim here has been to write a book that is thematic in structure, taking common aspects of medieval urban life but looking at them by making comparisons across both time and space, across Europe between 1000 and 1450. In this respect I have been much influenced by the approach of three particular academic historians whose books show a sensitivity to both geography *and* history. One of these is Beresford's compendious volume on *New Towns in the Middle Ages*, now over 30 years old but really a milestone in the study of medieval urbanism for its bringing together of fieldwork and archival research, and taking an international comparative approach.[7] More recent, and equally valuable for its international dimensions, is Hilton's book, *English and French Towns in Feudal Society*.[8] Though in size it is much more lean than Beresford's *New Towns*, Hilton's book is no less ample in terms of what it contains, and with its immediate style and critical nature it makes for a particularly refreshing read; so too does Dyer's *Standards of Living in the Later Middle Ages*.[9] Dyer, a student of Hilton's, provides us with similarly lucid accounts of urban life in the Middle Ages. Though ostensibly about life within English medieval towns and cities, his book brings out the everyday and the ordinary aspects of urban living, a much needed antidote to the sometimes dry and rather legalistic accounts of medieval urbanism that have come to characterise the subject.

I have been keen to ensure that this book not only includes comparisons between the different towns and cities of Europe, but also that it makes comparisons between towns and cities from across the Middle Ages, as well as comparisons which bring out the *internal* differences within individual towns and cities. In other words, I like to try and think about the *spaces* within and through which medieval urban life was played out, as well as what it was that characterised urban life at particular *times* within the Middle Ages. This preoccupation with space and time no doubt comes from my training as a historical geographer, coupled with my long-held fascination for the Middle Ages. I hope it will make for a book that will be of interest to students from a wide variety of academic disciplines, including history, archaeology, sociology, geography, architecture and politics. At the same time, I also hope that the book will be a useful travelling companion for those wishing to explore the medieval towns and cities of Europe in the field, as it were, rather than at a desk in a library or study. Indeed, I would urge readers to go and look for themselves at the rich European heritage of medieval urban life; to seek out market places where medieval townspeople gathered, gaze at the vestiges of town walls that poke through buildings in gloomy backstreets, stand before the façades of great cathedrals, muse upon the bridges spanning the same rivers where people once loaded and unloaded boats with merchandise from all across the continent. If this book inspires but a few to go out and explore for themselves, to imagine urban life in the Middle Ages and appreciate its richness, then it will have succeeded.

In the course of researching and writing this book I have incurred many debts of gratitude. It will become apparent that I have made use of my own research as well as the labours of others. I am grateful to the Economic and Social Research Council for the funding they provided for me to research in detail the origins and development of medieval Coventry, as well as the Leverhulme Trust for their grant that funded my work on Norman towns in England, Wales and Ireland, and most recently, the British Academy. A British Academy postdoctoral fellowship provided me not only with an opportunity to study in detail the topographical evolution of two important English medieval cities (Bristol and Norwich), but also the time necessary to prepare this book and read more broadly about urban life in the Middle Ages. I am grateful, too, to my colleagues who helped my research while at the Universities of Birmingham and London, particularly Nigel Baker, Denis Cosgrove, Christopher Dyer, James Higgins, Richard Holt, Terry Slater and Jeremy Whitehand. Without their help and support this book really could not have been written. I am also grateful for ideas, comments and criticisms received from Jeremy Black, Wim Boerefijn, Harold Fox, Peter Larkham and Anngret Simms; and to Maura Pringle for her work on my many illustrations. Thanks especially to Richard Holt for his probing queries and critical commentary on a draft of the whole text, and also to the anonymous reader, for without them the book would have contained many embarrassing blunders (though of course any mistakes that remain are solely my responsibility). Last, but by no means least, I acknowledge the consistent support and encouragement I have had from my friends and family, who have, to varying degrees, endured being hauled around numerous medieval sites all across Britain and the continent, in particular, Catherine, to whom I dedicate this book.

K. D. L.

INTRODUCTION

This book is about urban life in the Middle Ages. It is a study of the *life of towns*, and *life in towns*. The purpose of this chapter is to set out some preliminary context for the issues covered in the subsequent chapters; to introduce the subject of medieval urbanism by thinking about, on the one hand, how towns and cities have an animate, lifelike quality themselves, and on the other, to think about how medieval people lived their lives. The idea here, then, is to take a general overview of the life of medieval towns, and the life in medieval towns, while at the same time introducing topics that form particular themes for the book. To this end, this introduction concludes with a comment on how the book might be read, with an explanation of its chapter structure and some account of the content of each of the chapters.

Town and City: the Life of Medieval Towns

At the turn of the first millennium AD, in an age of intellectual and political ferment, when population and trade were both increasing, when the frontiers of Latin Christian Europe were being pushed out and tracts of moorland, marsh and waste 'improved' and settled, the map of urban Europe saw a major transformation, a renaissance of urban life. Not only did existing towns and cities grow larger and more prosperous, but numerous new towns were also added to the landscape. The development of these towns and cities, both old and new, ran side by side to create a new urban network, which by the end of the thirteenth century made Europe more urbanised than it had ever been.

A map of urban Europe in 1000 would show many of the same large towns and cities that we are familiar with today, including

1

London, Paris, Rome, Dublin, Bruges and Riga, to name but a few. Although this book is not about how these towns and cities first got to be on this 'map', some consideration needs to be given here to the emergence of urban life in Europe in the early Middle Ages, the period between the decline of the Roman empire and the start of the urban renaissance that marked the passing of the first millennium. The origins of urban life in medieval Europe have long vexed historians, particularly the issue of whether urban life in north-west Europe ebbed away with the disintegration of imperial Roman rule, or whether it survived. In an attempt to sift through the various theories of medieval urban origins that historians have put forward during the twentieth century, Benton derives a list of eight possibles, and remarks that none of the theories are mutually exclusive.[1] For Ennen, too, the key to understanding urban origins in medieval Europe lies in not assuming that there is any *one* explanation to account for differing patterns of urbanisation. She proposes that we should consider 'the diversity of conditions at the very beginning of medieval European towns', and suggests that 'three different regions of town life can be distinguished in Europe' depending on the degree to which elements of Roman urbanism survived into the early Middle Ages.[2]

The first of Ennen's three 'regions of town life' is 'the north German area, to the east of the Rhine and in Scandinavia', an area 'which was not directly influenced by the urban culture of the Mediterranean'.[3] This was the area north-east of the Rhineland frontier of the Roman empire, taking in eastern Germany and the Baltic states, as well as other areas of 'non-Roman Europe', including Ireland.[4] The second region covers what Fleure called the 'cities of temperate Europe', that is 'the zone which corresponds to northern France and the valleys of the Rhine and the Danube, where the remains of the towns of antiquity disappeared to a large degree, but not without leaving some evident traces'.[5] As well as including areas of the later Merovingian and Carolingian 'empires', such as Neustria and Austrasia, this area also includes Britain, as well as Spain. Finally, the third area Ennen suggests covers 'the southern regions where Roman urban traditions continued with respect to the possession of the land, housing, and manner of life'.[6] Here, for example 'in Italy, economic and social development continued without a break', from the Roman era into the Middle Ages.[7] These three regions provide us with a useful framework within which to consider the evidence for early medieval urban development, and thus deal with the thorny issue of post-Roman 'continuity' of European urban life.

Ennen's threefold classification of 'regions of town life' is predicated on the absence or presence of classical precedents in early-medieval urban life. In essence, regions two and three both saw urban life developed during the Roman period, the difference between them is to do with questions of how far urban life continued into post-Roman Europe. With region one, however, the issue is rather different. The important question here is over understanding what the origins of urban life are in 'non-Roman Europe'.[8] In both respects, the problem of 'continuity' is key, as Ennen herself recognised. She drew a distinction between 'functional' and 'topographical' continuity; that is, whether continuity means continuous urban activity on the same site, or simply continuous occupation on an urban site.[9] Over the past 30 years, since Ennen formulated her geographical model of urban origins, much new historical research has addressed this issue of Roman and non-Roman urban 'continuity'. What this has done is to broadly confirm Ennen's regional differences of medieval 'town life', but at the same time further add to our understanding of the subtle changes that actually took place in the urbanisation process in each of these three regions, particularly during the so-called 'dark ages', from the fourth century AD through to the eighth.

To understand what Roman and non-Roman urban continuity means requires us to get to the heart of the very tricky issue of what actually constitutes 'urban life' in the first place. How medieval urbanism is defined will clearly have a consequent bearing on how we might identify a medieval *town*. Sometimes, the definition of urban life is couched in terms of *Kriterienbündel*, or '"bundles" of urban criteria', but not all historians are in agreement over the use of this particular approach.[10] Leaving aside purely legal definitions of medieval urbanism for the time being (see Chapters 2 and 3), what we might say is that 'an urban community is a settlement of some size and population which is markedly larger than communities concerned with subsistence alone; the majority of its inhabitants, moreover, are not engaged in full-time agrarian pursuits', and that 'such a community should include the presence of more than one institution, so that a monastery or palace can only be termed urban if it is the focus of more people than merely monks or ministers and royalty'.[11] With this working definition in mind, though not to the exclusion of other such definitions, we may approach the issue of Roman and non-Roman urban continuity, and ask ourselves what changes were taking place in each of Ennen's three regions of 'town life' in the period prior to the year 1000.

Within her 'southern regions', the parts of the Mediterranean world where classical urban precedents survived into the Middle Ages, Ennen is sure that 'there is no argument about the basic continuity . . . of the legal form of the urban community'.[12] Studies of the physical urban landscapes of former Roman cities in Italy would at first seem to confirm this conclusion. The survival of Roman street plans in the layout of towns such as Lucca, Pavia and Piacenza suggests direct continuity of usage and maintenance of the urban fabric, while archaeological excavations of house sites have likewise revealed post-Roman continuity.[13] Lately, however, historians have pictured urban life in Italy in the fifth and sixth centuries rather differently. They have begun to point out that actually there is evidence for 'considerable decline' in the state of urban life after the 'sack of Rome' in 410, and that in some cases, as at Milan, 'a virtual break in habitation' occurred during the early centuries of the Middle Ages.[14] Perhaps, then, the distinction drawn on the basis of urban continuity between regions two and three is less hard and fast than it would at first appear. Indeed, as we move further north, into region two, the complexities of urban life in the early Middle Ages become no less marked.

In the area of Europe covered by her second region of 'town life' Ennen is again confident with her evidence, and writes that here 'the disappearance of Roman municipal organisation is a certain fact'.[15] Certainly, there is much to support this point of view. Along the Danube for example, it would appear that 'at the time of the Romans' withdrawal, the great majority of people who lived in the towns and fortresses had left, most of the *municipia* and *coloniae* were already deserted (and often plundered and devastated), whilst the *castra* were reduced to places of refuge for the inhabitants of the surrounding region'; and in the mean time, 'the ruins of the buildings could still be seen', either 'serving as quarries for new structures, or being reused in part as small fortresses because the Danube remained a border'.[16] In Vienna, the Roman *municipium* 'had almost vanished by the sixth century', and the nearby *castrum* was for the most part 'undisturbed by building activity for hundreds of years'.[17] More or less the same story was true north of the Alps for many former Roman towns and cities, but not for all. For example, at Cologne, on the banks of the Rhine, it seems that 'when the Franks finally occupied the town in AD 460, they did not destroy it, but settled within its walls', a factor that surely accounts for the survival of the Roman street pattern.[18] With Cologne, then, not only was there 'topographical continuity' in the early-medieval period, but 'functional continuity', too. It was because the 'bishops took over the government of the town in the immediate post-Roman period' that Cologne's administrative functions continued.[19]

The continuity of administrative functions in some cities, from the Roman period into the early Middle Ages, is also evident in areas further westwards, too. For example, 'the majority of cities in Gaul retain[ed] their status as *civitas*-capitals, and latterly bishoprics, throughout the Roman and early-medieval periods', while recently cases have also been made for similar functional continuities in former Roman cities in northern and western Britain.[20] Here, it has been suggested that bishops might well have been responsible for keeping alive urban institutions at Chester and Wroxeter during the fifth and sixth centuries, for 'without them, they would lose their congregation and their *raison d'être*'.[21] In contrast, the situation in south-eastern parts of Britain seems to have been somewhat different, especially in southern England, 'for these are undoubtedly the areas most likely to have been taken into Anglo-Saxon control at an early period, and so disruption, and even abandonment [of urban life], need not occasion surprise'.[22] In former Roman cities such as Canterbury, while Roman defence circuits were later reused in the Middle Ages, the current thinking is that urban life was all but abandoned, for archaeological evidence shows reoccupation in the later sixth and seventh centuries in the form of 'groups of rough timber buildings' within 'the ruins of old Roman masonry buildings'.[23] Even so, despite this evidence for discontinuity in urban life in southern and eastern Britain, the consensus now is that 'the Roman centres were not deserted overnight', and that urban life ended not as a 'violent bang' but with more of a 'feeble whimper'.[24]

In certain parts of Ennen's second region, the first two centuries after the Roman withdrawal thus saw folk reoccupying areas of abandoned Roman cities, while in other parts the administrative role of former Roman cities persisted into the Middle Ages through the continued activities of the Christian Church. At the same time as these topographical and functional continuities were occurring, new forms of urban life were emerging in northern Europe which straddled both regions one and two. These emergent urban centres, known as *emporia*, were to be found along the coasts around the North Sea basin and the Baltic, in some cases sited close to former Roman town and cities, and in others located on previously unoccupied settlement sites.

Often also referred to as '*wic* sites' because of their place names (for example, *Hamwic, Lundenwic*), the *emporia* were coastal trading centres, some of which had origins in the fifth and sixth centuries.[25] For Ennen, the *wic* sites were not in themselves definably urban, rather, in her view they later on 'acquired an importance which would be decisive for the origin of the medieval town', particularly where the *wic* was sited close to the surviving remains of a former Roman *civitas*, as was the case with *Lundenwic* – London.[26] Whether or not '*wic* sites' should really be labelled 'urban' is debatable, particularly those early in date. Ennen maintained that 'towns were not known in the northern German zone', and that the *wic* was 'an original element that pre-figured urban life'.[27] Dealing in detail with this issue, Hodges suggests that there were three sorts of *emporia*: the earliest type, he says, were sites of fairs where traders met periodically; the second type came later and was a development of the first into a permanent settlement engaged with long-distance trade and craft production; thirdly, and later again, was where the *wic* lost its international pre-eminence, and either faded away completely or became a regional market centre.[28] *Wic* sites have thus been referred to as 'proto-urban', that is, places that are on the way to becoming urban. Although Hodges himself rejects the idea that a place can be proto-urban (for him, a 'site is either urban or it is not'), in the context of studies of medieval urban origins in non-Roman Europe (Ennen's region one), the idea of proto-urbanism has attracted support.[29]

In an extended treatment of medieval urban origins in 'non-Roman Europe', Clarke and Simms propose 'a typology of proto-towns'.[30] They suggest four types, but nevertheless recognise that 'there will always be a tendency for some towns to slot easily and convincingly into one or other of the categories, whereas other towns will appear to have shifted historically from one category to another, or to belong to more than one category, or both'.[31] The first of their types, the 'trading centre', takes in the *wic* sites, including Birka and Haithabu. In this they also echo Hodges's view that these *emporia* formed part of a vast north European trade network, connecting the Merovingian and Carolingian empires with the North Sea basin, and that these trading centres 'were placed on or near territorial boundaries'.[32]

The second kind of proto-town that Clarke and Simms identify is the 'stronghold settlement', such as those that existed in Slavic lands that were the origins of Lübeck and Gdańsk, or the Viking *longphorts* of early-Scandinavian Ireland.[33] Associated with these strongholds was the *suburbium*, a place inhabited by craftspeople and/or merchants outside the defences of the stronghold.[34] This arrangement, of a stronghold (often referred to as a *burg*, or *castrum*) closely juxtaposed with a suburban settlement (sometimes called *portus*), was widely prevalent across Europe during the early Middle Ages, and was not just confined to non-Roman regions. For Pirenne, writing in the 1920s and 1930s, the *castrum/suburbium* arrangement 'was considered to be an essential feature of the medieval town', and in his view emerged 'out of purely military, not economic needs'.[35] In Flanders (Belgium), however, Verhulst has shown that Antwerp, Ghent and Bruges all emerged in the tenth century as urban centres with fortified *burgs* alongside a suburban market settlement (*portus*), and that here, *contra* Pirenne, 'the merchants sought [their] proximity not for military protection, but for trading possibilities'.[36] The issue of which came first – *burg* or *suburbium* – stronghold or trading place – is one that has long created heated discussion among historians.

With their third proto-town type, the 'cult settlement', Clarke and Simms suggest that 'the temple, episcopal church or monastic church with an attached *suburbium*, or equivalent', becomes the focus of emergent urbanism.[37] The examples they cite from Ireland include the case of Kildare, which 'as early as the mid-seventh century' appears 'as a *civitas* without a wall, but with suburbs (*suburbana*)'; as well as other episcopal and monastic centres, such as Armagh and Derry, which from 'the mid-tenth century onwards . . . had urban attributes, [even] though their main function was still religious'.[38] The duality of *civitas* and *suburbium* also characterised 'Carolingian episcopal and monastic centres in western Germany', such as Hamburg and Bremen, from the ninth century onwards.[39] Such 'cult' proto-towns were not confined to Christian sites, however, and neither were they only to be found in parts of non-Roman Europe. For example, cathedral and monastic 'cities' are also known to have acted as urban foci in early medieval Wales.[40]

Last in Clarke and Simms' list of proto-town types is the 'market settlement'.[41] This, unlike the other three types, appears to be associated particularly (though not exclusively) with Ennen's 'north German region' of non-Roman Europe.[42] In 'the area between the Rhine, Danube and Elbe', for example, market settlements were established by Ottonian and Salian rulers during the tenth and eleventh centuries, while further north, particularly around the Baltic and North Sea coasts, some medieval towns appear to owe their origins to markets set up before 1000, in the Viking Age.[43] Depending on whose definition of a town is being used, it might well be argued that these market settlements were really intended to function as towns from the outset, though many market settlements did not subsequently develop a wide range of urban functions (see Chapter 4).

The four types of proto-town outlined here provide a useful framework for discussing the origins and early development of medieval towns in Roman and non-Roman Europe alike. Indeed, as Clarke and Simms make clear, 'we should not exaggerate the distinction between Roman and non-Roman Europe' in our discussions of medieval urban origins.[44] Similarly, while the three regions of town life that Ennen proposed have some validity in understanding the pattern of urban evolution during the early Middle Ages, the regions ought not to be treated simplistically, as variations in how and why towns and cities emerged exist within each of them. Like Ennen, then, we should avoid trying 'to find an explanation for the origin of *the* medieval town', for 'there were many towns, and diverse factors influenced their origin and growth', and in discussing early-medieval origins and growth, much rests on what constitutes 'urban life' and 'continuity' of urban life.[45] What is certain, however, is that urban life in later medieval Europe rested 'on the solid foundations laid before 1000'.[46]

The idea that towns are 'born' is fundamental to narrating the life of towns in the Middle Ages. However, it raises an important issue which has only recently received the attention that it deserves from medieval historians. In a period like the Middle Ages, when historical evidence is often thin on the ground, knowing who was responsible for first bringing a town to life is often difficult to establish. In the past, some historians were content to talk about medieval towns as having 'spontaneously' appeared, as if they were the products of 'natural' development. But of course, it was *people* who brought towns into being; it was people who made the decisions about when and where a new town should be sited, what it should look like, how big it should be, and so on; and it was people who subsequently made the town succeed or fail. The question, though, is how this process worked: whether, as some social historians of the Middle Ages are now suggesting, there was a 'bottom-up' approach, with ordinary people taking the initiative themselves and negotiating with their social 'superiors' the need for a new town here or a market there; or whether instead, as is often assumed, urbanisation was a process driven by and for the medieval social elite, the kings, princes, dukes and other lords who sat at the higher levels of the social hierarchy.

When we look in detail at what was actually going on when new towns were being brought into being, we find a complex social process in action, with negotiation between different social groups and individuals, with delegation of duties across the medieval social hierarchy (see Chapters 4–6). Whatever the actual complexities were, it is wholly clear that urban life in the Middle Ages did not just 'happen' – it was made to happen. In some cases the towns prospered, many indeed are still urban places today, but others rose to prominence all too briefly and then passed away either towards the 'end' of the Middle Ages, or during the post-medieval period. Like the ghost towns of the western United States, these medieval 'ghost towns' were born out of optimism, and perhaps, it might be argued, selfishness. Similarly, too, the traces of these failed towns are still to be found in the landscape, a lasting reminder that in the drive to urbanise Europe in the Middle Ages, as in so many things, there were some winners and many losers.

Already it will be clear that there is something to be said for conceptualising the life of towns using organic, 'biological' metaphors. That towns and cities were at some time born, whether it was in the Roman period or in the Middle Ages, that they then either grew strong and healthy, or became periodically weak and frail. Not all towns died of course, but even here we might think of the survival of a town in Darwinian terms, of a survival of the fittest. What made one town 'fitter' than another opens up a lot of questions, some relating to what people were doing in the town, in terms of their livelihoods, as well as what extrinsic factors came into play, such as war or famine.

There is nothing new in conceptualising the life of towns in these terms. It has been popular ever since Patrick Geddes used it in his book called *Cities in Evolution*.[47] More recently, there has been a renewed interest in how organic metaphors are useful for exploring questions about how and why towns grow. However, there is also a danger that if these metaphors are taken too far, and taken too literally, they will engender a misleading sense of 'objectivity'. Medieval urbanism is not something that simply exists 'out there', but is instead a product of human imagination and industry. On the one hand, the medieval town is a product of modern-day imaginations (because we no longer live in the Middle Ages), while on the other, it is also the product of people's ingenuity and dexterity in the Middle Ages. In effect, if thought about in the context of current ideas on the 'socially constructed' nature of knowledge, an uneasy tension exists between ourselves, and *our* views of urban life in the Middle Ages, and the people of medieval Europe, and *their* actual engagement with contemporary urban life.

Townspeople and Citizens: Life in Medieval Towns

Having offered some thoughts about the life of towns in the Middle Ages, it is appropriate to turn next to the 'lived' lives of medieval townspeople, and to take a look at how they made sense of the world around them, and what informed their 'sense of being'. Of all the many things one has to keep in mind when thinking about life in the Middle Ages, one of the most important is the extent to which Christian belief was all-pervading and boundless: medieval Europe was Catholic Europe.[48] Outward expressions of this belief were to be seen, felt and heard everywhere: it was made visible by the multitude of religious buildings in both town and country, and in the countless shrines and wayside crosses placed along roads and streets; and it was made audible in the words of priests reading liturgy at mass, and through the voices of pilgrims, preachers and paupers, as they moved around from place to place proclaiming the way of the Lord to all who listened.

By 1000, society at large was conceptualised (by some in the Church) in terms of 'three orders'. In 995, an English churchman called Aelfric wrote: 'in this world there are three *endebyrdnysse* [three social categories]: *laboratores, oratores, bellatores,* . . . the *laboratores* are those who by their labour provide our means of subsistence, the *oratores,* those who intercede for us with God, the *bellatores,* those who protect our cities and defend our soil against the invading army'.[49] Later, in 1005–6, Aelfric further tells us that the *laboratores* are the 'ploughmen and husbandmen', the peasantry; while the *oratores* are the clergy, those 'who serve God through spiritual labour', and the *bellatores* are noblemen, 'who guard our strongholds . . . engaging in armed combat with any enemy who might invade it'.[50] Aelfric pointed out that these three orders had to work together in harmony and that chaos would result if one of them failed in their duties.

These orders, or 'estates', were hierarchically defined, according to their relationship with God. The living person closest to God was the head of the Latin Roman Church, the Pope, followed by his brethren; the archbishops, bishops, abbots and priors, monks and nuns. The nobility were also understood as guardians of the Christian faith. At the basis of medieval kingship was a belief that the king would 'assure "the defence, exaltation, and honour" of the holy Church'.[51] A king's noblemen assisted him in this respect by offering military allegiance in return for land – the essence of feudalism. The remaining lay population, the 'ploughmen and husbandmen' who tilled the fields, and provided the 'means of subsistence' in Aelfric's words, occupied the third and lowest order in the hierarchy. Later, in the mid-twelfth century, John of Salisbury said 'the husbandmen correspond to the feet' of society, that they bore the 'weight of the entire body' of people above them, the higher social orders.[52]

The 'three orders' represented an *idealised*, patriarchal conception of medieval society. The social reality of the later Middle Ages was really much more fluid and dynamic. For example, as Duby points out, townspeople did not fit easily into the theory of the 'three orders'; indeed 'for the ecclesiastical social theorist of the eleventh century they had no proper place in the functional hierarchy'.[53] Nevertheless, what the *idea* of the three orders articulates, very clearly, is a medieval ecclesiastical desire to make sense of earthly life by placing it within a hierarchical and ordered Christian cosmology, at the centre of which was God – all seeing and all hearing. His omnipotence could not be avoided.

Throughout the Middle Ages, Christianity really was a way of 'being'; it structured all aspects of all people's lives – their working day, their calendar year, their own life cycle. At the same time, Christian doctrine also determined the course of medieval history itself, by the way it provided nobles and churchmen with a *cause célèbre* for their moral crusades and territorial conquests. To make sense of how Christian belief ordered and organised the things medieval people did, the way that they did them and the decisions they took, the following discussion briefly examines the reciprocity between religious observance and patterns of medieval urban life by introducing three 'interlocking planes of time'. The first of these is the *durée*, that is, 'day-to-day existence'; the second is the *dasein* of 'the human being's life-space', and third is the *longue durée* of 'institutional time'.[54]

First the *durée*, a townsperson's daily routine. The routine working day for those living in medieval towns and cities was set by the canonical hours – the times of the day at which mass was held in church. In summer, as daylight lasted for longer, the hours of the working day 'lengthened', the more so in northern Europe. The hours were rung out across the rooftops by the sound of church bells. The canonical hours would determine meeting times, when the gates into a city were opened and closed, and the times at which traders could buy and sell in the market place (see Chapters 6 and 7). Work was not permitted on holy days, of course, and those who worked on Sundays would face penalties. Most important was Eastertide, which often marked the beginning of the medieval year. Also, punctuating the townsperson's year, were saints' feast days, of which there were an abundance.[55] The patron saint of a town's principal church or cathedral was particularly revered, as at Bury St Edmunds. The appropriate feast day would be marked by the whole town in pageants, fairs and in worship. A person's day-to-day life was thus plotted out according to religious observance, throughout their working week and year. The same was also true for an individual's life cycle.

The *dasein*, the 'life-space' of medieval townspeople, began and ended with vigil and prayer. At birth, at the baptism of infants, during the ceremony of marriage, and at death, townspeople were reminded of their subservience to God, as well as their own mortality.[56] In addition to these life events, regular attendance at mass, and for some, pilgrimage to religious sites and shrines, were further reflections of this vocation. Pilgrimage was a fundamental part of medieval urban life. In 1188, for example, Gerald of Wales accompanied the Archbishop of Canterbury on a journey through Wales, and at certain points during their itinerary, invariably in towns at market crosses, the archbishop encouraged people to 'take the cross', and embark on a 2000 mile Crusade to the Holy Land.[57] Often the distances travelled by pilgrims, by foot and by sea, were long and arduous. Some of the most well-known and celebrated vernacular written accounts surviving from the Middle Ages are in fact directly associated with pilgrimage journeys, usually to particular towns to see important holy shrines in churches and cathedrals – Chaucer's 'Canterbury Tales', and the 'Book of Margery Kempe', both exemplify this.

The pilgrim's search for salvation swelled the population of medieval towns and cities, while their journeys along the highways and byways of Europe were understood as an allegory of life itself. Christian morality also determined broader political events, and consequently permeated 'institutional time', the *longue durée* of the later Middle Ages. During the twelfth and thirteenth centuries, as population levels rose across the continent, ambitious aristocratic lords acquired new lands through conquest and colonisation. Although their methods were usually decidedly military in nature, their motives were underpinned by deeply felt religious beliefs, and aided by a supportive Church (see Chapter 1). This was true whether the conquests were aimed at non-Christians, the Muslims of southern Spain and the Holy Land, for example, or people who practised Christianity. Either way, the Church gave the nobility the means to justify their acquisition of territories and people; while at the same time, aristocratic lords endowed the Church with new lands from those areas that they had acquired. What this did was not only shape the geography of medieval Europe, but also the course of its history. It created 'frontier' lands, dotted with new towns intended to encourage people to come and settle and to take up new lives. While this process of territorial conquest and colonisation empowered some groups of people, it disempowered others – the consequences of which are still being felt in many parts of Europe today, including Ireland, Spain and the Baltic states (see Chapters 1 and 3).

That Christianity was a way of 'being' in the Middle Ages is unquestionable. It relates to what Bourdieu called the *habitus*: 'the production of a commonsense world endowed with the objectivity secured by consensus on the meaning of practices and the world'.[58] The *habitus* conditions the way that things are done, and makes things the way they are. In the mind of the medieval townsperson, the values and customs of a Christian way of life were 'commonsense', the way things were. In the course of reading this book, this medieval *mentalité* ought not be overlooked. To paraphrase the words of Frayling, for the medieval townsperson, 'everything stood for something else, and that something else was God'.[59]

A Map of the Book

This brings me finally to the book's structure, its themes and content, and how it might be read. Broadly, the chapters pivot around the two issues raised in this introduction: the life of towns and life in towns. Chapters 2–6 are more skewed towards addressing the life of medieval towns and cities, and discuss the role that law, government and lordship had on the process of *urbanisation*. In Chapters 6 and 7 the emphasis gradually shifts more towards life in towns and cities, and I address the role that towns played in shaping urban society. Of course, these two issues are closely interconnected, and in the course of writing the chapters I have sought to highlight the dialectical nature of urban life in the Middle Ages: to demonstrate that towns 'shape' people and people shape towns.

To set the scene for the main part of the book, Chapter 1 outlines some of the things that I consider to be important when thinking about medieval urbanism, namely the way that medieval urban life is understood, and made sense of, by people today. This gives me an opportunity to say a little about how aspects of medieval urbanism live on in the modern, twenty-first-century world, about how medieval urban life is represented. This chapter thus forms a context within which the other chapters should be read – as it is intended to offer a pause for self-reflection, to raise questions about why it is that the later Middle Ages (1000–1450) is an important period for Europeans, and to question how the fragments of evidence for medieval urban life are pieced together by historians archaeologists and others.

The subsequent chapters then take the reader through various aspects of medieval urban life, starting with some account of the way that urbanism was institutionalised in the Middle Ages by social and political elites. Here, I introduce the legal dimensions of medieval urbanism, the means by which towns and cities were ruled and governed. This requires some patience! The subject is a difficult one, fraught with legal terminology and somewhat complex and alien ideas about the constitutional make-up of 'chartered towns'. The chapter covers some of the important work of constitutional historians such as Ballard, Tait and Stephenson in the early part of the twentieth century. They opened up the constitutional complexity of medieval urban life, and though it might not make for particularly easy reading, some grasp of this subject nevertheless remains an essential and fundamental part of the story of urban life in the Middle Ages.

The constitutional dimensions of medieval urban life are further explored in Chapters 3 and 4, but in different ways. In Chapter 3, I set out some ideas about how the laws that governed urban life helped social and political elites to further their exploitation and control of land and people, particularly during the twelfth and thirteenth centuries in the context of territorial expansion and frontier colonisation and settlement. Chapter 4 is less concerned with these political motives of urbanisation and more with the economic returns that lords gained from promoting towns. The close connection between lordship and the process of urbanisation is explored by looking at the social dynamics of the process. In both of these chapters, I try to keep the discussion as broadly European as possible, to bring out the many similarities that existed between the life of towns in different parts of the continent.

In Chapters 5 to 7 I start to take a closer look at what was actually going on in towns and cities. The emphasis thus turns to how people living in towns influenced the built environment around them while at the same time the surrounding built environment, the townscape, affected them. Chapter 5 examines the physical dimension of the urban landscape, how it changed through the Middle Ages and why. Closely connected with the content of Chapter 5 is the subsequent chapter on urban property. Here I examine the social and spatial patterns of urban landholding, to show that ways people held properties in towns had a bearing on the organisation of urban society. Urban property-holding included not just the high-status people, but all sorts of townsfolk, all of whom had the potential to acquire and alter land in a town and so influence the physical appearance of the townscape. Finally, in Chapter 7, I look at the places inhabited by the townspeople themselves, their homes and their workplaces. Here I examine what 'ordinary' people did in towns and cities on an everyday basis, and consider how their identities were shaped through not only what they did but where they lived and worked.

Overall, then, the latter part of the book deals more with the lives of ordinary people and with the spaces they inhabited within towns and cities. The earlier part of the book deals more with the roles that social and political elites played in cultivating urban life in the Middle Ages, and their influence on the evolution of towns and cities. With this in mind, those readers who are looking more for aspects of 'everyday' life within medieval towns and cities should turn to the chapters towards the end of the book, while those seeking to understand the processes involved in the urbanisation of medieval Europe should content themselves more with the first few chapters. However, really to understand urban life in the Middle Ages both aspects need to be given equal attention.

1

URBAN LEGACIES

[People want so much] to search the world and cities, and
lands, and especially the young go to see all the cities and
castles, if they can. If it were not for the uncertainties of travel,
and for the fatigue and cost, if it were certain that is, and easy
and cheap, they would like to visit all the cities of the world.
Why? Because there is one city of men they have never seen
and yet desire, and believe that they will find in searching
the cities. So they go in haste, and when they have seen one
city, they wish to move on to another.

Giordano da Pisa, 1302–5[1]

Through what has been handed down to us from the Middle Ages
in the form of contemporary accounts about urban life and vestiges
of material culture, medieval urbanism continues to 'live on', not
only in books such as this one, and all sorts of other contemporary
media such as film, theatre, television and so forth, but in the very
towns and cities that Europeans live and work in today. In this
chapter I am concerned with how medieval urbanism impinges
upon the modern age. I shall look at the legacies of European
medieval urbanism in two ways. Firstly, by considering the contested
nature of medieval urban heritage, and secondly, by discussing
what evidence for urban life we have inherited from the Middle
Ages. One reason for doing this is to question 'how we know what
we know'. This means looking at the ways in which medieval urban
life is 'packaged' in contemporary culture, at how particular views
of medieval urbanism are presented and 'popularised', and what
implications arise from this. It also means looking at the ways in

which knowledge about medieval urbanism is constructed, how academic research in history, archaeology and other cognate disciplines combines to present a story of urban life in the Middle Ages.

A Medieval Heritage

The Middle Ages has long been popular with writers, artists, film producers and vacation tour operators. The Middle Ages sells – it is a saleable commodity. Its popularity in contemporary European culture can be traced back over two centuries, to the Romantic Gothic revival of the early nineteenth century, and the writing of Carter, Pugin, Viollet le Duc and Ruskin, and then Morris and Sitte.[2] It made its presence felt in architecture, as well as in art, design and literature. This 'Victorian' medievalism popularised Europe's medieval towns and cities, as a more mobile and affluent middle class sought the sublime and picturesque delights of those places that the industrial revolution seemingly passed by – Bruges, Florence, Venice, Carcassonne, Nuremberg.

Even today, the popular destinations of the nineteenth-century traveller are still on the tourist's map. Week-long tours from Britain will take you to Venice, Florence and Siena, while cities such as Bruges, Prague and Tallinn sell themselves as 'medieval cities', full of narrow streets, tall churches, and ringed by city walls. What is often overshadowed by this commodification and hype is how these cities and towns came to be the way that they are: the roles they played in the Middle Ages and the nature of urban life in them seven or eight centuries ago. My aim here is not to deride the pleasure that people get from going to visit 'medieval' towns and cities, far from it, but what I do hope to expose is, first, how 'popular' conceptions of the medieval city derive from twentieth-century imaginings, and second, how Europe's medieval urban heritage is a constantly 'contested' one.

Modern conceptions of the medieval city

One of the twentieth century's greatest architects had a vehement dislike for the Middle Ages, a prejudice that shaped his view not only of what he thought the medieval city was like, but also how he thought modern urban life ought to be. His name is Édouard Jeanneret – though he is better known as Le Corbusier. Le Corbusier's writing on modern architecture and city design became highly influential in design circles during the 1930s, and subsequently became a manifesto for the Modern Movement as a whole. There is no doubt that Le Corbusier was widely read, and though always controversial, greatly admired.

In writing about the 'city of tomorrow', the city of the future, Le Corbusier was at pains to point out how, in his view, the medieval city represented all the bad aspects of urban living. For him, the Middle Ages were a 'dark age', a time of disorder and chaos which he believed was most vividly represented in the forms of medieval towns and cities. Looking at small-scale maps and plans of 'medieval' towns, Le Corbusier emphasised how in the Middle Ages towns and cities were irregular and organic. With their narrow, winding streets they appeared to him to epitomise haphazard urban growth, and he regarded them a product of a disordered mentality:

> At cross-roads or along river banks the first huts were erected, the first houses and the first villages; the houses planted along the tracks, along the Pack Donkey's Way. The inhabitants built a fortified wall round and a town hall inside it. They legislated, they toiled, they lived, they always respected the Pack Donkey's Way. Five centuries later another and larger enclosure was built, and five centuries later still a third yet greater. The places where the Pack Donkey's Way entered the town became the City Gates and Customs officers were installed there. The village has become a great capital.[3]

What Le Corbusier was trying to do here was contrast the towns and cities of the Middle Ages with those of the Renaissance, doing so in order to justify his claims that the medieval city was not an appropriate model on which to base the plans of modern towns and cities. Thus, in his quest to make the 'modern city' a paragon of geometry and 'order', Le Corbusier projected a negative image of the 'medieval city' – an image that endures.

Le Corbusier's 'anti-medieval' stand was in large part a reaction to architects of the time who, unlike him, were advocating that the medieval city was a model from which a more worthy form of urbanism could be designed. In the early part of the twentieth century, in France, Belgium, Austria, Germany and Britain, architects such as Camillo Sitte, Camille Martin and Raymond Unwin visited, drew and mapped some of Europe's most picturesque medieval towns and cities, and emphasised that their beauty derived from their irregular forms; from the winding, narrow streets, from the over-hanging jetties of timber-framed buildings, and from the focal position of spires and pinnacles on churches and cathedrals.[4] Although there was some discussion over whether the 'irregularities' in the medieval townscape were deliberate or not, over whether they were the product of gifted masons and craftsmen, or simply happy chance, the consensus was nevertheless that the medieval townscape represented a visual joy to modern eyes, and repre-sented a suitable basis for creating new, more fulfilling urban communities and landscapes. So it was that during the early twen-tieth century the perceived irregularities of the medieval city were built into the designs for new urban landscapes, and thus they appear in the street layouts and architectural details of houses in Europe's garden suburbs and garden cities.

In favouring the medieval city as a 'model' for modern urban design, the likes of Unwin and Sitte were themselves promoting the idea that the Middle Ages were characterised by a certain backwardness, a simpler way of life, and that the medieval townscape, with its irregularities and informality, pointed to an urban society at ease with itself. Le Corbusier subsequently reinforced these idealised conceptions of medieval urban life even further, parody-ing them in his arguments for a Modern architecture. In sum, whether viewed positively or negatively, in the 'modern mind' the medieval city became oversimplified and idealised, caricatured.[5] The caricature is persistent, for many of the attributes that Le Corbusier ascribed to the medieval city are still used, in tourist guidebooks to cities such as Bruges and York, as well as in more specialised literature on the history of European urbanism.[6] What will become clear during the course of reading this book is that urban life in the Middle Ages bears little relation to these idealised views, and that far from being a squalid, chaotic and unrefined sort of place, the medieval town was highly organised, politically, socially and economically, and evolved not as a 'pack donkey' town but as a result of careful and considered judgement.

What I hope to have highlighted here is that the medieval town and city has long been appreciated within Europe, and put to use in certain ways. However, how we make sense of medieval urban life today is closely intertwined with the ways in which it has been represented in the recent past. Prejudice against the Middle Ages continues, and like all prejudice it is born from ignorance and naivety, something that all medievalists have had to battle hard against. It is thus important to recognise where our imaginings of the medieval city come from, and to challenge such preconceptions. This is all the more important in the context of the recent ('postmodern') boom in heritage tourism, and the popularity of medieval sites for heritage centres and place marketing.

A contested heritage

The Middle Ages is a contested heritage – it means different things to different people. This is why the role that towns and cities played in Europe's medieval past have to be recognised today. It is no use simply thinking that the medieval heritage is a plaything, a bit of fun; it is, in fact, highly charged. In the 1980s and 1990s academics were engaged in a debate over whether the many new heritage centres and museum displays (that were then appearing all over Europe) were guilty of 'watering down' history; whether they were presenting 'the whole story', or just parts which made for good entertainment. Latterly, this academic snobbery received short shrift from Samuel, a cultural historian who realised the value of making history (and heritage) more accessible and interesting.[7] Nevertheless, the 'heritage debate' continues to rumble on, with some arguing that heritage tourism misrepresents the past, and others arguing that heritage centres put on display material that would otherwise be consigned to dusty shelves in a museum store. This is not a debate I want to engage with here, not in any direct sense anyway. Instead, my concern is with highlighting the politicised nature of Europe's medieval urban heritage, pointing out how this heritage is contested today, and how it is built upon past conflicts that date back to the twelfth and thirteenth centuries.

In Europe, since 1945, it would be fair to say that almost every sizeable town and city of medieval origin has, to some degree, been subject to modern redevelopment. Whether for new office blocks, shopping malls or car parks, the European urban landscape has been utterly transformed over the last 50 years. Some of this 'creative destruction' (as Marxists call it) occurred following wartime damage, particularly in Russia, Poland, Germany, France, the Low Countries and in Britain; but equally much new development has taken place as a result of ever rising demands for more shopping and office space, and to provide space for parking an ever increasing number of private cars. Such redevelopment is a vital, though contentious part of modern urban life, providing opportunities for investment, profit and urban renewal. At the same time, this redevelopment offers a chance to understand what lies below the ground, in archaeological deposits (see below). Indeed, because developers are often obliged by local authorities to evaluate the archaeological potential of a site before construction work, redevelopment can potentially lead to important discoveries for urban archaeologists. However, the relationship between developer, local authority and archaeologist is not always a happy one, and although in many European countries the situation has now improved, in the past, redevelopment on archaeologically sensitive sites led to quite serious conflicts – a contest over medieval urban heritage.

There are numerous cases of developers and local authorities conflicting with archaeologists and local people over development proposals. One of the most well documented concerns the redevelopment of a site in central Dublin during the 1970s, which caused a storm of local and national protest.[8] This arose as a result of the city council initiative to build a new civic centre at Wood Quay, between the River Liffey and the cathedral of Christ Church. Evidence for a Viking settlement came to light in initial archaeological evaluations, but still the city-led redevelopment was going to go ahead. In response to this, in March 1979, 20 000 people took to the streets of Dublin, protesting against the threat to *their* urban heritage. The result was a stay of execution, and seven years' of excavation ultimately produced some of the most important evidence for Viking urban life in all Europe.[9]

What is significant about the Dublin case is how the discovery of the Viking urban settlement fed into contemporary Irish cultural and national identity. The evidence for Viking urban life was significant because it said something about where the Irish themselves had come from. Right up until the 1950s and 1960s, historians (and others) maintained that the English brought urban life to Ireland. This idea originally came from English chroniclers who were writing disparagingly about the Irish in the twelfth century. What the Viking evidence in Dublin did was give the Irish a claim to an urban history that preceded English rule. To understand why this is significant it is necessary to think about what England's relationship was with Ireland in the past, not least in the Middle Ages, when the English (or more precisely the Cambro-Normans and Anglo-Normans) first attempted to take control of Dublin, and Ireland.

During the twelfth and thirteenth centuries, aristocratic lords throughout Latin Christendom were engaged in a drive to acquire new lands. Through a process of conquest and colonisation, urbanisation and settlement, these lords pushed out the territories of their dominions, subjugated indigenous people, and got conquered leaders to submit to their control. This medieval expansionism – almost colonialism – has been well studied by historians in recent years, most forcefully in Bartlett's *The Making of Europe*.[10] This expansionism was an expansion of Western Christendom, and it thus affected large parts of 'frontier' Europe.

The English incursion into Ireland in the 1170s was at first an 'invited' invasion, for the King of Leinster had asked the English king, Henry II, for help.[11] As a result of this, there followed a contingent of lords, of Norman descent, in Leinster. One of them, Gilbert fitz Gilbert of Clare, otherwise known as 'Strongbow', married the daughter of the King of Leinster, and was granted a lordship in the south-eastern corner of Ireland. The 'Norman adventurers', as they have been romantically called, pushed north to Dublin and again further north into Ulster. Henry II, wishing to ensure that the renegade lords were under his control, had them swear allegiance to him, and at the same time took Dublin for his own. The English acquisition of lands in eastern Ireland was thus different from the Norman conquest of England under William the Conqueror 100 years before. In the 1170s, the English got into Ireland by a 'back door'; they were, to use Bartlett's phrase, an 'invited aristocracy'.[12] 'Invited', or not, the Anglo-Norman and Cambro-Norman lords quickly settled and urbanised their lands, creating towns where none had been before, and seizing those cities that had been established by the Vikings, like Waterford and Dublin (see Chapter 3).[13]

Colonisation went hand in hand with urbanisation in other parts of medieval Europe, too. Under such expansionism, towns and cities were built upon the political ambitions of conquering lords (in both a literal and metaphorical sense). One region of Latin

Christendom which was subject to a particularly aggressive form of expansionism was the area now covered by Poland and the Czech and Slovak republics. Here, during the eleventh, twelfth and thirteenth centuries, a 'conquering aristocracy' of Germanic origin pushed into Slavic lands east of the River Elbe. Again, Bartlett examines this process in some detail, noting particularly the importance played by towns in the German lords' attempts to consolidate their position in what were, initially, hostile lands.[14] Although there were Slavic towns throughout this region, some of long-standing importance as defensive and administrative centres, as with Ireland, historians had conventionally attributed the earliest urbanisation of Slavic lands to colonising German lords of the twelfth and thirteenth centuries. In particular, during the 1920s and 1930s, German-speaking historians mapped this eastward spread of urbanisation and, in so doing, furthered German nationalist claims over Poland and Czechoslovakia.[15]

Since 1945, excavations in towns and cities in east-central Europe have shown the extent to which urban life existed well before the medieval German lords had arrived, not least in Poland.[16] Again, as with Dublin, this became significant, for it revealed to the Polish people that their country's urban history *pre-dated* German colonisation. In the context of the Nazi occupations of Czechoslovakia and Poland in the 1930s and 1940s, this revised post-war view of Polish urban history was especially important, for it asserted a renewed sense of national identity, and helped to reverse the claims that had been made by inter-war German historians. This 'reclaiming' of medieval Poland was happening at a time of post-war reconstruction, when the country's bombed towns and cities were being rebuilt. The Polish authorities looked to the past for inspiration to build anew (unlike in Dublin), but in doing so they were presented with a difficult issue. The historic medieval towns that they were looking to rebuild were, for the most part, the very same towns that had been created by German lords in the twelfth and thirteenth centuries.[17] Although evidence for earlier, Slavic towns was unearthed as a consequence of this reconstruction, and although much was learned about the life in them in the Middle Ages, the rebuilt towns were restored to their pre-war appearance *despite* their German heritage.

The purpose behind this discussion was simply to point out that not only is Europe's medieval urban heritage contested, but that what we see today, when looking at some of the celebrated medieval towns and cities of Europe, is a picture of harmony that covers up the very conflicts that made them what they now are. The way in which the medieval past is presented and understood in local and national contexts has a profound influence on the built heritage of Europe's medieval towns and cities. This heritage is selectively packaged and presented for consumption, particularly for the international tourist market. Because what is presented is selective, it advocates not only a particular view of the medieval urban past but also a particular way in which to view it. This 'way of seeing' the Middle Ages reflects the modern fetish for the old, a nostalgia for the bygone. It is worth keeping in mind that heritage has been and always will be contested: it was contested in the Middle Ages, by the way that certain urban histories were marginalised and silenced in the aftermath of conquest and colonisation; and it remains contested because, politically, controlling the urban past is a way of manufacturing a sense of cultural identity and belonging.

Urban Inheritances

My concern so far has been with how the medieval urban past is understood in the context of what might be termed 'popular' conceptions of urbanism. For the remaining half of the chapter, I shall look more at where knowledge about medieval urban life comes from, how it is constructed from historical records. Academic ideas about medieval urban life do of course feed into 'popular' conceptions of it, and vice versa. Academics' interest in the Middle Ages is no doubt often first fuelled by early childhood encounters, perhaps through books and films, with 'medieval' stories and tales. The outcome of academic research and teaching also contributes to how museums, art galleries and heritage centres display 'the past' to the public. Here, though, I am principally concerned with two things. First, with how urban life was represented in the Middle Ages by contemporaries, and second, with how medieval urban life is pieced together by academics from documentary, archaeological and cartographic records.

Urban life in the 'medieval mind'

One thing that will become very clear during the course of reading this book and this chapter in particular, is how much we are
directed by what records have survived through from the Middle
Ages. In comparison with later periods, especially the nineteenth
and twentieth centuries, what we have in the way of contemporary
accounts of urban life in the Middle Ages are rather meagre. However, medieval representations of towns and cities do survive, as
written descriptions, images and sculpture, although some care is
needed in interpreting them. For one thing, medieval descriptions of cities and towns were almost always allegorical, that is,
they were intended to be symbolic. A case in point are the murals
of 'Good city government' and 'Bad city government' painted by
Lorenzetti in the mid-fourteenth century in the Palazzo Pubblico
in Siena.[18] Furthermore, medieval images of cities and towns were
created whether or not the narrator or artist had first-hand experience
of the places they were depicting. Descriptions were readily passed
on by word of mouth and then written down, or they were copied
from manuscript to manuscript, or from illumination to illumination.
This was especially the case for descriptions of Jerusalem and Rome,
because of their immense significance for the medieval Christian,
and because for many they were such difficult places to get to.

Doubtless far more descriptions and portraits of urban life were
made in the Middle Ages than those which have survived through
to the present day. Even with those images and accounts that have
survived it is not always possible to know why they were produced,
or indeed who produced them. It is even more difficult in many
cases to know who they were produced for, who their intended
audiences were. Even so, I think it is important to take a look at
what people in the Middle Ages thought about urban life, to give
them their say before turning to see what modern-day academics
have made of the historical evidence. It is unfortunate that much
of the modern academic writing on medieval accounts of contemporary urban life is highly specialised and difficult to get hold of
(and much of what is available on the subject is not written in
English). In the limited space available here, the examples of contemporary accounts of medieval urban life I have selected are but
a few of many: as with the other subjects I deal with in this book,
to do them proper justice would require a series of separate volumes.

During the Middle Ages, the wealthy and populated cities of Europe often attracted the attention of chroniclers writing about their times. Here I have chosen two well-known descriptions of major medieval cities, one from northern Europe and one from the south. One is from the end of the twelfth century and the other is from the end of the thirteenth. It will be clear that, despite their different origins and contexts, both share certain similar concerns to do with the appearance of the cities, from both outside and within. The first extract is part of William fitz Stephen's description of the most important city in the kingdom, London, dating to the period 1170–83, just over 100 years after the Norman Conquest:[19]

> Among the noble and celebrated cities of the world, that of London, the capital of the kingdom of the English, is one which extends its glory farther than all the others and sends its wealth and merchandise more widely into distant lands. Higher than all the rest does it lift its head. It is happy in the healthiness of its air; in its observance of Christian practice; in the strength of its fortifications; in its natural situation; in the honour of its citizens; and in the modesty of its matrons. It is cheerful in its sports, and the fruitful mother of noble men. . . .

Following this, the description turns specifically to address London's holy qualities:

> In the church of St Paul there is the episcopal seat. Once it was metropolitan [an archbishopric], and some think it will again be so. . . . As regards the practice of Christian worship, there are in London and its suburbs thirteen greater conventual churches, and besides these, one hundred and twenty-six lesser parish churches.

Having thus established its credentials as a holy place, fitz Stephen then points out that the city is well defended and secure:

> On its east side [the city has] the Palatine castle, very great and strong; the keep and walls rise from very deep foundations and are fixed with a mortar tempered by the blood of animals. On the west side there are two castles very strongly fortified, and

from these there runs a high and massive wall with seven double
gates and with towers along the north at regular intervals. . . .

He then stresses the city's mercantile connections, both regional
and international:

Immediately outside of one of the gates there is a field . . . on
every sixth day of the week, unless it be a major feastday, there
takes place here a famous exhibition of fine horses for sale . . .
by themselves, in another part of the field, stand the goods of
the countryfolk: implements of husbandry, swine with long flanks,
cows with full udders, oxen of immense size, and woolly sheep.
There also stand the mares fit for the plough, some big with
foal, and others with brisk young colts following them closely.
To this city, from every nation under Heaven, merchants delight
to bring their trade by sea. The Arabian sends gold; the Sabean
spice and incense. The Scythian brings arms, and from the rich
fat lands of Babylon comes oil of palms. The Nile sends precious stones; the men of Norway and Russia furs and sables; nor
is China absent with purple silk. The Gauls come with their
wines.

But not only is London a commercial melting pot, it is also a
lawful and orderly city:

The city, like Rome, is divided into wards; it has annual sheriffs
instead of consuls; it has its senatorial order and its lower mag-
istracies; it has drains and aqueducts in the streets; it has its
appointed places for the hearing of cases deliberative, demon-
strative, and judicial; it has its several courts, and its separate
assemblies on appointed days.

In all, then, fitz Stephen represents London as a righteous place,
confident and full of vitality and purpose. His message is clear:
London is on a higher plane than other English cities – it 'ex-
tends its glory farther than all the others'. This emphasis on the
holy is partly articulated literally by fitz Stephen. For example, by
the way he tells us about the many churches in the city 'and its
suburbs', and 'in its observance of Christian practice'. More subtly,
though, the description also makes use of Christian metaphors

and allegory. For example, the strength of the city's walls, built on sure foundations (like the Christian Church), and the exotic merchandise brought to London from the east, elevate the city by echoing the motifs of biblical stories.

In the Middle Ages, descriptions of cities often made an explicit connection between the earthly city and the Heavenly city of Jerusalem, with its circle of walls (Plate 1.1).[20] In the medieval mind, there existed a continuity between Heaven and Earth, such that what existed in Heaven also existed on Earth, albeit as an imperfect copy.[21] This idea was articulated cosmologically in medieval descriptions of the Heavenly Jerusalem and European cities. Between the ninth and twelfth centuries, images of the Heavenly Jerusalem typically depict it as it is described in the Book of Revelation – lying four square and surrounded by walls. This perfect, ideal city was 'mapped' onto earthly cities in the hope of elevating them, thus securing their salvation. We see this more explicitly in the case of a description of Milan, written 100 years after fitz Stephen's description of London, in 1288.

The description of Milan comes from Bonvicinus de Rippa.[22] He was a schoolmaster and wrote his description *De magnalibus urbis Mediolani* 'in order that "all lovers of this city should glorify God" on account of her greatness'.[23] In seven books, he praises Milan's location, its dwellings, the honesty of its inhabitants, its 'fertility and abundance', the city's 'fortitude', the people's 'fidelity' and their 'liberty'. The extract here is from Book 2, about its dwellings, starting with an account of citizens' houses and the city's streets:

In regard to housing . . . the truth is there before the eyes of those who see. The streets in this city are quite wide, the palaces quite beautiful, the houses packed in, not scattered but continuous, stately, adorned in a stately manner. Dwellings with doors giving access to the public streets have been found to number about 12,500, and in their number are very many in which many families live together with crowds of dependants. And this indicates the astonishing density of population of citizens. The roofed commons [open to all] neighbours in those squares which are properly called *coperti* almost reach the number of sixty.

Plate 1.1   *The Heavenly Jerusalem*

From here, Bonvicinus turns to the city's public buildings:

> The court of the Commune [city government], befitting such a great city, spreads over an area of two *pertiche* or thereabouts. And in order to make this more understandable perchance to some people, [it] measures 130 cubits from east to west, and 136 from north to south. In the midst of it stands a wonderful palace and in the court itself is a tower in which are the four bells of the Commune. On the eastern side is a palace in which are the rooms of the *podestá* [see Chapter 2], and of the judges, and its end on the northern side is the chapel of the *podestá*, built in honour of our patron, the Blessed Ambrose. And another palace prolongs the court on the north; so similarly on the west.

To the south there is also the hall where the sentences of con-
demnation are publicly proclaimed.

Having considered the city's civic core, Bonvicinus turns to Milan's
suburbs, walls and churches:

> Outside the wall of the moat there are so many suburban houses
> that they alone would be enough to constitute a city. . . . The
> main gates of the city are very strong and reach the number of
> six. The secondary gates, named *pusterie*, are ten. . . . The sanctu-
> aries of the saints . . . are about 200 in the city alone, having 480
> altars. The steeples, built in the manner of towers, are about
> 120 in the city. . . .

The sequence in which Bonvicinus describes the various characteristics of Milan's appearance is the reverse to the sequence fitz
Stephen follows in his description of London. Thus, Bonvicinus
first describes the city's administrative buildings before addressing
how many churches there are, whereas fitz Stephen is content to
first discuss London's churches and then turns to the city's public
offices. On the face of it, the sequence that Bonvicinus uses in his
account appears to make it rather more 'secular' in outlook. Moreover, Bonvicinus' abundant use of statistics gives his descriptions a
factual and 'scientific' appearance which fitz Stephen's rather more
vague account of London lacks. This apparent shift in emphasis
suggests a 'secularisation' in how cities were imagined in the later
Middle Ages. Indeed, Frugoni has argued that between 1000 and
1400, images of the medieval city become ever more secular.[24]
However, be that as it may, Bonvicinus's description of Milan is
stuffed full of Christian symbolism and is in fact no less allegorical
than fitz Stephen's description of London 100 years before.

Bonvicinus sought to praise Milan just as fitz Stephen had with
London. If anything, Bonvicinus' account is more explicitly cosmological than fitz Stephen's. He uses the cardinal points to describe
the area covered by the court of the Commune of the city, and
comments on the city's strong gates and walls. These are attributes
associated with the Heavenly Jerusalem. The central location of
the Commune's palace and court, and their arrangement on a
four-square principle, closely mirrors the medieval image of the
Heavenly Jerusalem which show it as a circle of walls, with gates at

the cardinal points, with Christ, the Lamb of God, sitting in the centre.[25] By depicting the city's administrative buildings in this way, by showing them to be a micro-cosmos of the Christian world order, Bonvicinus was, I believe, making an attempt to elevate the city closer to God, projecting it as a living symbol to 'glorify God'.

This all too brief incursion into contemporary medieval descriptions of towns and cities shows how fundamental the Christian world-view was in the Middle Ages in constructing people's sense of place and purpose. To make sense of medieval urban life, this outlook, or *mentalité*, needs to be kept in the forefront of our minds. Indeed, throughout the book I shall keep coming back to how Christian beliefs were 'mapped' onto, and out from, the medieval town and city (see Chapters 3, 5 and 7). To conclude this discussion of 'urban inheritances', the final section of this chapter examines how, by assembling and studying documentary, archaeological and cartographic records, modern academic observers have pieced together what urban life was like in the Middle Ages.

Fragments from the medieval past

It is rather artificial to start dividing up medievalists according to particular academic disciplines, for the Middle Ages is truly an interdisciplinary field of study, involving many scholars studying a range of different sources and using a variety of methods and approaches. Nevertheless, all too often books about medieval urban life neglect to tell readers about the difficulties encountered by academics in trying to recreate the Middle Ages from fragments of historical evidence. Here, all I am attempting to do is acknowledge that all historical sources pose problems of interpretation, and that scholars from different disciplines use particular sources in particular ways to ask particular sorts of questions. The most I can do in the space available is simply set out some of the main sources of evidence for reconstructing what urban life was like in the Middle Ages, and point out that these sources have been used by historians, archaeologists and geographers, alike. Inevitably, what I cover here is influenced by the sources and literature that I am most familiar with, which tends to be biased more towards a northern European (and North American) historiography. I shall start with some discussion of the documentary record of medieval urban life.

Usually understood to be the realm of historians, documentary sources provide a view of the Middle Ages which represents the view of those who created the documents in the first place. Only a fraction of medieval documents have been published, many more exist in libraries and repositories around the world awaiting study and publication. Most written documents surviving from the Middle Ages are written in medieval Latin rather than in vernacular (local), everyday languages.[26] This is because writing in the Middle Ages was largely the job of clerics educated according to rules of Latin grammar. Latin was the language of institutions across medieval Europe, in the Church, in the royal court, and in the aristocracy. Latin was thus the lingua franca of medieval Europe.

Much of the medieval documentary record relates to the activities of elites, for they could afford to pay scribes to produce written records. Thus medieval documents typically relate to aspects of institutional life, and arise out of practical concerns such as collecting taxes, finding out how much land people held, and keeping accounts of one's own expenditure and income. These sorts of concerns are the *raison d'être* behind some of Europe's most celebrated medieval written records, not least the Domesday Book (1086). Such fiscal records served those for whom they were created – the social and political elite of medieval Europe. During the twelfth and into the thirteenth century, the quantity of written records increased dramatically, as Clanchy has shown, largely as a response to secular and ecclesiastical institutions raising more revenue from lands and people under their control.[27] In England, for example, Henry I instituted the Exchequer to oversee monies owed to and paid by the Crown. During this period, too, the administration of many towns and cities was set down in writing for the first time (see Chapter 2). Particularly from 1100 onwards, more is known about the inner workings of town councils because they were making records about what they were spending money on, and where their income was coming from.

It is important to recognise that the documentary record represents only certain aspects of medieval urban life. There are wide spatial and temporal variations in the availability of documentary records, such that some towns and cities are well documented from a comparatively early date (the Italian city republics for example), while others only become well documented later on in the Middle Ages (the towns of Ireland, for example). These differences obviously mean that some places are better represented than others, that more is known about urban life in the fourteenth century than in the eleventh. As well as having temporal and spatial variations, the documentary record is also socially uneven. We know much more about the wealthy and the powerful – be they kings, bishops or leading merchants – than we do about 'ordinary' townspeople (see Chapter 7). Not only were large sections of the medieval population illiterate (in the conventional sense of the word), and thus made little impact on the documentary record themselves, most would have had little time or inclination for putting things down in writing. However, by the 1200s, many urban property-holders used written records in the form of private charters and deeds to record agreements with neighbours and to register transfers of land between parties (see Chapter 6). What people were doing in their houses on a day-to-day level is sometimes brought to light when one of these 'formal' documents makes reference to some personal aspect of someone's actions or activities.

Medievalists' use of written records has changed during the past century. In the late nineteenth and early twentieth century, British, French and German historians were particularly interested in medieval legal records from which they could write about the institutional and constitutional development of towns and cities in the Middle Ages. 'Constitutional historians', such as Ballard, Stephenson and Tait, sought to understand the origins of medieval towns and cities by looking at the rise of municipal government.[28] They were writing at a time when towns and cities in many parts of Europe were undergoing dramatic expansion, accompanied by municipal reform. Urban constitutional history was more about the higher-level political and economic institutions that controlled urbanism in the Middle Ages than the ordinary and everyday aspects of medieval urban life. Debates raged between these historians over the constitutional origins of urbanism in medieval Europe, and the circumstances in which characteristically urban institutions, such as guilds, councils and 'communes', were first formed. These matters are still of vital importance in any discussion of medieval urban life, which is why they are examined in some detail in Chapter 2.

During the middle part of the last century, a shift in focus took place as economic and social historians (and historical geographers) started to use medieval fiscal records to find out more about the demographic and economic characteristics of medieval urban life. Their concern was more with reconstructing changes in the pattern of medieval trade and population movement, both in and between towns and cities. Classic studies of this sort include Braudel's *Capitalism and Material Life*, as well as Darby's historical geography of *Domesday England*, and Beresford's *New Towns of the Middle Ages*.[29] At the core of much of this work is the analysis of statistical data, typically derived from taxation records and the like. This they tabulated and mapped in order to show temporal and spatial trends. The 1950s and 1960s were a period when positivism and empiricism underpinned most data analyses. Latterly, computers have revolutionised quantification techniques, by speeding up analysis and increasing the quantity of data processed. Not all medieval socio-fiscal records were subject to this sort of number-crunching study, however. At the same time, there was a growing interest among some historians and geographers, particularly in Britain, in reconstructing patterns of medieval urban topography using property rentals and surveys. Piecing together the physical layout of English medieval towns and cities this way from written records developed through the 1950s and 1960s in studies of Oxford, Canterbury and Southampton.[30] It has since been adopted by both urban historians and archaeologists, and in the 1970s and 1980s formed the basis of major studies on the topography of medieval Winchester, Norwich and Bristol.[31]

Like all things, academic study of the Middle Ages is subject to changes in fashion. Particularly popular at the moment are studies of medieval social attitudes (*mentalités*), largely inspired by French social historians (some with Marxist leanings) writing in the 1950s and 1960s, and the 'ordinary' and 'everyday' aspects of urban life. Exemplary studies in this vein, such as those by Le Goff and Duby, deal with the medieval view of the world, and draw upon a wide range of contemporary written sources, especially literary accounts, such as chronicles, theological and philosophical writing, and poetry.[32] The result is a rich, sensuous form of historical writing; subtle, nuanced and 'in touch' with the minds of medieval people. It helps to expose views and attitudes prevalent in the period, and engages with complex social matters such as heresy, sexuality, deviance and domesticity.[33] Recently, the French tradition in this sort of medievalism has become very popular among anglophone historians in Britain and North America. It reflects a growing concern with how the Middle Ages are represented in the discourse of history itself. The 'social construction' of everyday life in the Middle Ages is also something that has absorbed archaeologists, particularly those who seek to make use of critical theory to interpret material culture.

The archaeological record of medieval urban life was, until the latter half of the twentieth century, largely unexplored. Some urban medieval sites had been excavated (by 'amateur' archaeologists) in the nineteenth century, but most of these were concerned with institutional buildings, particularly monasteries, cathedrals and castles. 'Below ground' urban archaeology at this time was directed much more towards the recovery and recording of Roman artefacts. This often meant digging through medieval occupation layers, destroying the evidence in the process. Underpinning this 'vandalism' was the then prevalent idea that the medieval city represented a barbarous interlude in the evolution of urban life, a 'dark age' between Classical and modern civilisation (an Enlightenment 'myth' that dates back to the time of Petrarch). Also, the vestiges of medieval urban life, the fragile objects made of wood and leather, were either not recognised for what they were, or failed to survive once exposed to the air, unlike the objects recovered of Roman date. Thus, excavations in European towns and cities in the early part of the twentieth century revealed much about Roman buildings, streets and defences which lay beneath the medieval urban landscape, but relatively little about the medieval urban landscape itself.[34]

After the Second World War, medieval urban archaeology became more widespread in Europe. As bombed towns and cites were rebuilt, and the pace of redevelopment exposed more of what lay beneath modern streets and buildings, urban archaeology became all the more systematic and 'scientific'. During the 1950s and 1960s, as more was learned about medieval ceramics, it became possible to date archaeological contexts more closely. This transition is especially apparent if one compares the published report of an excavation undertaken in the 1950s with one from the 1990s.[35] The amount of material in some archaeological reports today is staggering, and indeed the enormous weight of evidence produced by modern archaeological excavations is often a factor in slowing down the rate at which excavation reports can be published. This means that the results of many urban excavations are unfortunately never published, but instead rest in the repositories of local authorities, usually in varying states of completion. On the other hand, more and more books are appearing on the archaeology of medieval towns and cities, some of which do an excellent service in bringing together the results of archaeological studies of sites in towns and cities all over Europe.[36]

Of course, archaeological work is not all about digging holes, despite this common perception. Indeed, there is now a widespread (and contentious) view among many archaeologists that excavation should be avoided unless a particular site is under threat. As a result, non-destructive 'above ground' archaeology has become as important as 'below ground' work. This involves the survey and evaluation of standing remains, recording the external and internal fabric of buildings. This sort of archaeological work has much in common with architectural history (which, incidentally, has long been concerned with buildings of medieval date). Medieval archaeologists will also typically undertake their work in collaboration with historians, using documentary study to establish a fuller picture of what the archaeological record itself reveals.[37] Over the last decade, however, some archaeologists have started to criticise the way in which medieval archaeology has seemingly followed an agenda set by historians. They have suggested that the archaeological record should be used to redefine the history of the Middle Ages, and that archaeologists should look at medieval material culture for what it says in its own right, rather than trying to make it 'fit' into the history that comes from the documentary record.

One of the major advantages of the archaeological record is that it reveals aspects of medieval urban life that are otherwise not well represented by written records (or sometimes not represented by them at all). Although most urban excavation sites are restricted in the amount of area that they can cover (due to external constraints), as a result of centuries of deposition on the same site, urban deposits are often very deep, deeper than their rural counterparts. This provides urban archaeologists with an opportunity to reconstruct the changes taking place in urban life in the Middle Ages, and map how urban landscapes changed over time. For a given site, therefore, its medieval development can be traced in terms of changes in the intensity and type of occupation.[38] This is especially useful in seeking to establish how ordinary townspeople lived and worked in the Middle Ages, as well as for trying to work out when and how a particular urban landscape developed. For example, recovered artefacts (such as ceramic vessels) and structures (such as walls and floors) reveal when urban occupation first appears, as well as what form it took, what activities were carried on there, and how the site became built up subsequently (see Chapters 5–7).

Since the late 1960s, developments in environmental archaeology, particularly with the analysis of organic material in waterlogged, anaerobic deposits, have revealed many aspects of everyday medieval urban life that are generally not well represented in written sources. The food people ate, the vessels they used to eat and drink from, the clothes they wore, the colour of their hair, the internal arrangements of their houses, are all aspects of medieval urban life that have become better understood thanks to environmental archaeologists studying the contents of the more unromantic features of the medieval townscape, such as middens and rubbish pits.[39] All of this has allowed archaeologists to visualise more clearly what medieval townscapes might have looked like all those centuries ago, as well as how they changed over time. The reconstruction drawings that come from this sort of work provide a very vivid and immediate impression of scenes that have long since gone. Of course, bearing in mind how very little of the urban landscape can be excavated at any one time, these artists' impressions have to be viewed critically, and recognised for what they are – products of someone's imagination.

For me, one of the most exciting opportunities that archaeology offers is the chance to see what medieval townspeople saw (even though what we see in these things might be very different from what people saw in them in the Middle Ages). It is not just the objects that are retrieved, important and interesting though they often are, but the broader picture that emerges – a town's streets and alleyways, the backyards of buildings, and the vaulted undercrofts beneath merchants' houses – all unseen for centuries.[40] When excavations open up this hitherto 'hidden' medieval world, they open up all sorts of possibilities and help us to picture what urban life was like in the Middle Ages. Archaeology also has the power to show that the streets we walk along in towns and cities all over Europe, are often the same streets that people walked upon in the Middle Ages; that buildings along these streets often have foundations dating back to the twelfth or thirteenth centu-

ries; that the boundaries of property parcels that divide up today's
townscape might have been in position (*in situ*) for 800 years or
more.[41] This remarkable continuity in the European urban landscape is important: it means first of all that we should endeavour
to protect the surviving vestiges of medieval townscapes for the
future. It also means that today's urban landscape is a 'palimp-
sest', a record in its own right because it fossilises its medieval
ancestry.

Finally here, not least because of my geographical inclination,
something needs to be said about the medieval cartographic record,
and the visualisation of medieval urban life in 'pictorial maps'
(drawings and images). Cartographic historians have on the whole
been rather conservative (at best) and dismissive (at worse) about
interpreting medieval mapping. Such mapping is usually seen as
unsophisticated and unscientific, particularly when compared with
later, Renaissance mapping.[42] This view has partly come about because
mappae mundi, idealised cartographic representations of the medieval
world-view, produced during the twelfth and thirteenth centuries,
have been taken as typical forms of medieval mapping. However,
divorcing these 'maps' from their cosmological purpose, and
comparing them with Renaissance world maps, is misleading to
say the least. Fortunately, more subtle readings of these symbolic
cartographic representations (including those of 'ideal' cities) have
recently begun to redress this iniquity, and the relationship between
medieval cosmology and cartography has been explored with greater
sympathy and nuance.[43]

Medieval cartographic representations of towns and cities per se
are without doubt rare, particularly before the fourteenth century.
However, they do exist, often having been produced for some practical purpose, for example, to show how land should be divided or
improved. One of the earliest English examples of a 'local map' is
of mid-twelfth-century date and shows how water was supplied to
Canterbury cathedral. Two centuries later, on a document recording
the transfer of a property in Exeter, a sketch map was inserted to
show what was there.[44] By this time, medieval surveyors were quite
capable of accurately measuring landscapes and setting out buildings
and streets to precise measurements (see Chapter 5). However,
instead of producing maps from their survey work, it seems that
one of the medieval surveyor's jobs was to record in writing what
was on the ground. Moreover, the few 'local' maps and plans that

have survived from the Middle Ages suggest that the surveyor's concern was less with visually representing what was already there on the ground, even though their knowledge of mathematics and the instruments used for surveying could have been put to this purpose, and more to do with using their expertise to create new landscapes.

For the most part, cartographic representations of medieval towns and cities are actually *post-medieval* in date. These depictions are widely used by urban historians and geographers, but because of their small scale and 'inaccurate' co-ordinates they present a highly simplified view of the medieval townscape, something that has unfortunately contributed to the idea that towns and cities in the Middle Ages were typically 'irregular' in form and thus the product of 'uncontrolled' and 'unplanned' growth (see above). Not until the middle part of the nineteenth century do Europe's medieval towns and cities first become accurately surveyed and represented in detailed cadastral plans. Although these plans depict the urban scene some 500 years or more after the Middle Ages, enough of the medieval townscape usually survived into the 1840s and 1850s (largely in the form of inherited streets and plot (lot) patterns), to make these plans and surveys a useful source from which to reconstruct what medieval urban landscapes looked like, and work out how they evolved (see Chapter 5).[45]

In all, it is only through combining the various fragments of documentary records, archaeology and cartography, that we can piece together an impression of urban life in the Middle Ages. Interdisciplinary work, linking the expertise of historians, archaeologists, geographers and the like, is now increasingly the norm in studies of medieval urbanism, and it is the basis of this book too. Unfortunately, in the limited space available here, it has not been possible for me to examine sculptural and artistic representations of medieval urban life, and discuss the work of art and architectural historians. What has been possible is just a brief treatment of the problems and issues involved in trying to reconstruct and represent urban life in the Middle Ages. These problems and issues need to be borne in mind when reading this book, for the survival and handling of the fragments of the medieval urban past continually affect our interpretations of it.

Conclusion: 'Inventing' the Middle Ages?

This chapter has examined some of the legacies of medieval urban life. The Middle Ages lives on in the modern world in all sorts of ways, and it is forever being (re)formulated and (re)encountered. Cantor has shown how, during the twentieth century, historians continually sought to understand what we call 'the medieval period', and how in the process of writing about what they think they see, have in fact *invented* the Middle Ages.[46] This sort of critical self-reflection is both refreshing and necessary, yet it also seems to reflect a 'crisis of representation', in which perhaps it has become no longer desirable (perhaps least of all possible) to represent *the* Middle Ages as an objective, historical 'reality'. Rather, we have to accept instead that today, the Middle Ages exists subjectively, within us, that we all 'invent' our own version of the Middle Ages. In the course of writing this book, in deciding what work to include and what to exclude, I have been highly conscious of this and the tension that exists between *my* Middle Ages and the (external) Middle Ages that I seek to represent faithfully.

Because the Middle Ages lives on in all sorts of ways, not just in academic texts but in the landscape all around us, and in the experiences of our everyday life, it seems especially invidious to claim, as some do, that the medieval town and city is irrelevant to modern living, merely history. The legacies of medieval urban life, whether in the form of ongoing European political and social conflicts, or artefacts viewed in a museum visit while on vacation, should always serve to remind us that the Middle Ages is still there, still very much alive. For me, the most potent living legacy of urban life in the Middle Ages is the European urban landscape. So many of us (in Europe) encounter the medieval urban landscape during the course of our day-to-day lives. Whether in busy capital cities or sleepy market towns, we continue to walk and drive along 'medieval' streets; to worship in medieval churches and cathedrals; use medieval market places for car parks; and shop for clothes or drink coffee in 'medieval' buildings (which now function as boutiques and cafés). These lasting, tangible reminders of Europe's medieval urban heritage put many of us in daily contact with the people whose activities shaped these very same towns and cities so many centuries ago, and whose lives were, like ours, shaped by the surrounding townscapes which they encountered.

2

INSTITUTIONAL URBANISM

Henry, King of England and Duke of Normandy and Aquitaine and Count of Anjou, to Archbishops, Bishops, Abbots, Earls, Barons, Justices, Sheriffs and all men of his land, greeting. Know that I have granted to my burgesses of Bristol that they shall be quit of toll and passage and all custom throughout my land of England, Normandy and Wales, wheresoever they and their goods shall come. Wherefore I will and firmly command that they shall have all their liberties and quittances and free customs, fully and honourably as my free and faithful men, and they shall be quit of toll and passage and all other custom.

King Henry II's charter to Bristol, 1155[1]

In the centuries that immediately followed the passing of the first millennium, urban life in Europe became increasingly subject to legal and institutional measures of order and control. All across Europe, from the Baltic to the Black Sea, kings, princes, bishops and abbots were all busy issuing charters to their towns. These town charters were a defining characteristic of urbanism in Europe between the eleventh and fifteenth centuries, and indeed Europe's towns and cities are still granted charters today to grant and confirm rights and privileges. By granting special laws, privileges and customs, chartered towns in the Middle Ages were set apart, legally and constitutionally, from the villages and hamlets that were dotted around the surrounding countryside.

Historians have debated the complex development of medieval urban institutions since the latter half of the nineteenth century.

Their work on the formation of medieval urban constitutions still remains a critical foundation in urban history, though today it is overlooked by many students. However complex, some grasp of constitutional history is vital in any discussion of medieval urbanism, and so it is the purpose of this chapter to cover some of the fundamental issues concerning the development of urban government in the Middle Ages. There are a number of readable commentaries on the animated debates that went on during the early part of the last century between influential constitutional historians such as Adolphus Ballard, James Tait and Carl Stephenson.[2] Despite its apparent antiquity, this urban historiography continues to influence how medievalists interpret the institutional organisation of urban life in the Middle Ages, and therefore it needs to be followed through diligently.

Today, historians' views of medieval urban institutions differ somewhat from those held by their predecessors writing at the start of the last century. The emphasis now is much more on how power was shared in medieval society at large, and with how urban institutions were simply an agreed machinery for urban government. There is thus a greater sensitivity towards the role that people played in regulating urban communities in the Middle Ages, and to the possibility that self-regulation and self-government emerged through complex social relations because power was being forever shared and negotiated.[3] The urban institutions under discussion in this chapter are thus simply an expression of the outcome of these ongoing negotiations and relationships, and in this context it is important to remember that 'charters were one method by which medieval kings could recognise or increase or restrict local autonomy: they did not create it'.[4]

What changed during the course of the Middle Ages was the balance of power in urban government. This becomes apparent if municipal histories are looked at across long periods of time, and if different towns are compared. This is the focus of the second part of the chapter, which considers how medieval municipal governments were formed and organised, and examines in some detail the changing internal political structure of four medieval cities. To start with, however, the first part of this chapter simply introduces aspects of the machinery of medieval urban government, in particular the contents of charters that specified urban privileges and institutions, and the constitutional make-up of specially

enfranchised towns known as 'boroughs'. Having established what
the legal foundations of medieval urbanism were, we can then go
on to examine the political uses to which these laws were put to
by feudal lords in Europe, as well as the implications that these
legal frameworks had for urbanisation and urban property-holding
(Chapters 3, 4 and 6).

Chartered Towns and Town Charters

The concept of a 'chartered town' is perhaps a difficult one for us
to understand today, yet it remains an important element of Europe's
medieval urban heritage. For many European towns and cities, great
significance is still placed on having a charter dating back to the
Middle Ages. Such charters, granted sometime in a town's remote
medieval past by some important patron, continue to give local
people a sense of pride.

On entering a historic town in almost any country in Europe, it
is common to find a sign which proudly proclaims when the town
was first chartered. Take, for example, Marlborough, a small but
lively market town famous for its college, nestling below the white
chalk downlands of Wiltshire in southern England. Descending
into Marlborough, on the road through Savernake Forest, there is
a blue-painted sign welcoming travellers to the old market town.
Written beneath the words 'Borough of Marlborough', the more
observant visitor will also notice that the town was first 'chartered'
in 1204. Although this event occurred 800 years ago, it is still
remembered and commemorated by the words on this sign. Why
should this be so? What does it mean for a town to have been
chartered in the Middle Ages? Answers to such questions lie within
England's constitutional history, and the complex institutional and
political development of medieval towns more generally.

The reason why 1204 is an important date for Marlborough is
because it was the occasion when King John granted a *borough charter*
to the town's inhabitants, a charter which contained special legal
and economic privileges making Marlborough constitutionally different from other, nearby settlements lying around the town.[5] The
legal distinction, between 'town' and 'borough', raises an important terminological problem, one which Maitland observed long
ago when he wrote: 'a legal, though a wavering, line is drawn

between the borough and the mere vill or rural township'.[6] In 1204, Marlborough was both a 'town' *and* a 'borough'. That is to say, it was a settlement that had commercial and administrative functions which characterised it as a town; while at the same time it also had special constitutional status making it a borough, and providing its inhabitants with social, political and economic privileges. The purpose of this part of the chapter is to discuss the character and nature of these privileges. First of all, though, it is necessary to acknowledge that the terms 'town' and 'borough' have distinct meanings in the context of medieval urbanism.

Defining 'town' and 'borough'

The range of different words which were used in the Middle Ages to describe an urban place is at first rather bewildering. The medieval scribes who wrote about towns, and compiled legal documents, used Latin terms to describe the status and character of a particular place. There is a good example of this to be found in Domesday Book, the great survey of England that William the Conqueror commissioned shortly following the Norman Conquest.

It is now well known that the compilers of Domesday Book had difficulties in knowing how to deal with towns, for towns did not easily fit with the rubric that they were working to.[7] The English Midland town of Stafford has a comprehensive entry in the pages of Domesday. Stafford was the seat of a shire before the Norman Conquest, a county town. It had important administrative and judicial functions dating back to the early ninth century, when the shires in central England were first being fashioned from earlier Anglo-Saxon kingdoms.[8] The scribe who wrote the Domesday entry for Stafford used three different Latin terms to describe the place: *civitas* ('city'), *burgus* ('borough') and *villa* ('town').[9] In 1086 this was no contradiction in terms, for Stafford was in fact all three at once: constitutionally and legally it was a *burgus*, and yet it was also a sizeable fortified place, a *civitas*. The word *villa* was employed broadly during the Middle Ages to describe more or less any place that was a habitation, whether it was urban or not. In Old English *villa* equated with 'tun', from which the word 'town' is derived.

When using the term 'borough' to describe a town it is important that we are clear that the place was so defined in the Middle Ages. There are cases where the chartering of a town could actually lead to a change in the term used to describe it. In Poland, for example, Duke Barnim I granted the law of Magdeburg to the Slavic settlement of Stettin (Szczecin) by means of a charter. His charter had the effect of making the place a *civitas*, whereas before it had been reckoned an *oppidum*.[10] To complicate matters more, not all *towns* in the Middle Ages were legally defined as *boroughs*, so although some settlements functioned as an urban centre, they did so without actually having borough status. Yet, on the other hand, there were also places that were granted borough status but which failed to develop urban functions, and consequently these places faded from the landscape.

Chartering a borough: the case of Portsmouth

The towns I am dealing with in this chapter are those that were chartered as boroughs. They acquired special legal and economic privileges from their lords, the details of which were set out in specially drawn up legal documents called charters. An examination of one such borough charter will provide a useful start point.

On 2 May 1194, just before he set sail to France, King Richard I dated and signed a borough charter for Portsmouth, a port-town located in Hampshire on the south coast of England. In his charter Richard set out the legal and economic privileges that were to make Portsmouth a borough.[11] First, the king pointed out that the borough ultimately belonged to the Crown, to him. The charter thus records the king's wishes: 'know that we have retained our Borough of Portsmouth in our hands'. Then the charter states, 'we have also granted that our burgesses in the same borough may have a market on one weekday in every week, namely on Thursday, with all the liberties and free customs which our citizens of Winchester, or Oxford, or others of our land have'. The right to hold a weekly market was a fundamental privilege for a borough. It was usually accompanied, as at Portsmouth, by the right of townspeople to also 'be quit and free of toll, and "pontage", and passage, and "pedage", and "payage", and "stallage" and "tallage"' (all forms of taxation levied in other boroughs), throughout the realm. The king's borough charter asserted one other important right: 'that the said town of Portsmouth, and our burgesses holding thereof, shall have and hold their houses and possessions . . . with all liberties and free customs . . . and forbid that they should be impleaded for any tenement of the same town except before us'.

In essence, Richard's charter to Portsmouth may be summarised on three counts: the right to hold a weekly market; the right to hold tenements by burgage tenure (often 12d. or 6d. a year in English boroughs); and the right to be tried in a special court within the borough (in which the lord usually had only a limited hand). As a burgess (*burgensis*), a person held a plot of land ('burgage', or *burgagium*). They could build upon it, subdivide it, rent it out, sell it or hand it on to their offspring. Whatever they did with the burgage, the annual rent remained fixed. According to Beresford and Finberg, the possession of burgage tenure was the 'lowest common denominator of boroughs', for boroughs 'large and small, early and late, corporate and incorporate, royal, seigneurial, or ecclesiastical'.[12]

As a royal borough, the profits accruing from rents and trade in Portsmouth went to the Crown. It was clearly in the king's interest to make the place as attractive a place to live in as possible, but it was also in the townspeople's interest to have a charter that enabled them to run the town in a way to suit themselves. The charter thus satisfied the needs and requirements of the king and the urban community, and the liberties and privileges that Richard granted in 1194 ensured that further artisans, traders and merchants would migrate to Portsmouth and take up the opportunity of holding properties in the town. The royal grant of the borough charter might easily be mistaken to mark the foundation of the town. However, the charter marks a formal recognition of the *borough* of Portsmouth, and not the foundation of the place as a *town*. To find out when the town was first created it is necessary to look to the activities of a Norman merchant called Jean de Gisors. It was he who, in the 1180s, created a new settlement called Portsmouth. Ten years before Richard granted Portsmouth's borough charter, de Gisors had established a *villa*, and laid out streets there, together with a place for a market and plots for houses.[13]

The example of Portsmouth serves to make a more general point about medieval town charters and chartered towns. Charters could either be drawn up to grant new borough privileges and customs to a settlement ('constitutional charters'), or they could be used simply to confirm existing borough privileges ('charters of ratification').[14] Portsmouth is a case where a charter founded a new borough, even though the settlement was already there. In other cases, charters were granted to existing boroughs, to confirm already existing privileges. An example of this is the borough charter issued to Bristol by Henry II in 1155, cited at the start of this chapter.

The distinction between the two uses of borough charters has been neatly drawn by Bartlett.[15] On the one hand, he says, the grant of a borough charter could reflect a 'recasting' in 'the organisation of an existing town', and 'not the foundation or establishment of the town'. Meanwhile, on the other hand, the grant of a borough charter might equally 'constitute the foundation of a town, and the transformation of a rural settlement or even the birth of an entirely new place'. Put another way, urban charters were used to define or enhance the privileges of an established urban community, as well as to set out rules for a 'new' town. Thus charters granting borough status were sometimes 'a stimulant' to urban development; they 'were not always issued at the outset of the process of town foundation, but often in the course of building or even at the end'.[16] (Aspects of the process of town foundation are considered in Chapter 4.)

Common borough privileges

It is worth looking in a little more detail at the content of borough charters and identifying their common elements. A borough charter usually consisted of five parts; an address, a conferment of privileges, a 'volumus' clause, a prohibition of disturbance, and a dating clause.[17] The contents of both 'constitutional charters' and charters of 'ratification' (that is those charters that confirmed existing burghal privileges rather than granting new rights and customs) were mainly composed of these five parts.

Although broad similarities exist in the constituent parts of borough charters, the details of particular privileges conferred by each charter often differ. For example, the annual rents paid by burgesses for their burgages usually form an important feature in the conferment of borough privileges, but the amount they paid in rent to the lord could vary from one place to another, according to the grantor's wishes. Also, burgess rights to land outside the area of the borough, for example in marshlands and woodland, are frequently mentioned in charters, but obviously the details of these vary according to local circumstances.

As Stephenson noted, a useful, general distinction may be drawn between those town charters that granted 'advanced liberties', which usually embraced aspects of municipal government; and those that gave 'elementary liberties', which conceded borough privileges but not special rights of self-government.[18] In the case of both 'advanced' and 'elementary' liberties, borough privileges and rights of burgage tenure were largely similar:

> In the first place, burgage tenure enabled the burgesses to dispose of their houses in the borough almost as easily as their chattels . . . then, by having a court of their own in which they were tried by their fellow townsmen they were more favourably treated: there was often some limitation of the amount of fines that could be levied in a borough court, for instance, in the boroughs that received the law of Breteuil, whereas there was no such limitation on the fines imposed by the manorial court [of the lord]: in many places the burgesses were free of toll, not only in the market of the borough but also throughout the possessions of the lord.[19]

However, in those charters which granted towns more 'advanced liberties', such as the charter that William Clito gave to St Omer in the early twelfth century (when he was trying to buy support to establish himself as Count of Flanders), two important and fundamental concessions were made in addition. First, the right to have a gild merchant ('a union of prominent merchants'); and second, the right to have a board of magistrates (*échevins*) – whose job it was to administer justice within the jurisdiction of the town.[20] The more advanced liberties are considered later in this chapter in the discussion of medieval municipal government.

Urban privileges: a European perspective

The content of a town charter was not simply decided upon by the grantor alone. It was instead a product of compromise and negotiation between the urban community and their overlord.[21] Together, they determined the political constitution and legal orientation of the chartered town, sanctioning and defining specified 'urban' privileges. To study the nature of these privileges further, it will be useful to adopt a broad, pan-European perspective. Comparing charters of one town or borough with those of another reveals certain similarities and differences between the sorts of urban privileges that were being drawn up in the Middle Ages by Europe's feudal aristocracy. In this and the following section, examples of urban privileges from different regions of Europe are compared to help draw out some general observations.

Throughout medieval Europe, from north to south, the term *burgus* was used in charters to confer basic urban rights and privileges. By noting that there are similarities between borough charters in twelfth- and thirteenth-century England and France, Hilton compiled a list of the 'most frequently included' urban privileges:[22]

1. Legal security for the burgesses, personally, against arbitrary feudal jurisdiction. This was implied by the personal freedom conveyed by burgess statutes and by there being no obligation to attend (with few exceptions) courts outside the town.
2. Simplified legal processes in urban courts. Decision by duel and ordeal, if not entirely abolished, was limited. There were reduced and fixed penalties.
3. Tenure of urban real property was a form of free tenure. It was expressed as 'burgage tenure' in Normandy and England. Rents were normally paid in money only.
4. Burgesses were exempt from seigneurial impositions such as tolls, *banalités*, *gîte* and tallage.
5. Property was secure against arbitrary seizure, though measures against debtors from outside could include the right of distraint on the debtor's goods, and even on goods of fellow townsmen of the debtor.
6. There was a varying degree of financial autonomy, usually by giving the townsmen the right to collect various dues previously collected by royal and seigneurial officials, and to pay an annual lump sum to the king or the lord (*firma burgi* ['borough farm'] in England).
7. There were varying degrees of political or administrative government of the town by a number of elected officials, such as mayor, *échevins*, consuls and so on. The smaller the town the less likely was self-government – the urban court would be presided over by the lord's steward.

These basic medieval urban privileges are not only peculiar to France and England. Turning to medieval Germany, urban privileges set out in town charters of the thirteenth century include similar sorts of statements concerning: first, the relationship between the lord of the town and community, with the privileges they enjoyed outside the town; second, laws concerning the organisation of the town's constitution and administration; and third, the economic and material privileges to be enjoyed by the town's inhabitants.[23] Clearly, broad similarities existed in the characteristics of urban privileges, and in the basic content of town charters in Europe north and south of the Alps.

To get an impression of the ubiquitous nature of institutionalised urbanism in the Middle Ages it is worth looking in a little more detail at charters issued to towns by French, German and Spanish lords. As a starting point, the table drawn up long ago by Ballard provides us with some useful comparisons between urban privileges.[24] Although he was later criticised on the grounds of choosing only a limited sample of German charters and mixing the documents 'without regard to relative age and importance', his efforts have yet to be bettered, and so his table is reproduced here (Table 2.1).[25]

Table 2.1   *Urban privileges in European chartered towns*[26]

Type of privilege	British	French	German	Spanish*
Liberty to sell burgages	C	–	–	–
Sales to religious houses	Forbidden	C	R	F Teruel/ Cuenca
Pre-emption by lord	R	U	U	U
Pre-emption by kin	F	R	F	Teruel/ Cuenca
Possession for year and a day	C	C	C	Cuenca
Limitation of lord's credit	F	F	U	U
Franchise by year and day	C	C	C	U
No external pleas	C	F	F	U
Trial by battle	Forbidden	C	C	Teruel/ Cuenca
Distraint on foreign debtors	C	U	U	U
Freedom from toll	C	R	R	U
Firma burgi	C	R	U	Teruel
Destruction of house†	R	C	C	Cuenca
Lex talionis	U	C	C	U
Monopoly on trade	F	U	R	U

U = privileges unknown; R = privileges rare; F = privileges frequent; C = privileges that are common.
* Ballard considered only charters for Teruel and Cuenca; see below.
† Where a burgess had committed a forfeiture.

From his comparison, Ballard observed that in Britain, France and Germany 'the burgesses of many places were able to secure exemption from pleading or being impleaded at any courts other than those of the borough or town; that in all three countries there were towns in which possession [of a property] for a year and a day gave secure titles to the owners of landed properties; [and] in all three countries there were many places in which the borough franchise was acquired by residence for a year and a day'.[27] These common aspects of charters and borough laws are a useful basis for comparing European medieval urban privileges in a little more detail.

Urban privileges in France, Germany and Spain

Burgage tenure was a common feature of medieval town charters in the north of France, Normandy and Flanders. At Verneuil in Normandy, for example, Henry I set out the borough's privileges in a charter, permitting 'that each burgess shall receive three acres of land and a garden, for which, no matter how many houses he puts up, he shall pay twelve deniers yearly, and so enjoy the privilege of buying and selling in the town'.[28] As well as this, the charter stated that 'during the first three years, the men [i.e. burgesses] of Verneuil are to be quit of customs throughout Henry's dominions . . . and except when pleas are carried to the king in person, trials are to be held in the town'.[29]

A similar set of privileges was also used in chartering towns in the Midi, in the southern part of France, for example at a town called Montauban which was issued a formal charter of liberties in 1144 by Alphonse, the Count of Toulouse. His charter established liberties 'remarkably like those of Verneuil', and included 'guaranteed freedom from claims of outside lords' to all those who settled there, and fixed the rent of their building plots at twelve deniers a year.[30] Moreover, the charter also provided the future development of the town's liberties, for the count encouraged the townspeople to build a new bridge over the Tarn river, agreeing that when the bridge was finished he would determine the customs of the town 'by consultation with six townsmen of the better sort'.[31]

The origins of burgage tenure, it has been argued, lay in Normandy where the term *bourgage* (burgage) can be traced to the early eleventh century.[32] The term *burgensis* (burgess) has also be traced to eleventh-century northern France, from where it is thought to have spread eastwards and northwards.[33] The origins of the concept of burgage tenure are in fact difficult to determine, but clearly the essence of borough customs, the principles of burgess status and burgage tenure, were to be found in town charters in both north and south France, certainly by the middle of the twelfth century.

One important aspect of many of these French town charters is the 'practice of affiliation'. For example, the 'law of Beaumont-en-Argonne [of 1182] was adopted by more than 300 towns in Lorraine, Champagne and the Ardennes, and the *Établissements* of Rouen were the foundation of the constitution of sixteen towns'.[34] In France the affiliation of towns allowed disputes to be settled by calling upon the *chef de sens*, 'the mother town', which 'in addition to giving its opinion on disputed points often decided controversies between a commune and its lord, and between parties in the commune'.[35] Table 2.2 shows some further affiliations between French chartered towns.

The practice of using affiliations in town charters was not peculiar to France, for it is to be found in British and German charters, too. Already we have seen, in the case of Richard's charter for Portsmouth, the customs of Oxford and Winchester being used as models to define Portsmouth's liberties in 1194 (see above). In cases of dispute within English boroughs the custom was to appeal to 'mother towns'. For example, 'the charter granted to Oxford by Henry II, by which the citizens received the liberties of the citizens

Table 2.2 *Affiliated chartered towns in France (1128–1207)*[36]

Mother town	Affiliated town
Laon (1128)	Cerny, Bruyères, Montdidier
Mantes (1150)	Chaumont, Pontoise, Poissy
Sées (1153)	Chapelle-la-Reine
Lorris (1155)	Molinet, Dixmont, Chambly, Bois-Commun
Soissons (1181)	Crépy, Vailly, Sens, Compiègne, Senlis, Villeneuve-St-Melon
Amiens (1190)	Doullens
St Quentin (1195)	Chauny, Roye
Péronne (1207)	Athies, Tournai, Fillièvre
Rouen (1207)	Poitiers

of London, provided that in cases of doubt they should send to London, and that the decision of Londoners on any point should be considered firm and valid'.[37] Bartlett has noted that there were three different levels in the 'degree of dependence between mother and daughter towns':

> Sometimes the new town was simply granted the customs of an existing town and there was no further connection. In other cases the affiliated town might turn to the mother town for a ruling when some point in the customs needed clarification [whilst] an even closer bond existed in town families such as Lübeck [see below], whose mother town heard judicial appeals from the courts of the daughter towns.[38]

In Germany, the town of Freiburg im Breisgau was chartered and established by Conrad of Zähringen and from the start its inhabitants were to have 'the law enjoyed by the merchants of Cologne'.[39] Like the borough charters of France and England, Conrad's charter specified that the inhabitants of Freiburg were to have a defined plot (each measuring 50 by 100 feet) for which they paid one *solidus* in rent every year; they were also granted freedom from tolls in the duke's dominions, free use of pastures, forests and the river, and the right to elect a chief magistrate (*advocatus*): Freiburg was in many senses a 'free town'.[40]

The use of affiliations in German charters is well attested, and 'many of the charters contain clauses conferring on the donees the customs and laws of other towns'.[41] One example is Brandenburg where the charter of 1315 contained a clause 'that all the cities in "our" dominions [i.e. the dominions of the Margrave of Brandenburg] should repair to Brandenburg and accept their laws and decisions'.[42] Other German towns also passed their laws on in charters, and by this means sometimes the customs and privileges of a town could travel over quite large distances. Two well-known examples in this respect are the towns of Magdeburg and Lübeck, whose laws and customs were spread across eastern Europe from the twelfth century onwards as lords used their liberties and customs as models for drawing up subsequent charters (see Chapter 4).

In considering Spanish town charters, Ballard focused in particular on two places, Teruel and Cuenca.[43] The latter was granted its *fuero* in 1190, and the former in 1176. The *fuero* 'was the written

expression of a town's juridical status and degree of autonomy'
and 'usually rendered the towns privileges ... and some of the
regulations relating to the practical administration of urban life'.[44]
As elsewhere in medieval Europe, not all inhabitants of towns were
burgesses. At the town of Sahagún, chartered by Alphonse VI, 'the
burgueses were favoured by fiscal, military and market privileges',
and a divide drawn between burgesses and 'mere inhabitants'
(*moradores*).[45] Spanish *fueros*, in particular that of Cuenca, were also
copied as models for drawing up liberties in charters for other
towns in Spain, as was the custom in other parts of Europe. For
example, Béjar, Plosencia, Sepélveda and Teruel all had privileges
that were related to the customs and laws of Cuenca.[46]

Despite the apparent number of similarities there is an important difference between the privileges agreed in Spanish charters
and those of France, England and Germany. This concerns the
absence of 'tenurial privileges and exemptions of burgesses from
the rights of the feudal lord';[47] indeed it has been said that the
twelfth-century municipalities of León and Castile, for example,
actually show most affinity with the political and constitutional
organisation of mercantile towns in northern Italy.[48] Nevertheless,
it is clear that urban privileges in medieval Europe shared certain
common characteristics, and that town charters provided a vehicle
for the diffusion of particular models of burgage tenure and borough
customs during the eleventh, twelfth and thirteenth centuries.

Municipal Government and Urban Governance

The development of urban institutions which governed the administration of medieval towns and cities is an important though
complex matter. In this second part of the chapter, the rise of
medieval municipal urban government will be considered. That
is, those towns and cities that received 'advanced liberties'. The
following discussion focuses on some common aspects of medieval
municipal government, and considers how certain urban centres
obtained increasingly sophisticated structures of political self-
organisation with the power to oversee not only trade and commerce,
but also judicial and military matters.

Firstly, I provide an outline of medieval municipal organisation,
pointing out how elections were organised; who occupied positions

of authority; and what the responsibilities of particular officers were. This means looking primarily at the larger towns and cities, since they were the places which developed sophisticated and ever increasingly independent local urban governments from a relatively early date (in some cases from the eleventh and twelfth centuries, but more commonly from the thirteenth and fourteenth, particularly in northern Europe). Secondly, I chart the constitutional evolution of four municipal urban governments. Two examples of towns are taken each from north and south Europe: Norwich (England) and Cologne (Germany), and Toulouse (France) and Florence (Italy). The purpose of this discussion is not only to highlight some parallels in the municipal development of these cities, particularly in terms of their corporate and civic institutions, but also to raise the historiographical differences that exist between historians' accounts of medieval municipal organisation and evolution.

Municipal organisation and self-government

The internal political organisation of self-governing towns is indicated by the vast quantity of written material created by the bureaucratic procedures of the towns themselves. Towns with charters allowing them some element of self-government came to be organised by appointed officials. These officials together constituted a corporate body, able to represent the interests of the urban community at large, yet to some varying extent answerable to them: but who was involved in this self-government; how were people chosen to represent others; why did lords give certain towns the ability to create their own laws and governments; and what stimulated political changes within the government structures of towns?

These are difficult questions to answer, yet during the twentieth century urban historians dedicated themselves to addressing such fundamental matters. Among them, Weinbaum, Petit Dutaillis and Ennen, have in particular searched contemporary records of towns in England, France and Germany to establish an idea of how municipalism grew in Europe during the Middle Ages.[49] In this context, Stephenson's approach, distinguishing towns with 'advanced liberties' on the basis of urban self-government, still provides a useful starting point.[50]

At the most fundamental level, those towns and cities that were self-governing took on the responsibility of administering local justice. Rather than leaving matters of law and order to the lord's own officials, justice in towns with advanced liberties was overseen by one or more magistrates who were nominated by representatives of a town's citizens or by the citizens themselves. Stephenson put it like this:

> In spite of minor variations, early municipal administrations tended to follow one simple plan . . . everywhere the chosen magistrates, through themselves or through appointees, administered justice; collected tolls; held charge of walls, gates, bridges and streets, and other public works; laid taxes; and saw to the payment of the lord's dues.[51]

Similarly and more recently, Hilton sees the ability 'to organise municipal finance, and to use the crucial instrument of power in feudal society, jurisdiction, over the town's inhabitants', as two defining functions of a self-governing urban community in English and French enfranchised towns (see above).[52]

The essence of self-government is to be found in town charters. In France, in the twelfth century, the 'grant of the Prévôté' commonly allowed urban communities 'the right of electing a prévôt' whose task was to 'collect rents and tolls and other dues, including fines and forfeitures'.[53] A charter of 1196 granted to Bapaume authorised 'the election of a mayor and échevins (scabini) and jurats' and stated that 'the échevins shall judge all quarrels arising within the precincts of the town of Bapaume except those which related to the king's bailiffs and the men of his household'.[54] At St Omer in 1100, a charter gave the town's citizens the right to 'have their own board of échivins', 'a commission to govern the town combining in their hands all political functions – judicial, financial and executive'.[55]

In the south of France, too, in the Midi, towns such as Montauban (see above) 'secured not only fundamental liberties . . . but also autonomous administration under elected consuls – magistrates exactly corresponding to the échevins and jurés of the north'.[56] These échevins and jurats in French towns usually stood in judgement in tribunals: hence 'many of the communal charters speak of bodies of men, known sometimes as échevins and sometimes as jurats, who were magistrates of the town and sentenced offenders and assessed damages'.[57]

Electing a town council

Although magistrates in municipalities went by different names, in essence their task was the same: to exercise justice over fellow townspeople and to take responsibility for organising a town's economic and political affairs. But *who* were the magistrates, and *who* chose them? This varied from town to town, as did the process of selection.

Sometimes, those already in office had the privilege of selecting new members. For example, at Arras, 'the twelve outgoing échevins elected four men and co-opted twenty others; of these twenty-four, twelve were the échevins for the following year, and the other twelve were entrusted with the administration of the town' for a term of office lasting 14 months.[58] Otherwise, it might be that a list of names was drawn up, and a selection made from it. This was the case at Rouen in the twelfth century, where the well-known *Établissements* record how the king made the final choice in selecting a mayor, a process which subsequently formed the basis of electing civic officials in other towns in France, from Poitou to Normandy.[59] In English monastic boroughs, too, 'the chief municipal magistrate [usually called the mayor but sometimes known as reeve or alderman] was rarely elected independently of the abbot and convent', but rather 'chosen by the abbot or prior from three candidates presented by the burgesses'.[60]

The mayor was, primarily, the chief magistrate, but the mayor's main function was to act as the head of a municipal government and its citizens. He was the virtual leader of a self-governing town. The title of 'mayor' was not always used in charters however. In 1120 at Freiburg im Breisgau the chief magistrate was termed *advocatus*, and was accompanied by a council of 24 *conjuratores*, the terms of the town's constitution having been derived largely from Cologne.[61]

The municipal bodies of chartered towns were often formed of 12 or 24 men. In Pisa in 1164 a council was formed by including 6 men from each of the city's quarters giving a total of 24; while at Toulouse in 1175–76, 12 chaptermen, otherwise known as judges or consuls, formed a council to 'define in order of judgement matters of common interest to the City and Suburb brought before them'.[62] Often there were 'inner' and 'outer' councils too, the latter being composed of a greater number of members than the former. At Norwich, in 1404, the Mayor's Council initially consisted of 24 citizens, but these came to be supplemented by a 'Common Council of 60 citizens annually elected to attend assemblies'.[63]

The arrangement at Norwich was reasonably commonplace in some Italian towns as well, albeit on a different scale. From the twelfth century onwards, there were some 'great councils' consisting of as many as 4000 men, though round numbers of between 200 and 1000 were more frequent.[64] Inner councils usually consisted of 'higher status' citizens, were often oligarchical in nature, and relatively small in size. At whatever level, all town councils were select bodies and throughout medieval Europe they were the typical constitutional basis of urban self-government.

The practice of electing officials to serve on inner and outer councils was clearly complex and varied. In the case of late-thirteenth-century Florence, for example, as many as 24 methods of electing 'priors' were considered by the guilds in 1292. In essence, however, three basic principles of election can be identified: 'one is indirect election, that is, the system whereby election takes place in two distinct phases, the first election determining the personnel of the electors who make a final choice. Another is election by the outgoing councillors or officials at the end of their term of service. The third is election by lot or "sortition".'[65]

The process of electing officials to form an English borough council is neatly contained in a royal charter for Ipswich. The charter, issued on 29 June 1200, permitted the election of reeves and coroners, and records how

the whole borough assembled in the churchyard of St Mary at the Tower and unanimously chose two good and lawful men . . . who were thereupon sworn as bailiffs. . . . In the same way they elected and installed four coroners. . . . Likewise on the same day it was ordained by the common council of the town . . . that there should be in the borough twelve sworn chief portmen . . . to govern and maintain the borough and all its liberties . . . and it was announced by the magistrates that for this purpose the whole town should reassemble in the churchyard on the next Sunday. . . . At the appointed time . . . by the consent of the town, the four bailiffs and coroners chose four good and lawful men from each parish. . . . The twelve thus selected were the four magistrates and eight others. . . .[66]

The Ipswich charter touches on a number of features common to the organisation of other medieval municipal bodies. In the appointment of individuals it was usual for contemporaries to use the phrase 'good and lawful men' or 'proud men' (*prud'hommes*), and the practice of choosing 'proud men' to represent individual parishes or administrative units was a common means of forming a town council (see below). The use of an open assembly of burgesses at a particular place and time is also to be found elsewhere in medieval Europe. In Italy, before the formation of 'great councils' became commonplace in the larger towns, assemblies included all of a town's citizens in order to decide on important matters such as the election of consuls.[67]

Although the term 'men' was used collectively to describe citizens and burgesses (whether or not there were female burgesses present), not all a town's inhabitants were part of the burgess community, and most borough franchises excluded 'virtually all women from the privileges of collective decision-making'.[68] 'Burgesses' and 'citizens' were sworn members of the urban community and election to serve on a council frequently depended on a person's citizenship. The town council could decide upon a person's citizenship; at Norwich in the thirteenth century the City Assembly admitted 'foreigners' to the 'freedom' of the city, and at Parma the General Council would admit a 'stranger' as a citizen providing they built a house worth 100 *libra* and swore an oath.[69]

There are thus a number of common aspects to medieval urban self-government. Despite differences in the titles of officials or in the methods of elections, there are enough similarities to indicate that in the Middle Ages European towns and cities with advanced liberties followed a more or less common set of formulae in drawing up municipal structures and organising civic affairs. Sometimes mutual aspects of government were explicitly stated in their charters, as it was in the case of Freiburg im Breisgau in 1120, which had a charter that took the customs of Cologne as a benchmark, or in the cases of those French and Norman towns that borrowed upon the *Établissements* of Rouen in the twelfth century (see above).

The formation of four medieval municipalities

To see parallels in the development of municipal government more clearly, and to reveal more of the similarities that existed between civic positions and duties, the following final part of the chapter follows through the evolution of selected urban governments from north and south Europe. The differences are not so great as some historians would like us to believe, and as Reynolds pertinently pointed out, those great city administrations of medieval Italy, with their advanced systems of municipal government, were in many ways quite similar, in principle at least, to those that were used in towns and cities in the 'foggy north', as she puts it.[70] To examine this I shall now consider, in turn, the development of urban government in two northern cities (Norwich and Cologne), and two from the south (Toulouse and Florence).

1. The case of Norwich

The early urban origins of Norwich are obscure, though it has been suggested 'that Norwich owed its legal status as a borough to Edward the Elder, after his subjugation of the East Anglian Danes in about 917'.[71] Alongside this English borough the Normans added a new one in the 1070s. No doubt there was a self-governing urban community in Norwich at this time: just 'because English towns did not have charters of liberties before the Norman Conquest it does not mean that their inhabitants did not have any autonomy, did not promote their collective interests and did not bargain with the government'.[72] Its just that without a charter it is difficult to work out how Norwich was governed during and before the eleventh century.

The development of urban government in Norwich starts to become clearer during the twelfth and thirteenth centuries thanks to a series of charters specifying the liberties and customs of the borough. In a charter granted to Norwich by Richard I in 1194 'the citizens obtained a grant of the city at fee farm [i.e. fixed] rent of £108'.[73] In addition to this move towards greater financial autonomy, the men of Norwich were also 'granted the right of choosing their own reeve and retaining the tolls, rents, fees, fines of court, and other profits of city business'.[74] Of course, as Campbell notes, 'some of these advantages may already have been enjoyed *de facto*'.[75] Subsequently, in 1223, the appointment of a single reeve was substituted by four bailiffs, each of whom was elected by 'the freemen of the four leets'.[76] The four leets were separate administrative areas covering the city, and each bailiff represented one leet. The duty of the bailiff was to preside over the courts held within each leet, but in addition they collectively heard pleas presented at the city court and presided over the city assembly, thus ensuring that the fee farm was collected and paid to the king.

The situation of 1223 remained largely unchanged in Norwich for nearly 200 years. The municipal government was organised around the city assembly, which all 'admitted' citizens could attend ('foreigners' were not allowed in), though in practice certain leading citizens no doubt controlled what went on. The assembly's tasks included raising levies, appointing committees, and sending representatives to Parliament. During the fourteenth century the four bailiffs at the head of the city's government came to be supported by an elected 'council' of '24 citizens'. These were bound to attend the assemblies (but not to the exclusion of other citizens), and by 1378 became known as the Council of the Bailiffs. In 1404, this system of municipal government changed under a charter issued by Henry IV. His charter permitted the election of a mayor, supported by two sheriffs, who replaced the four bailiffs. In addition, the Council of the Bailiffs became the 'Mayor's Council'. Those appointed to sit on this council were soon to be termed 'aldermen' and were elected for life, while a Common Council was formed beneath it comprising 60 annually elected citizens who sat on their council to the exclusion of others.[77]

The 1404 charter also made the city of Norwich into a county in its own right. Its 'incorporation' followed a formula that was becoming widespread in England during the fifteenth century. The idea behind it was that 'the process of incorporation unites and emphasises all the tendencies contained in the mass of rights and privileges usurped or granted in the heyday of charter giving and building of new towns'.[78] In England, the first city to be incorporated was Coventry, in 1345, while others were soon to follow suit. It was only the larger, incorporated cities that received independent county status, as Bristol did in 1373.[79]

In the case of Norwich what we see is the structure of municipal government remaining largely unchanged for long periods, and that when changes do take place they mainly affect the process by which the municipal officers were selected rather than the overall hierarchy of the city's government: in other words, although the formal expression of power changed between 1223 and 1404, in effect the power base of municipal government in Norwich remained largely unchallenged. With incorporation in 1404, the previous institutions that made up Norwich's urban government were regularised, 'as if a common roof had been found for a massive and irregular building'.[80]

It is also evident that any major changes in the constitution of the city's government were by and large ratified by royal charter, although it is important to bear in mind that the point behind having self-government was that it allowed the municipal body itself to decide how to manage its own affairs, and so precipitate change. For example, in Norwich the late fourteenth century saw the rise of a religious guild called St George's Gild. The guild became closely entwined with the city corporation, especially after 1452 when an agreement settling disputes between the citizens and elected officials was made in which the guild was united with the municipal corporation.[81] This same pattern of changes can to some extent be matched with the case of Cologne.

2. The case of Cologne

At Cologne the development of urban institutions in the twelfth and thirteenth centuries initially allowed for greater citizen participation in government and justice. Subsequently, this came to be replaced by more exclusionary and oligarchical forms of government. Unlike Norwich, however, the development of Cologne's municipal government did not proceed by means of formal charters. This makes it rather more difficult to piece together the municipal development of the city, though it is possible to identify four stages in the development of the city's government.

Initially, officials of the Archbishop of Cologne acted in the interests of their lord on legal and financial matters but by the early twelfth century there is evidence of a sworn association of citizens (a 'commune'), accompanied by guilds of parish masters whose authority was separate from the archbishop's. By the later twelfth century an exclusive political organisation, the *Richerzeche*, based on an emerging urban patriciate, seems to have taken responsibility for the city's administration, though 'by the following century a full-fledged urban constitution, with a chief *Burgermeister* and a council, had come into existence'.[82] It is worth looking in a little more detail at these changes.

According to Strait one of the main reasons why urban institutions developed in Cologne in the twelfth century was the archbishop's relative neglect of the city.[83] This neglect allowed 'competing bodies' to form and take responsibility for administering justice and regulating trade. The guilds, *Richerzeche* and town council each had an influence on the government of Cologne, but remained relatively independent from each other throughout the twelfth century.

Before 1100 the archbishop's administration of Cologne was overseen by two important officials, the *Burggraf*, who was a vassal of the archbishop, usually a rural noble, and whose task was principally to oversee criminal justice in the city, and the *Stadtvogt* (*advocatus*) who took care of civil justice and lesser cases in a lower court.[84] By the end of the century 'whether by choice or persuasion, the major judges, the *Burggraf* and *Stadtvogt*, were increasingly excluded from urban affairs', though their offices continued to exist.[85]

Supporting the archbishop's officials were the *scabini*. They initially helped in court sessions but gradually assumed roles of greater importance in Cologne's government such that by 1149 they were involved with regulating craft guilds, held meetings in the city hall and held the city seal.[86] The *scabini* are first mentioned in 1103 as the major judges delegated duties, and it seems that although the *scabini* were installed by the *Burggraf* they controlled the elections.[87] The *scabini* found a role in aspects of urban administration including the parish guilds and *Richerzeche*, and in 1218 were mentioned as leaders of the urban community.[88] What we see here is a change in those who became *scabini*, from archbishop's servants to leading burgesses.

The shift away from direct intervention in urban affairs by the archbishop took place in the early 1100s following a civil uprising against him initiated by Cologne's richer merchants (referred to as *primores*).[89] By 1106 there is evidence for 'some sort of community organisation with a degree of autonomy', as Henry IV, King of Germany at this time, asked the citizens to fortify their city for him, an act which it has been argued 'required common government'.[90] Subsequently, in 1112, we hear of a *conjuratio* at Cologne, a sworn association between citizens, and this seems to have involved those citizens who were propertied.[91] However, as Petit Dutaillis has shown, a sworn association was not a prerequisite for the formation of municipal government but rather 'the act of granting a commune to the burgesses of a town implied the permission . . . to form an association to bind themselves together on oath' (which is why, he says, 'the charter granting the commune so rarely sets out the workings of municipal institutions').[92]

At Cologne there is no surviving charter to reveal who or why the *conjuratio* was established, but the motives may have been similar to those behind the creation of a commune in Chateauneuf in France in the 1180s where 'a small bourgeois oligarchy insisted on forming a commune as a sure means of resisting an ecclesiastical lordship and of imposing its selfish wishes on the inhabitants as a whole'.[93] The *conjuratio* of Cologne is not mentioned again after 1112, but instead three urban institutions emerge and developed alongside each other; the parish guilds, the *Richerzeche* and the college of *scabini*. These did not form a 'unified administration, but a group of competing bodies, each with its jealously guarded privileges', which after the early twelfth century appear to have developed relatively peaceably without interference either from the archbishop or his officials.[94]

Cologne, like Norwich, was divided into separate administrative units. Each of these units, termed 'parishes', had a magistrate, or master, to oversee judicial matters, and although their activities related to particular parishes together the magistrates were an important group who were able to represent the citizens' interests.[95] There were 12 parishes and normally two masters served in each parish for a given period of time, probably a year, but after they left office they were still considered masters.

The magistrates formed a guild of parish masters and in 1150 the election of masters relied on the parish citizens and serving masters to decide and select a candidate.[96] At the same time and at the level of the city as a whole the 'college' of *scabini* was also in a position of some strength and like the parish masters they had formed a guild by the middle of the twelfth century. Twenty-two *scabini* are mentioned in 1178 and by 1235 the *scabini* had control over the election of their brothers.[97] By 1150, because the *scabini* met in the city hall and helped to establish a code of regulations for weavers, Strait pictures them as 'urban leaders' acting jointly 'as judicial officials in the archbishop's palace'.[98] The *scabini* were involved with the *Richerzeche*, which also regulated craft guilds by the end of the twelfth century and was formed of the city's richer merchants. This exclusive organisation developed as a powerful guild in its own right during the thirteenth century with a privileged membership of Cologne's patriciate that excluded 'common citizens'.[99] By 1258, in the so-called Great Arbitration, the Archbishop of Cologne conceded that 'the *Richerzeche* was a legitimate institution and had the right to elect the *Bürgermeister* because it was established by time-honoured custom'.[100]

Clearly the development of urban institutions at Cologne during the twelfth and thirteenth centuries is complex, and in certain ways quite different from the formation of municipal government in Norwich in the same period. No (extant) charters formalised the creation of Cologne's urban government, rather there is evidence for a collection of civic bodies that each represented the interests of certain groups of citizens in different and sometimes competing ways. However, despite this, there are some similarities to be observed between the two cities, particularly in the way that the administrative geography of Cologne, like Norwich, was divided into small units, each having its own jurisdictional privileges, while at the same time acting collectively, on behalf of all the citizens living within the city's 12 parishes.

3. The case of Toulouse

At Toulouse the development of urban institutions is rather more clear-cut than it is for Cologne, but there are some important similarities, particularly with regard to the role of a local patriciate in the formation of an urban government. Here I shall review the formation of urban institutions in Toulouse for the twelfth and thirteenth centuries, drawing on Mundy's work.[101] It seems that there were two significant shifts of political power in Toulouse: firstly, towards the end of the twelfth century, when the role of the Counts of Toulouse in urban affairs was diminished and replaced by an urban aristocracy; and secondly, in the early thirteenth century, when 'for a brief time . . . it passed into the hands of the many, the *universitas* of Toulouse'.[102]

Following the restoration of Count Alphonse-Jourdain in 1119 the two parts of Toulouse, the *Bourg* and the *Cité*, 'constituted a *de facto* association under the count', and the representatives of this association, the so-called Good Men, proceeded to perform public duties'.[103] Although the citizens of Toulouse were under the lordship of the count, it seems that he was advised by the Good Men who themselves formed the count's court in the town. By 1158 the

Good Men had judicial, executive and military powers within Toulouse and in 1152 'a formal assembly of representative Good Men from the community had been formed . . . called the Common Council of the City and the Bourg'.[104]

The Common Council was not part of the count's own administration yet it was subordinate to him. The count's interests were represented by an executive council or board of the Common Council made up of 'chaptermen' consisting of 12 notables chosen not by the count but elected for comital approval by the Common Council.[105] Here we can see a parallel with the role of the *scabini* in twelfth-century Cologne, who initially were at one and the same time able to function both as officials of the archbishop and the city. From the 1170s the chaptermen of Toulouse became known as 'consuls' and formed a consulate. The 12 consuls were allowed to judge in matters of interest to the Cité and Bourg by the consent of the Common Council and the Good Men.

In 1189 the town rose against the count giving more political strength to the consulate in matters of jurisdiction, though by this time the consulate was essentially oligarchical in nature and 'the Common Council became a relatively small and aristocratic council of the consuls'.[106] In *c*.1202 a consulate election changed its social composition. Mundy calls this a 'landslide' victory for a 'popular party', but really the change was not the result of a unified political struggle between two clearly defined parties but rather a gradual assimilation of merchants into an organisation that had previously been principally composed of landholding families, a patriciate.[107]

In the latter part of the twelfth century the consuls were able to legislate on a variety of economic matters, such as setting weights and measures, as well as social concerns, such as the expulsion of prostitutes; fines levied by the consuls went to help with the maintenance of the city's fortifications, which like the roads and bridges also fell within their jurisdiction.[108] Although the consulate was momentarily suppressed by Simon de Montfort in 1216 it was soon re-established after he was deposed in 1217, and soon afterwards 'a consular ordinance of 1222 . . . issued with the express consent of the Common Council and the count . . . proposed that consuls and *comunarii* [finance and taxation officers] were to be elected from among the Good Men' and it was 'further ordered that no elector could choose either as consul or treasurer any relative or dependent'.[109] The Good Men in this context included artisans and traders, and although the 'retiring consuls elected or nominated the succeeding consulate' it seems that, 'as in many other towns, the basic electorate was probably the *universitas* meeting in the general assembly'.[110]

As Mundy points out, the consulates of the 1220s were not only elected by men of different social positions but the consulate itself could also occasionally be composed of 'quite humble men'.[111] By 1226 the city had a common seal and also in this period the Common Council had been replaced by a larger Common and General Council, described as 'Many Good Men' or 'Many Wise Men' by contemporaries, which was summoned by the sound of a trumpet or cry.[112] By the 1230s, then, Toulouse was governed by a municipal organisation elected by or on behalf of the town's citizens, that is those inhabitants who were paying taxes to the municipality and who obeyed the city's laws and customs.

All in all, the evolution of urban government in Toulouse follows a somewhat familiar pattern in which successive yet closely related civic bodies were able to determine not only their own internal political organisation but also rights of external jurisdiction. In the case of Toulouse these bodies encompassed the whole town, both the Cité and Bourg.

The consulate, despite its clear political solidarity towards the end of the twelfth century, was in fact a constantly changing institution which actually lacked a formal constitutional document that set out its rights. As a result, although in 1180 the number of chaptermen was doubled to make a college of 24, six years later Count Raimond V was able to reduce the college to the earlier number of 12.[113] The chaptermen represented the two parts of Toulouse. In 1175–76 the 'twelve chaptermen were explicitly described as six of the City and six of the Bourg' and 'were characterised as constituted and charged under oath "diligently to hear and faithfully to watch over, deal with, and define in order of judgement, matters of common interest to the City [Cité] and Suburb [Bourg]"'.[114]

Although these chaptermen (or consuls) were initially concerned with watching the activities of the Common Council, they gradually involved *themselves* in the council's affairs. In this respect there is a common pattern to the development of medieval urban councils. It seems that as councils change in terms of their social composition

and political agenda, and as they develop greater degrees of autonomy and narrower, oligarchical structures, new, larger and more
general town councils are created either to sit beneath them or in
place of them. We see this at both Norwich and at Toulouse. The
council of 24 citizens at Norwich became an elite Mayor's Council
in 1404 only to be subsequently supplemented by a new council
comprising 60 citizens, whereas at Toulouse in the 1220s the smaller
and politically select Common Council was replaced by a more
encompassing and larger General and Common Council.

4. The case of Florence

Finally, let us turn to the case of Florence, a 'city republic' whose
urban government changed dramatically over the course of four
centuries. Here, the focus is on the municipal governments of the
thirteenth and early fourteenth centuries, admirably discussed by
Najemy and Lansing, largely because it is in this period that interesting developments take place in the organisation and election
of successive civic institutions.[115] Florence at this time had a complex social structure and economy which continually made it difficult
to strike a balance between opposing class factions. As a consequence the municipal organisation of Florence was especially
contentious and highly sophisticated.

As at Cologne, before 1200 in Florence 'formal political
organisation had begun in voluntary associations of leading townsmen, private and strictly limited in powers'.[116] These private
associations gained power with the collapse of episcopal jurisdiction but only gradually did they assume public duties. For example,
there were neighbourhood associations based on parishes, each
with judicial and fiscal responsibilities, which Lansing suggests
may have joined together to create a basis for Florentine urban
government.[117] There were also consular officers and these formed
another important commercial and judicial authority, particularly
in disputes between neighbourhoods.

By the middle of the twelfth century the consuls 'answered to a
general assembly of about 150 men, and to the popular assembly
or *arringum*, which met in the cathedral and presumably voted by
acclamation [an oral vote]'.[118] However, the consular system was
weak because 'in practice, most consular offices were held by members of a small group of patrician families', and because early

Florentine 'civic government was based on a fragile balance between ruling families . . . when that balance tipped it was unable
to maintain order'.[119]

One of the most celebrated aspects of Florentine medieval municipal government is the creation of the *podestá*. In common with
other Italian cities, in 1200 a salaried executive officer was appointed by the council in Florence. The *podestá* was made accountable
for expenditure at the end of his term (which lasted for a year),
and by being impartial and neutral was intended to prevent any
one class faction gaining power so that, 'in effect, the *podestá* resembled a hired city manager'.[120] After 1207, the *podestá* could not
be a citizen of Florence but had to be a 'foreigner'. In juridical
matters, such as a pact sworn in 1204, he was joined by 'consuls of
the commune, consuls of the merchants, priors of the guilds, and
the general council of Florence', all of whom 'assembled at the
sound of the bell'.[121] According to Waley, though 'it was the very
essence of the *podestá*'s standing that he was an official, an executive administrator, above all the head of the judiciary, he was not a
ruler, but rather stood for the rule of law'.[122]

With the economic development of the city during this period,
'popular associations' were formed and in 1250, at the end of
imperial control of Florence, the first popular regime, the Primo
Popolo, was established by the 'society of the people', the *societas
populi*.[123] This group had developed to represent those citizens who
were merchants in the city, whose interests were in opposition to
the patrician families or 'magnates' that had dominated Florentine
urban government for the last century.

The Primo Popolo lasted for ten years in which time for the
most part the original structure of Florentine urban government
was left more or less intact. It was led by the *capitano del popolo* who
was advised by two councils. One of the councils represented the
greater guilds while the other represented the *sesti*. These were
quarters of the city that had been reorganised by the Primo Popolo
to form the basis of new neighbourhood companies, called *gonfaloni*,
whose primary task was to maintain peace within the city.[124] As a
political organisation, the Popolo of Italian cities such as Florence
was formed 'with two different but related aims; the general one
of seeking to counterbalance the social weight of the powerful
and lawless, and the more specific one of achieving for the *popolani*
a considerable constitutional role in the commune'.[125]

In Florence, the Primo Popolo may have started as an organisation to protect mercantile interests in the city but it ended up creating new powerful families itself. In its ten years in office, the Primo Popolo was responsible for moving the city's government into a purpose-built civic palace and also saw to the abolition of the *societas militum*.[126] In the years that followed a series of different urban governments ruled in Florence. During this latter part of the thirteenth century, 'from the Primo Popolo of 1250–1260 to the Ghibelline government of 1260–66, the popular revival of 1266–7, the Angevin protectorate of 1267–80, and finally to the papally sponsored government of the Fourteen [*Quattordici*] in 1280–2, no Florentine regime had succeeded in sinking firm institutional roots into the shifting sand of communal politics' in the city.[127]

In 1280, following conflict between two local aristocratic factions, the Guelfs and the Ghibellines, Cardinal Latino Malabranca, legate of Pope Nicholas III, installed a new government in Florence, the *Quattordici*, made up of eight Guelfs and six Ghibellines. The latter group had ruled in Florence (for six years until 1266) and during that time they imposed restrictions on Guelfs, but Cardinal Latino's plan relied on using Florence's powerful guilds 'to serve as formal guarantors of the reconciliation and as defenders of the new constitution'.[128] This put the guilds, each of which had its own system of election and representation (headed by a consul), in a strong position, and over the following half-century the major guilds of Florence played an important role in determining the organisation of the city's government.

The guilds represented the interests of both elite and non-elite families, the difference being, according to Najemy, that one 'tended to see themselves, despite their guild affiliations, as a class apart, united by business, patronage and family ties that transcended their association with the various guilds'; while for the latter, 'the guilds were primarily professional and occupational associations' and were seen to constitute 'a sovereign federation . . . with each guild free to elect its own representatives to governmental committees' at the communal level.[129] The difference between the two views concerned 'the constitutional role of the individual guilds in the electoral process' and hinged on whether communal society was seen as being 'the sum of autonomous parts' (a 'corporation') or 'an organic harmonious whole' (a 'family').[130]

By 1282, the *Quattordici* was losing its potency as an institution but the office of the priorate (*priores artium*), which was also created at this time, continued to act as 'the pivotal magistracy of the republic for the next two centuries', though the processes and basis by which this position was held were constantly debated between the two groups, between those who advanced 'corporate' and 'consensus' ideas of electoral politics.[131] In 1293 the Ordinances of Justice attempted to define the election of the priorate and ensured that 'magnates were excluded from most civic offices, including the councils of the commune, the leadership of the guilds, and then from the priorate itself'.[132] However, the patriciate of Florence, the elite magnate families, cut across corporate guild lines, and in the following century a long political conflict ensued, 'between the corporate approach to political organisation advanced by the Florentine guild community and the consensus-based approach developed by the oligarchy'.[133]

In all, the complex development of municipal government in Florence demonstrates very clearly the difficulties that faced urban institutions in the Middle Ages, particularly over such matters as who should participate and influence urban politics. This dilemma was precipitated in the later thirteenth century as external influences in urban governance diminished and internal struggles among those groups, whether patriciate or not, became increasingly vocal. This state of political flux and conflict continued into the fifteenth century. By this time, 'the Florentine upper classes had succeeded in working out a clear vision of the nature of communal government and its ruling class, a vision reflected and refined in the optimistic pronouncements of civic humanism'.[134]

The municipalities compared

What can be learned by setting the development of urban institutions in Norwich, Cologne, Toulouse and Florence side by side? At a fundamental level certain common patterns are evident, particularly in the twelfth century with the rise of private associations, especially guilds, and their ability to make inroads into matters of urban government by adopting public functions and representing local citizens. One aspect of this, which seems to have been common, is the use of small administrative units, whether they be parishes, leets or quarters, to structure and organise local urban government. The diminishing role of external authorities, such as episcopal and ecclesiastical lords, is also marked, but whether this was caused by the rising powers of municipal authority is difficult to determine. It may be that a demise in lords' external intervention in urban affairs was a cause of greater local municipal autonomy. What is also difficult to establish, in all cases, is the constantly shifting balance of power between the urban community at large and a small but powerful merchant oligarchy. All the same, the four cities considered above developed quite different municipal governments, at differing rates of change, sometimes sanctioned and condoned by outside authorities, sometimes not.

The four case studies presented here also raise another problem. This is to do with how municipal histories are written, for interpretations will differ between historians. Since so few European medieval municipal histories are available in English this problem becomes an acute one, and needs to be taken into consideration. To summarise four municipal histories is a risky venture in itself, and is all the more so when it becomes necessary to rely on only one or two historians' work. I would thus urge any diligent student to look at the case studies in more detail, for it is the detail of municipal development that reveals so much about the individuals and officials who were involved in governing cities in the Middle Ages. Although some general comparative observations can be made, particularly with regard to the processes of election and municipal organisation, the evolution of medieval urban governments requires careful and considered study.

Conclusion

The institutional nature of medieval urbanism presents a somewhat difficult and complex picture. Yet, it was through an elaborate, interwoven fabric of laws, customs and privileges that medieval urban life was structured. The evidence for this is to be found in constitutional documents that emerged more particularly during the twelfth and thirteenth centuries throughout Europe 'as a manifestation of the striking development of government control and above all of record-keeping at the time'.[135] Often dry and formulaic in nature, these documents reveal many common elements in the privileges that distinguished and defined those enfranchised towns which they termed *burgi*, boroughs. Though not all towns were boroughs, and not all boroughs were towns, the fundamental organisation of medieval urbanism came to depend upon these legal structures. However, it is important to remember that in the Middle Ages self-government could exist in towns which were not boroughs, and that self-regulation in urban communities might occur well before charters were negotiated between the townspeople and their overlords.

Through from the twelfth century onwards, the development of 'advanced liberties' can be traced in towns across medieval Europe. Some of these were the wealthiest of Europe's cities, but not all. Having self-government was no guarantee of commercial success. To understand the significance of chartering towns it is necessary to move from looking at the customs and liberties enshrined in the charters themselves, and instead consider some of the political and economic motives for institutionalising urbanism.

3

GEOGRAPHIES OF URBAN LAW

Englishmen and Frenchmen, having a more civilised way of life, dwell in cities and are familiar with trade and commerce.

William of Malmesbury, *c.*1125

The lands and tenements within the borough [of Shrewsbury] shall be dealt with according to the law of Breteuil and the law of the barony and the law of the Englishry.

Shrewsbury borough charter, 1205[2]

The previous chapter introduced the legal frameworks that structured urban life in the Middle Ages. The purpose of this chapter is to show how urban laws and privileges enabled ruling lords to extend their control of land and people across often large and scattered territories. The political motives that lay behind chartering towns were closely linked with a dual process of urbanisation and colonisation, especially in territories acquired by those lords who were busily seeking to expand the compass of their dominions during the later Middle Ages. This may be seen in the way that urban laws were used by lords to extend their power, particularly across the 'peripheral' regions of Europe during the twelfth and thirteenth centuries.

The idea that urban laws helped medieval lords to colonise parts of Europe is not new. In his book, the *Making of Europe*, Bartlett notes that

The town, as envisaged in innumerable borough charters, *Stadterechte* and *fueros*, was a picture, a set of norms that could be adapted to, rather than swamped by, local situations . . . hence, German law formed the model for towns far into eastern Europe, Norman customs could be transplanted to Wales, and the *fueros* of Christian Spain could be introduced into the towns of the Reconquest.[3]

As colonising feudal lords redefined the frontiers of their territories, they needed a method of ensuring political stability. One way in which lords tried to achieve such stability was to attract people to settle in chartered towns; towns enfranchised by lords using urban laws that they themselves were familiar with. In this respect, the urban privileges discussed in the previous chapter should be seen in the context of a politically motivated project, driven by ambitious lords whose aim was to settle and colonise the physical and cultural frontiers of Christian Europe.

'Families' of urban law

In his discussion of how urban privileges were duplicated and copied from one town charter to another, Bartlett uses the phrase 'families of urban law'.[4] It is a useful concept, for it reinforces the point that urban laws were passed from 'mother' towns to (usually more distant) 'daughter' settlements. Mother–daughter relationships between chartered towns have long been recognised by urban historians.[5]

In the early 1900s, Mary Bateson first explicitly demonstrated the presence of 'mother–daughter' relationships between medieval chartered towns. Her particular interest lay in the widespread use of the urban law of Breteuil by Norman lords in England, Wales and Ireland. She recognised, as Stephenson later put it, that during the twelfth and thirteenth centuries the laws of Breteuil 'became also the laws of Hereford, Shrewsbury, Rhuddlan, Bideford, Haverfordwest and a host of similar foundations'. By studying the content of borough charters, and comparing urban privileges with one another, it became clear to Bateson that the borough customs and laws of particular towns bore 'a strong family resemblance'.[6] Bateson also made the important point that the laws of Breteuil served the needs of Norman lords in what she saw as their desire for 'burghal colonisation'.[7]

Although Bateson's ideas on families of urban law have since been developed by a number of urban historians, her interest in the spatial spread of the laws, and their connection with the process of settlement and colonisation, has been rather neglected. For this reason, this chapter looks at how chartering towns helped lords not only to colonise land but also to legitimise their possession of it. To examine how this was so, the following two sections consider aspects of what I term the 'geographies of urban law'. First, the supervisory qualities of urban laws are exposed, particularly the way in which urban laws put into place an institutional framework, or 'spatial network', that conveyed the external power of the town's lord to his local townspeople (while also maintaining surveillance over them). Second, I consider how urban laws were used by lords to divide and segregate spatially the populations of medieval towns, particularly those towns situated on lands newly acquired by colonising lords, and located in frontier territories. Urban laws enabled lords to make indigenous groups of townspeople more marginal, thereby reinforcing the dominant position of newcomers from outside the town who were more likely to be sympathetic to the interests of the colonising lord. The two geographies of urban law are each explored in the following two sections of this chapter.

Surveillance and the Spatial Diffusion of Urban Laws

Urban laws provided medieval lords with a means of 'watching over' the activities of townspeople without having to be personally present in the town. In this sense, surveillance using urban laws was 'indirect'. Clearly, such a device was going to be advantageous to lords, especially where they had estates scattered over large areas and could not be present everywhere at once. By using urban laws to institute codes and customs, and thus formalise a system of political organisation, the activities of people within towns were kept in check; lords could keep an eye on what burgesses were doing, and remind them of his ultimate authority.

To examine how urban laws were used as a form of indirect surveillance, the following discussion focuses on the geopolitical dimensions of the spread of urban laws, looking particularly at how they were used in the colonisation of two regions of medieval Europe. The first example to be considered here is the Norman colonisation of Britain and Ireland, and the spatial spread of the

urban law of Breteuil following the Norman conquest of England
in 1066. The second example is concerned with how the diffusion
of two German urban laws went hand in hand with German
colonisation of lands in east-central Europe during the twelfth and
thirteenth centuries.

The law of Breteuil and Norman colonisation in Britain and Ireland

Bateson recognised that, right from the start, the Normans knew
their urban laws had the potential to help them colonise newly
acquired lands in western parts of Britain, particularly in areas
that were hostile to them, such as south-west England and Wales.
She wrote,

> Not the *castellum* [castle] only, but the *bourg* [borough]; not gar-
> rison colonies only, but colonies of chapmen, garrison and market
> towns, were the Norman instruments to quell and to civilise the
> troubled or thinly-occupied regions.[8]

Those 'troubled' and 'thinly-occupied regions' were the parts of
the new Norman kingdom that William the Conqueror and his
successors were busily trying to subjugate and colonise in the first
century after the Battle of Hastings.

Although there were already towns and markets in Wales and
Ireland before the arrival of Norman and English lords, as far as
the Anglo-Norman aristocracy was concerned neither Wales or Ireland were seen to be properly 'urban'.[9] An indication of this attitude
is provided by the celebrated Norman historian, William of
Malmesbury, whose comment that the English and French were
more civilised than the Irish stemmed from the fact that Ireland
lacked chartered towns with laws and customs set out in borough
charters. Before the arrival of the Normans and the English both
Wales and Ireland did lack certain institutional forms of urbanism, though neither was lacking in urban life. Like Bateson, the
Normans saw urbanism in a particular way: for them it was something that relied on institutionalised and legalised urban life.

To assert their control over newly acquired territories in Wales
and Ireland, the Norman and English aristocratic lords employed
a strategy of using urban laws that they were familiar with. In doing so they put into place a web of new alien urban laws, customs

and codes, which not only legitimised their authority but also aided them in the process of colonisation itself. Even where there were already well-established towns, as was the case in Ireland, these colonising lords brought with them their own urban laws and customs, issuing charters to their own advantage. One Norman lord who settled and colonised parts of Wales in the late eleventh century, and who used urban laws that were familiar to him, was William fitz Osbern, cousin of William the Conqueror.

Norman lords and frontier colonisation

Shortly after the Norman Conquest, William fitz Osbern was granted lands along the disputed and contested border between England and Wales. The title Earl of Hereford was conferred on him by the king, and the castle and town of Hereford became the seat of his earldom. The town had been established long before the Norman Conquest in the early ninth century, as part of a defensive system of *burhs* set up by the Anglo-Saxons along the Welsh border.[10] In effect, the Normans were stepping into the shoes of earlier border, or 'marcher' lords, and like their predecessors they sought to colonise and stabilise the western frontier of England by placing experienced and high-ranking men in key strategic locations.

Along the Welsh marches, to the north of fitz Osbern's earldom of Hereford, were two other important frontier earldoms created in the early years after the Norman Conquest. One of these, held by Roger of Montgomery, was centred on Shrewsbury, while a second, further north at Chester, belonged to Hugh of Avranches. All three of these Norman marcher lords were very familiar with the difficulties of occupying border areas. Their experience of using castles and towns to establish authority and control came from having to stabilise the frontiers of the Duchy of Normandy in the eleventh century, before William the Conqueror's success in England. Roger of Montgomery, for example, held lands along the southern frontier of Normandy, in Maine, and studded it with new castles and towns.[11]

Fitz Osbern, too, was accustomed to the idea of establishing towns in newly acquired territories. Soon after *c.*1060, Duke William gave fitz Osbern a castle at Breteuil-sur-Iton (Eure). There he quickly established a new town, just as he had done before, earlier on in the century, at his castle of Cormeilles.[12] Before long, the influence of fitz Osbern's new town of Breteuil was to be felt far beyond

the shores of Normandy. By adopting Breteuil's laws in his subsequent town charters, fitz Osbern helped to pass on the liberties
and customs of this otherwise insignificant Norman town to towns
in Britain, starting with the seat of his English earldom, the town
of Hereford itself.

The spread of the Breteuil laws

The laws of the Normandy town of Breteuil have not survived in
their original form. However, by studying the charters of boroughs
created by Norman lords in England, Wales and Ireland, Bateson
managed to piece together the likely content of the 'lost' Breteuil
laws and customs.[13] Her 'draft of the laws' contains clauses concerning burgages (their size, their alienation, their rebuilding,
their rent), as well as clauses on free marriage; the collection of
tolls from 'strangers'; the taking of wood for building; the right to
'freedom of men who remain for a year and a day undisturbed in
the town'; and aspects of jurisdiction, such as the election of borough
representatives and collection of court fines.[14] All of these privileges
are familiar ones (see Chapter 2). What is important in the context
of this discussion is the regulatory use that these laws were put to
by the Norman lords.

The early diffusion of the Breteuil laws across Wales and England
was due largely to the colonising activities of fitz Osbern in the
1060s and 1070s. After fitz Osbern granted the law of Breteuil to
his French burgesses of Hereford, other Norman lords, such as
Roger of Montgomery, soon adopted them to grant privileges to
their towns.[15] Thus, once Roger had wrested Shrewsbury from Eadric
the Wild in 1069, he introduced the law of Breteuil; while at
Rhuddlan, in the earldom of Chester, the Domesday Book (1086)
records that Hugh of Avranches had granted the inhabitants there
the same Breteuil customs. From the little Normandy town of
Breteuil, then, Norman urban laws were taken across to England.
The favourable terms of the Breteuil laws, especially the low
amercements, proved to be unpopular with English burgesses already
living in towns such as Shrewsbury; but for the Norman lords, the
privileges of Breteuil provided a useful means of attracting new
people to come and settle in 'frontier' towns, especially along the
relatively unstable and fluid borders of Wales and England in the
last quarter of the eleventh century.

Once established in England, the Breteuil laws became the 'law of Hereford'. The latter was derived from the former, and from Hereford the Breteuil customs were taken west into Wales as the Normans pushed into Dyfed, Ceredigion and Brechyniog during the twelfth century (Figure 3.1). By this process of expansion and colonisation the laws of Hereford were replicated in the charters of other towns, newly enfranchised by the Norman lords. Thus the Hereford laws were used as the basis for chartering the new boroughs of Denbigh, Builth, Brecon, Cardiff, Haverfordwest, Carmarthen, Montgomery and Newtown.[16] Once the customs of Breteuil were passed to these 'second generation towns' they then became the basis of charters granted to 'third generation towns'. Hence, Carmarthen's liberties subsequently became replicated in charters for the new boroughs of Cardigan and Laugharn, in the thirteenth century. Similarly, in north Wales, the Breteuil privileges held by Rhuddlan were granted to the new boroughs of Flint, Overton, Caerwys and Hope during the course of King Edward I's advances into Gwynedd during the thirteenth century. The lineage of these laws and customs can all be traced back to the law of Breteuil and the marcher activities of fitz Osbern in the late eleventh century.[17]

By establishing chartered towns in lands taken from the Welsh, the Normans diffused their urban laws across the more remote areas of the kingdom, into regions that were at the very margins of Norman power. The political thinking behind this gradual diffusion becomes all the more apparent once the chronological pattern of new chartered towns is mapped onto the geography of Anglo-Norman lordship in England and Wales (Figure 3.1).[18] It then becomes apparent that the Norman colonisation of frontier areas, such as Wales, northern England and the south-west peninsula, was closely dependent upon using the law of Breteuil, or its derivatives, to grant borough privileges and establish chartered towns. Norman urban laws thus gave the town's lord an 'eye' through which to watch over the activities of the town's inhabitants. Moreover, the chartered towns formed a web of Norman urban law extending right across large parts of Wales and England. This network of chartered towns helped to articulate Norman authority far beyond the confines of the lord's manors and castles, the bastions of Norman lordly power. Hence, those people who lived in the Norman lord's newly enfranchised towns, particularly those who lived in 'Norman' towns in the 'troubled' frontier regions, could

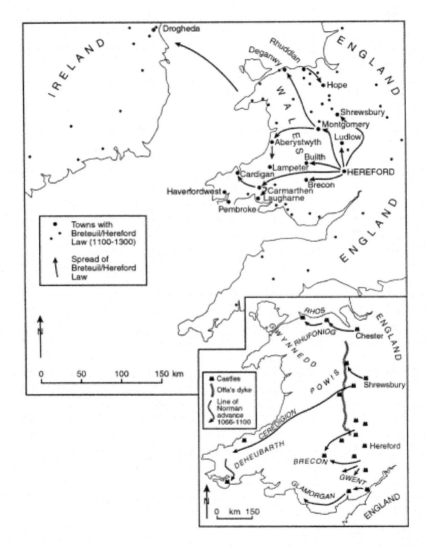

Figure 3.1 *Norman urban laws and the colonisation of Wales and Ireland*

not avoid being subject to the presence and authority of an extended Norman overlordship.

As well as having an important role in the colonisation of Wales, Norman urban laws also played a part in the subsequent English (Anglo-Norman) colonisation of Ireland (Figure 3.1). The Breteuil laws were used in Ireland during the late twelfth and thirteenth centuries, in charters drawn up, for example, by Walter de Lacy at Drogheda in 1194, and Maurice fitz Gerald at Dungarven in 1215.[19] Other 'Norman' urban laws were also used for the same purpose, particularly the laws of Bristol, which in Ireland formed the basis of important charters for Dublin (1171) and Waterford (1205).[20]

By encouraging migration into their newly chartered towns, Norman (and latterly English) lords were able to consolidate their political control of lands and people in Wales and Ireland. At the same time they were also able to ensure that they were the ones reaping the financial rewards of trade and commerce from towns in areas that were often situated far from a lord's head manor. As Bateson put it; 'there is a large class of burghal liberties not wrung from reluctant lords, but offered by the lords as bribes to secure their own ultimate enrichment'.[21] This enrichment had as much to do with political self-aggrandisement as it had about seeking financial gain (see Chapter 4). Furthermore, those people who lived and traded in towns chartered with Norman urban laws were themselves implicated in perpetuating and reinforcing the authority of their lords. The geography of urban laws that the Normans put into place therefore communicated and maintained their authority most effectively.

German urban law and colonisation in east-central Europe

Elsewhere in medieval Europe, urban laws were being similarly used by lords who were equally as ambitious as the Norman aristocrats in Britain and Ireland. Lords of German origins likewise sought to articulate their authority and facilitate frontier settlement and colonisation using urban laws that they were familiar with. In particular, during the twelfth and thirteenth centuries, urban laws played an important role in the German colonisation and settlement of large parts of east-central Europe, an area which today includes Poland, eastern Germany and the Czech and Slovak republics. Although in some ways similar to the experience of Norman

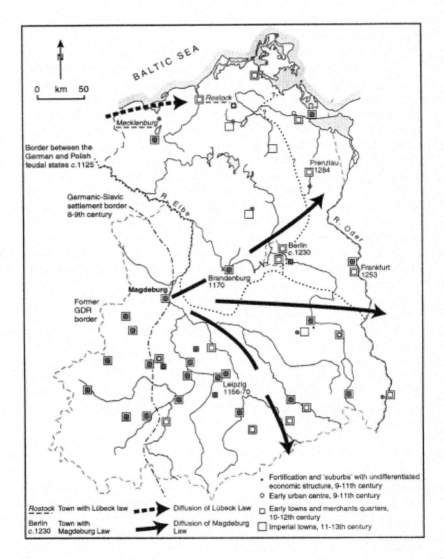

Figure 3.2 *The spread of Magdeburg and Lübeck laws in eastern Germany*

Britain and Ireland, the colonisation of this region of Europe, and its associated diffusion of German urban laws, can be seen to have been a rather more complex process.

Two urban laws were instrumental in spreading the influence of German lords across east-central Europe during the twelfth and thirteenth centuries: the law of Lübeck and the law of Magdeburg (Figure 3.2). Both proved to be highly influential and enduring models of urban law, just as the laws of Breteuil and Hereford were in Britain. Similarly, the spread of Lübeck and Magdeburg law was intimately connected with the colonising activities of particular lords. In looking at the actions of individual German lords, we can see that they, like their counterparts in Norman England, saw urban laws as a means of communicating their authority across large distances. However, in east-central Europe, the diffusion of German urban law was not just the result of 'conquering lords'; it was also encouraged by the activities of what Bartlett terms 'invited' aristocracies (see Chapter 1).[22]

The laws of Lübeck and Magdeburg

In 1157–58, Henry the Lion, Duke of Saxony, refounded Lübeck. By then, the town was an important centre for long-distance trade, and had been so for a number of centuries, having initially developed from a Slavic ring-work settlement.[23] Lübeck received its first formal charter of urban privileges in 1188. This came from Frederick Barbarossa, Emperor and King of Germany, and was followed, in 1226, by a more comprehensive charter granted by Frederick II. The charter of 1188 was concerned with the constitution, administration and economic affairs of the town, and it included laws on such things as inheritance, justice, fortification and coinage. It also laid down regional boundaries and exemptions from customs duties. The later charter, of 1226, confirmed the freedom of the citizens of Lübeck, the boundaries of the city and its *Weichbild* (the area of urban jurisdiction), and made the city answerable only to the emperor.[24]

The law of Lübeck (*ius Lubicense*) was a formidable piece of medieval legislation. No wonder, then, that other lords called upon the law to draw up their own charters of urban privileges and liberties. In 1226, for instance, Duke Sambor of Pomerelia used Lübeck law to establish the 'law of the city of Danzig [Gdańsk]'.[25]

Although important, the law of Lübeck was preceded by the law of Magdeburg (*ius magdeburgensis*), an especially popular urban law which became widely used in chartering towns all along the eastern frontier of the Holy Roman empire.

By the 1150s, Magdeburg was a town in the hands of Archbishop Wichmann, a man from a noble Saxon family who had a 'vision of development on a regional scale'.[26] He had acquired his position of authority from the German emperor and held his episcopal seat in Magdeburg, on the river Elbe (Figure 3.2). At that time, Magdeburg lay on the boundary between the duchy of Eastphalia, in the German kingdom, and Nordmark (the 'North March'), a fluid, frontier region divided between German and Slavic lordships.

The Nordmark formed part of a large tract of land which had formerly been held under German control. By the late tenth century it had been acquired by the Slavs. It was during the German reacquisition of this extensive territory, in the twelfth century, that new towns were established using Magdeburg law.[27] Magdeburg was by then an old, long-standing urban centre. As Stephenson notes, 'as early as 965, according to a grant of a local church, a group of Jews and other traders were living at Magdeburg, and ten years later such *mercatores* received a formal grant of privileges from Otto I'; 'by 1038 the law of the merchants of Magdeburg was famous enough to be given to those of Quedlinburg'.[28]

The law of Magdeburg, like the Norman law of Breteuil, was chiefly concerned with setting out urban constitutional and administrative matters. These usually confirmed the role of citizens (*cives*) in the urban community, and related to the administrative organisation of market business. The townspeople themselves could lay down their own statutes, providing they did not infringe those of the lord, while the lord guaranteed the peace of the market and the freedom to trade. The townspeople thus lived in *relative* freedom (hence the oft-cited German maxim of the time, *Stadtluft macht frei*). However, although they owned land in the town, and collectively formed a corporate body, the towns were by no means autonomous, 'the lord was always included too'.[29]

In essence, both Magdeburg law and Lübeck law shared certain common elements. All the same, the two laws came to be used by different people living in different parts of east-central Europe. During the two centuries following their earliest recorded mention, the two urban laws were spread eastwards and southwards from

Lübeck and Magdeburg through the actions and activities of ambitious men. In order to facilitate control over contested lands, men like Archbishop Wichmann used urban laws to set up networks of interlinked and dependent, enfranchised urban settlements.[30] In this respect, there are some parallels with the way that Norman lords used Norman urban laws to colonise Wales and its frontier with England. To understand the role played by German urban laws in the process of colonisation in east-central Europe, it is necessary to examine the town-chartering activities of individual lords.

The spread of Magdeburg law

During the German settlement of the march between the Elbe and Oder in the twelfth century, high-status German aristocratic lords chartered towns by repeatedly using Magdeburg law (Figure 3.2). In 1160, for example, Albrecht the Bear, Margrave of Brandenburg, granted a charter to Stendal in which he allowed the inhabitants the same rights as burgesses in Magdeburg, the *cives magdeburgenses*. Similarly, the Margrave of Meissen, Otto, granted the customs of Magdeburg to Leipzig in his *Stadtbrief* (a letter, or charter, presenting urban law). This charter defined the customs and privileges of the townspeople, for example, their property rights, criminal justice and inheritance laws, as well as rights allowing them to pasture their animals. The charter also prohibited markets from being held within one German mile of the town (*Bannmeile*), and defined the town's *Weichbild*.[31]

Archbishop Wichmann was himself involved in similar such schemes at this time. For example, in 1174 he granted the law of Magdeburg to a place called Jüterbog in the march of Lausitz. In so doing, he made Jüterbog the central place (*caput*) of its surrounding region (*provincia*). Jüterbog formed the focus for rural settlements in the town's hinterland and new settlements within this region were deliberately organised hierarchically. All the settlements were thus legally and economically related to each other. In turn, Jüterbog was itself legally and economically tied to the 'mother' town of the archbishop, that is, Magdeburg.[32] Market settlements (*villae fori*) that were subsequently established within the Jüterbog region were also subject to the law of Jüterbog, and so they too had laws that were originally derived from Magdeburg.[33]

During the twelfth and thirteenth centuries, Wichmann's *modus operandi* found its way into the economic and legal organisation of towns in the march of Meissen, as well as the Ascanian mark of Brandenburg.[34] Through the support of Wichmann, Albrecht the Bear had gained possession of Brandenburg in 1157, following the death of the last Slavic prince, Prebislav-Heinrich. Albrecht adopted the laws of Magdeburg in his charter to Brandenburg. He gave the inhabitants of the town customs exemption in 1170, and allowed them their own seal in 1200. By this time he had also established a new town of Brandenburg, adjacent to the old town, and had given that the laws of Magdeburg, too. The same policy was used in other towns within the Ascanian mark, and hence Magdeburg law spread further eastwards.[35]

Through the creation of interrelated chartered towns, the law of Magdeburg was gradually diffused across a wide part of east-central Europe. As with the law of Breteuil, the use of German urban law to enfranchise both new and old towns provided lords with a means of controlling the activities of townspeople and trade, in regions that were often remote from the lord's own power base. However, the degree of strategic planning evident in Wichmann's elaborate settlement scheme was more ambitious than anything attempted by the Normans in Britain. Wichmann's strategic approach soon had its followers and imitators in other parts of central and eastern Europe.

The continued popularity of Magdeburg law among German lords can be seen in the activities of the Teutonic Knights who took 'advantage of Silesian models, experience and even inhabitants of the area in creating their own version of German law'.[36] The Teutonic Knights were a religious military order, like the Hospitallers and Templars, and they acquired large parts of Prussia after Prince Konrad of Mazovia called for their help in 1226. He offered them Chełmno as fief but subsequently they seized Gdańsk (Danzig) in Pomerania and then 'proceeded to colonise the conquered Prussian and Slav lands with settlers from Germany and Mazovia'.[37] During the thirteenth century the activities of the Teutonic Knights helped to spread Magdeburg law even further east. In 1233, they granted it to both Chełmno and Torun and then after this the towns they chartered in Prussia and Mazovia were given the law of Chełmno (*ius culmense*). In essence this was of course still Magdeburg law.

In the same way that the Breteuil law was mediated through derivative laws (such as Hereford and Carmarthen), the law of Magdeburg bore a host of other, secondary urban laws. Sometimes this process appears to have been relatively straightforward, as it was, for example, in the laws of Berlin, Brandenburg and Stettin (Szczecin), which were all derived from Magdeburg. At other times the process of borrowing laws to enfranchise towns became slightly more complicated.

During the early thirteenth century Magdeburg law diffused southwards as well as east. The Silesian prince, Henry the Bearded (1201–38), seems to have borrowed Wichmann's model in his settlement programme of Silesia, and Great Poland and Little Poland. He granted the law of Magdeburg to colonists in Złotoryja, Lwówek, Wrocław (Breslau) and Krosno, and in the process was able to keep close control over his newly enfranchised towns. However, because Magdeburg citizens began to intervene in the affairs of his townspeople of Wrocław, Henry decided to turn away from Magdeburg law. When he first established a new market at Sroda, he initially opted for Flemish rather than Magdeburg law.[38] Subsequently, though, Henry turned again to Magdeburg law. In 1234, in a charter he issued to Sroda, he acquired a copy of the laws from Halle, a 'daughter' town of Magdeburg, rather than from the citizens of Magdeburg themselves. The Halle copy of Magdeburg law became, in turn, Sroda law.[39] Not all were content to follow Henry's tortuous route to establish their urban privileges. In Bohemia, the burgesses of Litoměřice (Leitmeritz) preferred to obtain the law of Magdeburg directly from the *cives magdeburgenses*, even though Halle was closer to their home town and had laws that were derived from Magdeburg.[40]

Another area where Magdeburg law proved to be popular was Pomerania (Figure 3.3). This region lay along the Baltic littoral, within present-day Germany. There, Duke Barnim I (1220–78) adopted Magdeburg law as the model for chartering his 'free' towns. Although Pomerania had not been seized by aggressive German lords, Barnim's policy of using Magdeburg law to charter his own towns nevertheless helped to spread the use of German urban customs. His charter to Prenzlau (1234) was the first recorded use of the law in the duchy. He 'entrusted eight men, of whom at least one (and possibly all) came from Stendal in the Altmark, with the *promotio civitatis* under Magdeburg law'.[41] Other town charters quickly

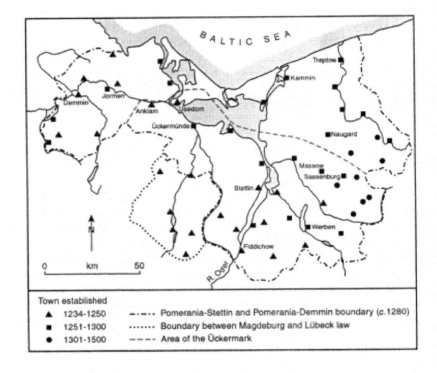

Figure 3.3 *German urban laws in Pomerania*

followed. In 1245 Barnim granted a charter to Szczecin (Stettin) and 'designated it as the superior court for all places with the law of Magdeburg in his territory', no doubt to avoid any direct intervention from the *cives magdeburgenses*.[42] Later, in 1260 for example, towns such as Damm had charters conferred 'along the lines of Stettin'.[43]

The spread of Lübeck law

Just as Magdeburg law had allowed Archbishop Wichmann to maintain control over distant territories across the German march, so too did it give Duke Barnim a means of watching over both towns and trade in his duchy of Pomerania. It was from the chartered town of Stettin (Szczecin) that Barnim governed the southern part of Pomerania, until its amalgamation with Pomerania-Demmin occurred, in 1264.

Pomerania-Demmin stretched along the Baltic coastline. Latterly it had been an area ruled by a Slavic prince, Wartislav III. For enfranchising his chartered towns, Wartislav had favoured Lübeck law rather than Magdeburg law. The geographical divide that separated the areas of Pomerania where the two German urban laws were used thus reflected a political divide between Wartislav's lordship and Barnim's (Figure 3.3). It was a division that continued to exist. Even following the political amalgamation of the two lordships under Barnim's rule, the duke continued to use Lübeck law to enfranchise towns in Wartislav's former lordship. Thus, when Barnim chartered the two towns of Kammin and Treptow in Pomerania-Demmin he called upon Lübeck law; whereas for the towns of Anklam, Fiddichow, Ückermunde and Usedom in Pomerania-Stettin he adopted the law of Magdeburg. This geographical divide between the two laws was respected by other, lesser lords, too. For example, Bishop Hermann of Gleichen (1251–89), who held land in both areas, gave Lübeck law to his towns of Naugard and Jarmen in the north, and Magdeburg law to Massow, Sassenburg and Werben in the south.[44]

In the case of Pomerania it is clear that lords who were chartering towns used the two dominant German urban laws in a consistent way. Kuhn suggests that this was because the choice of urban law was influenced by the legal traditions of those settling in the chartered towns. He argues that, because 'Barnim's settlers came above all from the marcher zone . . . [they] therefore brought Brandenburg-Magdeburg law with them'; and because those 'burgesses of the towns in Pomerania-Demmin were recruited from the coastal region of Holstein as far as Rügen, [they] were accustomed to Lübeck law'.[45] In all likelihood, however, it was primarily lords such as Barnim and Wartislav who were making the decisions to choose one particular urban law over another. They would have recognised that the German urban laws were the most useful means of establishing and maintaining political stability in their region; for attracting new settlers to take up plots in their newly chartered towns, and for getting them to engage peacefully in trade and commerce.

There were, of course, important differences between the laws of Lübeck and Magdeburg. According to Quirin, the *Stadtbrief* that Frederick II issued to Lübeck was a general description 'that offered an easy opportunity to modify Lübeck custom and to develop special local variants of it'.[46] On the other hand, he suggests, 'Magdeburg law . . . appeared narrower and more concentrated, with its systematic provision for civil and criminal law and its emphasis on urban freedom'.[47] Generally, as we have seen in the case of Pomerania, the law of Lübeck was the preferred choice for enfranchising chartered towns in regions along the Baltic coast.

One route by which Lübeck law was diffused eastwards was by coastal communication and trading, from Holstein, along the Baltic and into Prussia. Towns using Lübeck law included Kiel, Wismar, Braunsberg, Revel and Wesenburg, to name but a few. In 1218, Prince Borwin of Mecklenburg granted it to Rostock, and again subsequently, in 1225–26, in charters to Gadebusch and Parchuim.[48] The law of Lübeck also formed the legal basis for the Hanseatic league of towns, which by the fifteenth century comprised communities as far afield as Visby, Bergen and Novgorod. Indeed, the *ius Lubicense* was found to be a durable piece of legislation, and as a reflection of this 'its extremely sophisticated legal framework was recognised by towns which had already formulated basic laws of their own'.[49] The law was in many ways a common language: 'from Lübeck to Revel, merchants and ship's masters encountered the same council constitution and legal system; court actions, inheritances and contracts were dealt with in the same manner familiar everywhere'.[50]

Conclusion

The laws of Lübeck and Magdeburg, and their derivatives, served the economic and political interests of those lords who were responsible for granting them. The privileges associated with these laws encouraged the sort of settlement that Norman and English marcher lords were hoping for on their lordships in Wales and Ireland during the twelfth and thirteenth centuries. The similar uses to which urban laws were put in the Middle Ages are thus clear, but there are also important differences of course. The laws, while being widespread and often interrelated, were not all the same, and neither were the particular lords who used them. Some lords, such as Wichmann, were overtly strategic in their use of urban laws, while others appear to have been more pragmatic. Despite the differences, the duplication and diffusion of urban laws served a common objective: it was a means of watching over urban activity, even in remote regions. Urban laws allowed lords to put into place a network of chartered towns, and like a spider's web this network conveyed the authority of absentee lords from their centres of power to the very edges of their dominions, often across large distances. At one and the same time, the use of these laws encouraged and controlled urbanisation. The following part of this chapter looks at how urban laws were also used to differentiate the internal spaces of towns.

Social Exclusion and Differentiation in Chartered Towns

In the Middle Ages, lords could use urban laws to help them divide and segregate towns and townspeople. Where one set of laws provided favourable terms for one group of inhabitants, another group had to live by a different set of codes and customs. Urban laws were thus exclusive and exclusionary in nature. They marked out social boundaries. These social boundaries were often also spatially defined, in that burgesses following one set of customs might live in one area of a town, while those subject to a different set of laws lived in another. This part of the chapter examines how those towns acquired by an 'outside' group were internally divided, socially and spatially, by the use of particular urban laws. As with the previous section, two examples are considered, starting with another look at Norman urban laws. This is then followed by some discussion of the urban laws used by European settlers to divide up former Muslim cities in the Holy Land during the Crusades. In both cases, urban laws are found to have been applied to discrete areas of towns, and used as a means of marginalising existing townspeople and favouring newcomers. This method of social exclusion was reinforced by the spatial differentiation of groups of burgesses within chartered towns. It was a mechanism which allowed lords to oversee the conduct of different groups of townspeople – an important issue in towns situated in regions that were politically unstable.

Internal divisions in Norman towns

In some chartered towns a particular set of laws and customs applied to the whole urban area. This we have seen already in the case of Leipzig, where the Margrave of Meissen's *Stadtbrief* applied to the entire area of the town's *Weichbild*. However, in some towns, particular urban laws were applied differentially, accommodating some people while excluding others. Urban customs and laws created social boundaries between groups of townspeople, and these boundaries between groups were often reinforced spatially. The evidence for this usually comes from town charters, but sometimes the geographical divisions between different groups of burgesses were physically apparent in the towns themselves. Such internal divisions existed in English towns during the early decades that followed the Norman Conquest, for example in Norwich until the 1140s, though their presence was not always especially long-lived.[51]

Already some assessment has been offered of the impact of Norman urbanism on the Welsh borders of England. In some towns, such as Hereford and Shrewsbury, it is evident that Norman urban laws coexisted alongside already established English borough customs. In such cases, the town and its people lived with two sets of urban privileges, one belonging to the new immigrant townspeople (the 'French' who were being encouraged to settle by the Norman aristocracy), and another for existing inhabitants (the 'English' who were there before the arrival of the Normans). In simple terms, there were Norman urban laws for the newcomers, and English urban laws for existing burgesses. For example, at Shrewsbury, the Domesday Book makes it clear that 'the French burgesses were living under a law different to that of the English borough'.[52] This legal distinction between the two groups was very real. The Domesday assessors themselves note that 'the English burgesses state that it is very hard on them that they pay as much tax as they paid before 1066'.[53] The grievance of Shrewsbury's English burgesses was in part due to the destruction of some of their burgages caused by the construction of Earl Roger's new castle. But their complaint also reflected concern that more favourable urban privileges had been granted to the French burgesses, who were living in the town under the law of Breteuil.

According to the Domesday Book, by 1086 there were 43 French burgesses living in Shrewsbury. Although there is no reference to where these burgesses had actually taken up residence, toponymical evidence suggests that they may well have been living in a small 'bridgehead' suburb called Frankwell – a name that means 'the Frank *ville*' ('the French town').[54] If they were here, the location they chose was by no means an enviable one, for the suburb lay on the road to Wales, and would have thus borne the brunt of any

Welsh attack on the town. Nevertheless, unlike their neighbouring English burgesses, these new French burgesses had the distinct advantage of paying lower amercements. Under English borough law, for example, a burgess breaching the king's peace could be fined 100 shillings, whereas under Breteuil law a much lower fine was levied, a maximum of 12d.[55] A somewhat similar arrangement also existed at Hereford.

As at Shrewsbury, William fitz Osbern's strategy at Hereford was to likewise use the law of Breteuil to favour new burgesses coming from across the English Channel. The Domesday Book entry for Hereford records how 'the English who live there have their former customs, but the French burgesses have all their forfeitures discharged for 12d'.[56] As with Shrewsbury, the newcomers were clearly much better off than their English counterparts, and this was no doubt a deliberate incentive contrived by fitz Osbern to encourage outside settlers to take up plots. The question arising from this is how were the boundaries defined between the old English and new French burgesses? On this subject, Bateson makes the suggestion that when fitz Osbern arrived at Hereford he 'introduced the laws of Breteuil for his French tenants, his castle men', and that 'they, and only they, enjoy[ed] the privilege of a maximum amercement of twelve pence'.[57] The earl's new castle was inserted into the edge of the Anglo-Saxon town, just within the defences of the *burh*. However, the Breteuil customs brought over by fitz Osbern surely covered a larger proportion of the town than that which was occupied by the castle? Indeed, it seems likely that the legal differentiation which separated French from English burgesses applied to all those living in Hereford, and not just fitz Osbern's 'castle-men'.

The geographical distribution of Hereford's English and French burgesses is a matter which unfortunately is not recorded by the Domesday Book. In order to find out where the newly arrived French burgesses were located, it is necessary to consider aspects of the town's topography. The most likely area inhabited by Hereford's new French burgesses lay just outside the defences of the Anglo-Saxon town, a suburb consisting of a large open market place surrounded by spacious house plots (see Chapter 5) (Figure 3.4). For any incoming French burgesses this suburb would undoubtedly have looked an attractive place to take up residence. There was sufficient land for them to build their houses, and plenty of space for them to engage in trade. Taken together with the prospect of

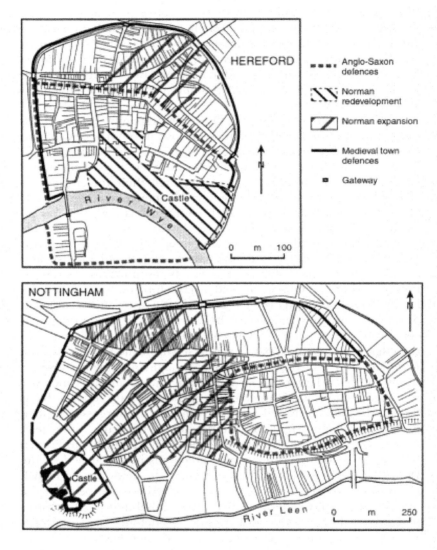

Figure 3.4   *Norman boroughs and English towns*

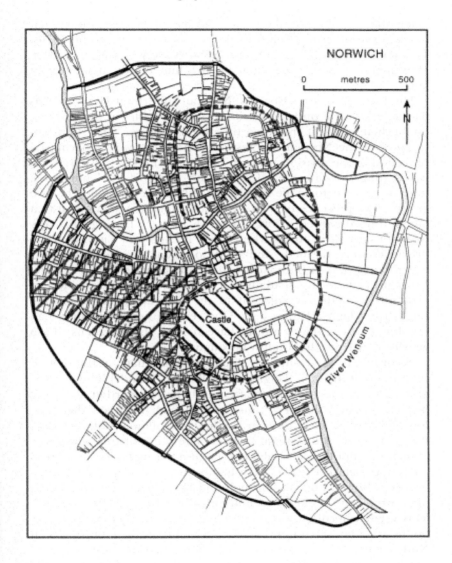

being able to live under the favourable laws of Breteuil, the French burgesses were clearly well provided for in Hereford in the 1070s. This was exactly what fitz Osbern would have wanted: an enclave of French burgesses, sympathetic towards him and the new Norman king.

The location of fitz Osbern's 'Norman suburb' at Hereford has parallels with the outlying position of 'Frankville' at Shrewsbury, established at about the same time by Earl Roger. The suburban location of the Norman burgesses in the two towns is perhaps a reflection of the division between them and the English burgesses. By creating separate areas for 'English' and 'French' burgesses, lords were able to make visible the difference between the two groups. The presence of such 'Norman' suburbs is something that Stephenson observed in other English towns.[58] During this early Norman period, in towns where both French and English urban privileges were defined, similar socio-spatial divides existed between burgesses. At both Nottingham and Norwich, for example, Norman lords set up spatially discrete, suburban 'Frankvilles' in positions immediately adjacent to the built-up areas of existing English boroughs (Figure 3.4). One reason they might have had for doing this is that it would have helped them refocus urban activity away from the English boroughs.

According to the Domesday Book, at Nottingham, at the time of the Conquest in 1066, 'Hugh, son of Baldric, found 136 men [burgesses] living there'. Shortly afterwards he is recorded as having himself 'erected thirteen houses which had not been there before'.[59] Other Norman lords in Nottingham followed suit, including Roger de Busli and William Peverel. The focus of this new development was not the old-established English borough, but was instead a large new market place which had been created by the Normans between the old English borough and Hugh's new castle, an area of Nottingham that later documents called the 'French borough'. This French borough was a definable legal and spatial unit. The boundary that separated the English and French boroughs at Nottingham did not fade after the Norman Conquest, rather it survived though the Middle Ages.[60] As we saw at Shrewsbury and Hereford, the area subject to French borough customs lay outside the English borough.

In the case of Norwich, the Domesday Book records the presence of new French burgesses as well as a 'new borough' (*novus burgus*) (Figure 3.4). The centre of this new borough was a large market place, still the commercial centre of Norwich today, and it was probably here that the French burgesses lived. The location of this new borough, outside the defences of an English town, matches the same spatial pattern of 'Frankvilles' to be seen at Nottingham, Hereford and Shrewsbury.[61] On this basis, it seems that the Norman efforts to refocus urban life away from the English boroughs was a deliberate attempt to marginalise English burgesses, both spatially and socially.

Recently urban sociologists and geographers have shown that one way social boundaries and inequalities are reinforced between different groups of people is by making one group spatially marginal to another.[62] In early Norman England this same principle was being used to draw a distinction between French and English burgesses. In what were once 'their' towns, English burgesses became socially marginalised, in effect excluded, by the urban laws sanctioned by Norman lords after the Conquest. Moreover, the Normans reinforced this marginality of the English burgesses by *physically* marginalising the area of the town where they lived. As the Normans created new areas for homes and for trade around the edges of existing towns, what had been the core of the English borough became its periphery. In the 1060s and 1070s, the French settlers who came and took up residency in these new suburbs further helped to recentre the focus of urban life away from the old English boroughs, while at the same time diminish the power and status of the English burgesses. The longevity of these social and spatial divisions obviously varied from place to place, but in some cases, for example Nottingham, the effects were long-lasting. In this sense, the new Norman urban laws that were attracting settlers to live in English towns were an important means of maintaining social order in a kingdom that in the later eleventh century was in a politically delicate state.

Internal divisions in Crusader cities

Using urban laws to divide and differentiate social groups within medieval towns was not just a practice of Norman lords in eleventh-century England. To end this part of the chapter, and to provide some comparative context that takes us away from Norman England, this section examines the geographies of urban law that created spatial and social divisions within Crusader cities in the Holy Land. In their conquest of the Holy Land during the twelfth and thirteenth centuries, European Crusaders and settlers seized control of Muslim cities. In 1099, Jerusalem fell to a Latin Christian army, and thereafter the former Islamic cities became crucial strongholds for European overlords seeking to consolidate their political control of the Crusader states.[63]

Four 'Crusader states' were established in the Levant, but with very rare exception, 'the Crusaders had no need to found and build new cities' in this territory.[64] Instead, they inherited a legacy of urbanism that owed its origins to centuries of previous development under Byzantine and Islamic cultures. What the Crusader overlords did was to adapt and extend these ancient cities to meet their own needs. Just as conquering Norman lords, such as fitz Osbern, altered English towns to suit themselves, so did the European Crusaders and settlers who occupied the Islamic cities of the Holy Land. One way in which they did this was to add on 'new boroughs' to existing towns and cities. For example, a 'novus burgus was added to the old city' at Jaffa, as were others, at Nablus in 1168, and Tyre, by 1190.[65]

The impact of European Crusaders on these cities was in part legal and political. Once under Christian control, the legal and jurisdictional organisation of the Crusader cities was very different from that which had existed before. The use of burgage tenure in the Crusader cities, for example, 'was a European institution imported wholesale from Europe'.[66] As Islamic institutions were replaced by Christian ones, the position of surviving Muslim inhabitants worsened. The legal geography of the Crusader cities thus changed dramatically during the 1100s. The cities came to be composed of separate but interlocking jurisdictions. These jurisdictions were based on individual communities of European settlers (merchants, pilgrims, craftspeople, as well as the Crusaders themselves), who had arrived in cities such as Acre and Antioch during and after the First Crusade. Each of these communities brought with them its own distinct brand of urban customs and privileges that were derived from its native city, as well as its own language and culture.

The European Christian settlers who arrived in the Crusader cities had largely come from the wealthy and well-established maritime cities along the northern Mediterranean coast, particularly Venice, Genoa and Marseilles. These cultural groups remained spatially coherent within the Crusader cities and each occupied a distinct 'quarter'. These quarters were areas within a city which had their own separate jurisdiction. Through them political life was controlled and organised. During the twelfth century, the individual 'quarters' came to assume a large degree of political autonomy in their own right. By 1136, for example, Venetians in Tyre had secured a third of the city, 'as a kind of autonomy', which Prawer suggests, 'we might regard, in accordance with the later Venetian interpretation, as a creation of a state within a kingdom'.[67] The *Pactum Warmundi* put it like this: 'Venetians will have the same rights of jurisdiction over burgesses of whatever origin, living in the quarter and the houses of the Venetians, as the king has over his own.'[68] Clearly, then, the Venetian quarter in Tyre was understood legally and socially as a distinct spatial area.

As well as having a strong presence in Tyre, the Venetians also set up their own quarter in Acre, another strategic coastal city. Acre was situated on a promontory and its defensive position enabled the Christians to survive Muslim attempts to regain the city, until 1291. Crusader Acre was a walled city comprising three Italian quarters. Following an initial grant of 1110, the Venetians managed to have their quarter extended with royal approval, in 1123. Along with the Venetians there were also Pisans and Genoese living within the walls of Acre. The Pisans had founded their own quarter after they received a royal charter from King Almeric I in 1168. Then, in 1182, Baldwin IV gave the Pisans a second charter which allowed them to extend their quarter. The Genoese had also been granted a quarter, but much earlier than the Pisans. The Genoese established their quarter in 1104, 'in return for their decisive participation in the conquest of the city'.[69] In addition to the three Italian quarters in the city there were also a further three: two of these belonged to military religious orders (the Hospitaller Knights of St John and the Order of the Temple), while the third was retained as a royal jurisdiction (Figure 3.5).

All together, the three Italian quarters in Acre formed discrete blocks of separate urban jurisdictions. All three were encircled by the quarters of the Hospitallers, the Templars and the king. In turn, all six of the 'quarters' were surrounded by a line of impressive city walls. By the 1260s, the outer limit of the Venetian quarter was visibly and physically marked by its own set of walls, thus visible reinforcing the boundary of the Venetians' jurisdiction. This walled area was itself divided into four subdivisions, each one containing

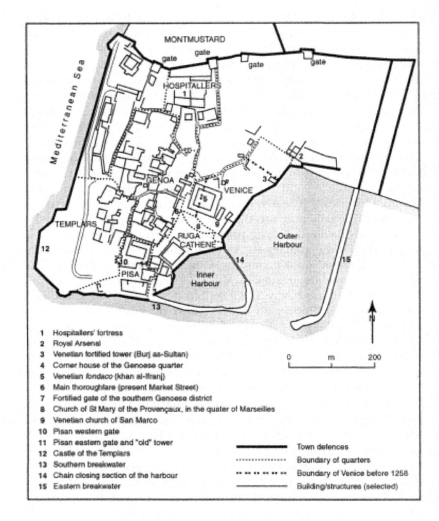

Figure 3.5 *Internal jurisdictions in Crusader Acre*

streets, a place for holding a market, a church, and an oven and bath.[70] Each of the Italian quarters had 'their own *funda* and their own *fondaci*', along with separate market jurisdictions (which required market inspectors) and systems of taxation. Also, in order 'to make sure that their respective nationals enjoyed their full privileges', the officials of the Venetian, Pisan and Genoese quarters 'were always present' at the 'market of the port' (*catena*).[71] Later on, by 1191, and following the reconquest of Acre, the three existing Italian quarters in Acre were augmented further by the addition of the quarter of Marseilles [or Provençaux], granted by King Guy de Lusignan.

Each of the quarters that divided the legal geography of the Crusader cities functioned as political units in their own right. Unlike the towns and cities of medieval Europe, 'no Crusader city obtained a charter or special privileges', and neither did their inhabitants 'live according to any common urban law'.[72] Instead, 'each component of the Crusader city's population lived within the special framework of their [particular] laws and customs', where burgesses lived according to 'their own body of rules'.[73] The number of quarters varied between the Crusader cities. In Jerusalem, for example, the number of quarters with separate laws and customs was much higher than at either Acre or Tyre. There were, for example, Spanish, Provençaux, Hungarian, German and Breton communities, to name but a few. Each of these groups was not only socially and spatially coherent and identifiable, but each also had its own legal unity and status. Their own particular urban privileges were defined in terms of the area of the city inhabited by the group. In other words, the groups' legal and political 'cohesion resulted from living in the neighbourhood alone'.[74]

In the Crusader cities, therefore, instead of urban laws and privileges being granted by a lord to a single body of burgesses, they were mediated at the local level through the political autonomy of the various 'quarters'. Courts of burgesses were present in the Crusader cities, but generally these were 'essentially an administrative and executive body (with a very limited legislative function)', and through them 'the lordship dealt with a given segment of the city's population and its particular property'.[75] In the Crusader city there was, therefore, a number of distinct levels of jurisdiction, some applying to the city as a whole, while others only encompassed particular quarters. What was the place for the cities 'former Islamic inhabitants in this interlocking framework of European urban jurisdictions?' Well, there was no place for them; not within the European jurisdictions. In fact, following the First Crusade, the Muslim population was expelled from the cities, and placed outside the legally privileged European quarters. The legal privileges which successive Levantine Christian kings endowed on these quarters thus served to politically and spatially marginalise the Muslim population. Although the means they used to do this differed from that of the Norman lords in English towns, the outcome was nevertheless very much the same.

Rather than leaving the existing Muslim population in place in the Crusader cities, together with their customs and institutions, European Christian settlers sought to remove them altogether, and replace them with their own laws and customs. The principle behind this strategy was pretty much the same as that used by the Normans in eleventh-century England. In both cases, lords used urban laws to exclude others, while at the same time encouraging settlement and colonisation to take place within defined urban jurisdictions. The authority conveyed by urban laws in European towns and cities allowed political elites to control individual and collective activity within towns. At the same time, this strategy also often complemented an orchestrated plan for overall political domination, particularly in newly acquired territories. What is more, it also had the power to create and shape the cultural identities of marginalised social groups, stigmatising some sections of the urban community while privileging others.[76] The role that spatial practices had in defining and shaping social identity is picked up again later on in the book, in Chapter 7.

Conclusion

The purpose of this chapter was to outline some of the ways that urban laws were used to achieve political ends during the Middle Ages. One way lords used urban laws was to charter towns and encourage the settlement and colonisation of lands and territories. In the context of colonisation in 'frontier' regions, such as western Britain and east-central Europe, there were particular advantages to be gained from spreading urban laws and putting into place a network of chartered towns. Such 'geographies of urban law' enabled lords to watch over what people were doing in their towns, while at the same time offer attractive and favourable terms for settlers to come and take up residence in the towns. The outcome of this process is still to be seen in Europe today, with many of the towns created by colonising lords surviving as a testimony to their ambition and zeal.

In the mind of the coloniser, urban laws not only facilitated colonisation but legitimised it, too. In regions where institutionalised urban life was absent (or simply not recognised), colonising lords used urban laws as an apparatus to justify their takeover of lands and people. This was the case in the late eleventh and early twelfth centuries when Norman lords sought to colonise parts of Wales. In the later twelfth century, when the Anglo-Normans started to colonise south-east Ireland, they used it again. William of Malmesbury's remark, cited at the start of the chapter, refers to how he believed the English and French were more civilised than the Irish because they lived in towns – towns such as Bristol, with charters, laws and customs. His prejudiced remarks against the Irish sadly continued to resonate in the work of later historians, including Bateson.[77]

There was also a second dimension to the role that urban laws played in the process of urbanisation and colonisation in medieval Europe. By using particular urban laws to favour certain groups of burgesses, lords were able to marginalise those townspeople who might cause them trouble by challenging their authority. We see this in the context of early Norman England and the initial attempts made by Norman lords to instil political stability in English boroughs. The Normans used their own particular urban laws to refocus town life away from the old-established English boroughs, while at the same time also marginalise English burgesses. In contrast, French and Norman burgesses were favourably provided for, by being offered urban laws that were more advantageous than their English counterparts, as well as new areas within which to settle. The social divisions created by differing urban laws were thus reinforced spatially, so as to further marginalise the place of English burgesses. In similar, though not identical ways, urban laws in Crusader cities defined and shaped social and cultural boundaries, and served to exclude the Muslim population. What we find, then, is urban laws being used to make indigenous groups of townspeople 'outsiders' in their own towns and cities.

4

LORDSHIP AND URBANISATION

Edward, by the grace of God, King of England, conferred on us the manor of Kirkham in free, pure and perpetual arms, and finally by his charter granted us that we might have a free borough in our manor.

Charter of Walter, Abbot of Vale Royal, 1296[1]

Because we desire the improvement of our manor of Chard, we will grant that the *villa* of Chard ... be a free borough forever.

Charter of Jocelin, Bishop of Bath and Wells, 1235[2]

The two extracts from borough charters cited above typify how lords were using chartered towns to raise profit from their lands. It is this process, the urbanisation of lordships, that this chapter seeks to explore.

In the Middle Ages, urban land almost always exceeded the value of agricultural land, as it still does today. Yet towns occupied only a fragment of the space used for growing crops and grazing livestock. Towns were thus important as generators of income on medieval lordships. Market tolls, as well as burgage rents and fines levied in borough courts, combined to create a vital source of revenue for lords. As well as gaining revenue from the town itself, the market provided an outlet whereby a lord's rural, agricultural tenants could sell their produce, and so pay him money rents. With a chartered town, a lord provided an incentive for further urban economic growth and yet at the same time kept people and trade under close surveillance (see Chapter 3). On lordships all over medieval Europe, lords were using town charters to develop and control urbanisation.

The role played by lords in urbanising their lordships was by no means a straightforward one. The commercial success or failure of a chartered town largely depended on the town's location, as well as the timing of its creation, and both of these factors were closely allied with the relative social status of the town's founder. There was a close relationship between all three of these factors. Urbanisation was indeed a complex *social process*, and the purpose of this chapter is to demonstrate how, when creating a town, it was not simply a case of a lord implementing plans of his own. A range of people were involved in setting up new towns. Some lords entered into partnerships with other, local lords, while some also used 'middlemen' to take care of things at the local level. The process of urbanisation thus required negotiation between different levels of the medieval social hierarchy.

This chapter considers the ways that such social relationships underpinned the urbanisation of medieval lordships. It does so by looking, firstly, at how particular groups of lords went about creating new, chartered towns on their lordships; secondly, at how some lords used partnerships and joined forces with other lords; and thirdly, how middlemen provided some lords with a way of creating their new towns. The aim here is to show that chartering towns was not simply a 'top-down' process, although in the past that has been the predominant way of thinking about the process of 'town foundation'. As with so many aspects of urban life in the Middle Ages, co-operation provided the key to urbanising lordships.

The need for towns

In their drive to urbanise their rural estates it may be said that medieval lords were acting as entrepreneurs, taking a risk with a commercial venture that might not succeed. If successful, urbanisation provided them with an additional source of consistent and regular cash income. Lordships all over Europe thus mushroomed with new towns. Sometimes these new towns were created when lords granted urban privileges to already existing settlements; while in other instances a grant of urban privileges went hand in hand with the founding of a wholly new town, created on a previously unoccupied 'greenfield' site (see Chapter 2).

Such new towns are to be found all over Europe – identifiable often by a generic form of place name: 'new town' (for example, Newton, Villeneuve, Nova Villa, Neustadt, and so forth). Before dealing with how both urbanisation and lordship were intimately linked together, it is worth looking at why lords would wish to have new towns on their lordships.

From what has been said in the previous two chapters it will have become clear that town charters primarily favoured the lord who granted them. As Hilton has noted, with town charters 'the interests and profits of the lord are always present'.[3] In theory, revenue generated through urbanisation ultimately passed to the town's overlord. Money was needed in order to help lords meet the military obligations that were demanded of them as knights. Right across Europe during the twelfth century, many lords were facing a growing need for cash.[4] Aristocratic life was, in general, a consuming and expensive business. To be able to practise favoured 'leisure' activities, such as hunting, hawking and feasting, lords needed money. For many, whatever their feudal rank, this growing demand for more money was met in part by creating new towns, or to be more precise, by creating newly chartered towns and granting urban privileges.

One noble lord whose aristocratic lifestyle is unusually well recorded by medieval standards is William Marshall. This Anglo-Norman magnate lived during the latter part of the twelfth century. In order to maintain his lifestyle he had to meet a variety of expenses. For example, there was the cost of buying and maintaining equipment and animals for battles and tournaments. Also, there were expenses to be met when Marshall took the cross and ventured to the Holy Land, and when he undertook expeditions to Ireland to acquire new lands there. Like his fellow magnate lords of the time, William followed the king's initiative and installed his own 'financial office',

> Storing up the ultimate source of the Marshall's power; the silver pennies that paid his knights and servants, bought their robes, horses and arms, the silks, furs, and precious vessels that displayed his dignity and grandeur to the world.[5]

Of course, all this money had to come from somewhere. It should be no surprise, therefore, to find William Marshall busily promoting towns on his many estates. In Ireland, for example, Marshall created *la Novele vile* (literally 'the new town'), on land lying on the banks of the Suir river. His 'new town', now known as New Ross, replaced an earlier manorial centre that was situated some distance away from the river. The foundation of this particular new town finds a place in Marshall's biography, written anonymously a few years after his death, an indication perhaps that the event was seen to have been of some significance for him, a measure of his 'achievement' perhaps.[6]

The burden of maintaining an aristocratic lifestyle was increased further by also having to provide support for the royal household. A king was able to call upon his vassals to provide him with military aid for wars and defence. However, in the twelfth century a gradual transition took place as lords increasingly had their knight services commuted to a cash payment. This made it all the more vital for individual lords to find larger amounts of cash. It has been suggested that in England, 'difficulty of raising the feudal levy led very early to the commutation of the service by money payment', and evidence shows that by the reign of Henry I (1100–35) this had become common practice, even among ecclesiastical tenants.[7] By way of comparison, in France, the Capetian monarchy were paying wages to household servants and clergy by the middle of the twelfth century, and collecting money rents in lieu of military service.[8]

Apart from dealing with their home affairs, in this period of the high Middle Ages (1100–1300), English and French kings were also leading armies of Crusader knights into the Holy Land. The Crusades were an enormous expense, requiring vast sums of money, not just for raising armies and feeding them in a hostile environment many miles from home, but also for meeting ransom demands. In 1250, for example, King Louis of France agreed to pay 1 million gold bezants, or 500 000 *livres*, in order to secure his release from capture by Egyptian forces in Egypt on his ill-fated Crusade.[9] Generally, during the twelfth and thirteenth centuries, as the value of coinage depreciated, royal demand for currency grew more and more. Money came to count for more than land, and so land had to be made more profitable.

Increased demand for money among the feudal aristocracy and royal *familia* of Europe also affected the lower levels of the medieval social hierarchy, including the rural peasantry. At a time when knight services were being replaced by lump-sum payments, lords in the countryside were placing ever greater emphasis on extracting money rents and cash fines from their agricultural tenants. Rather than simply relying on traditional servile obligations and labour, lords were looking to the peasantry to make payments in money. This was the case in east-central Europe, for example. During the German colonisation of the twelfth century, 'in general, new settlers were not subject to labour services, but paid rent in cash or produce', and of course they had to get the money from somewhere.[10]

Paying money rents to lords in return for holding land was a fundamental element of medieval social organisation. It was found all across Europe, especially in those areas that were being colonised and settled, where new tenants were needed to take up land. The Knights Templars used it on their lands in Aragon in Spain, for example, and in Ireland the Anglo-Normans used it on lordships in the thirteenth century.[11] Even in areas that were typically dominated by demesne working (where labour services were commonplace, as was the case in eastern parts of England), newly cleared land was being settled and put under the plough. In these cases, too, lords were offering agricultural tenants cash rents rather than asking for labour dues.[12] In these cases, 'it seems as if lords were prepared to sacrifice direct claims on their tenant's labour in order to encourage settlement and increase their rent revenues'.[13] Of course, lords were doing this not out of kindness but to supply themselves with necessary cash income. What it meant for agricultural tenants was that they had to find a means of raising the cash, so that they could then pay the money rents.

Recently, economic historians have shown the extent to which peasants in medieval England were involved in producing goods for sale in local urban markets, for country towns and market villages.[14] Market produce came from the peasant's fields and crofts, or from making items from locally available materials, such as baskets of wicker, or pots and tiles. By this means, cash was mobilised in the medieval countryside. The money raised by selling goods in the local market gave agricultural tenants the cash that they needed to pay fines and rents being levied by their lord. In turn, of course, these revenues provided lords with income that was sufficient to pay their commuted knight services. Ultimately, the circulation of cash coming from lords and peasants served the needs and demands of royal households.

For these reasons, on the estates of lords throughout Europe, there was a growing trend towards commercialisation in the medieval countryside. Colonisation (in both 'frontier' and 'interior' areas) required financial income, and commercial growth, via urbanisation, generated this income. If it was to profit the lords it was serving, commercialisation of the countryside had to be carefully administered and controlled. By chartering towns and markets on their estates, lords capitalised on this growing commercialisation. The following part of the chapter examines how this process urbanised lordships, and how lordship influenced the foundation of new towns.

Town Foundation in England and Wales, 1100–1300

The main source of historical evidence to reconstruct trends in medieval town foundation is borough charters. Although these rarely explicitly state what the urbanisation policy of an individual lord was, they nevertheless allow us to establish, occasionally with certainty, when a particular town was chartered and who chartered it. However, we should bear in mind that a borough charter was often granted some time after the creation of a town: town foundation and town chartering might be two separate events. This was the case with Portsmouth, referred to earlier (see Chapter 2), which was founded as a town *before* it became chartered as a borough. To complicate matters further, the earliest *surviving* charter is not necessarily going to be one granted first – it could be a later copy or a confirmation. Some early borough charters have not survived and might only be mentioned in later sources. In these respects, some caution has to be exercised when borough charters are used to reconstruct the chronology of town foundation. Generally in the Middle Ages, the chronology of *borough* enfranchisement lagged behind the economic development of *towns*.

The rate at which lords were creating (and/or chartering) towns obviously varied between different areas. At the regional level, however, it becomes easier to identify some trends and characteristics in the rate of medieval town foundation. For example, as Beresford has shown, during the last decades of the twelfth century in England and Wales there was a gradual, but marked increase in the number of newly founded, chartered towns (Beresford called these 'planted towns').[15] This growth reached a peak in England

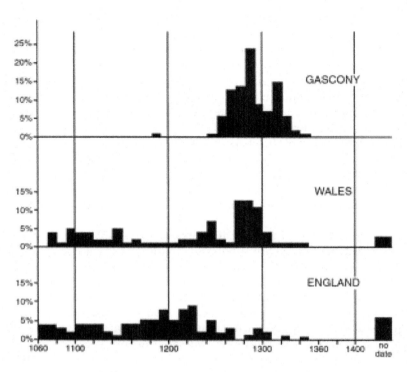

Figure 4.1 *Chronology of 'town plantation' in England*

in the 1210s, before then tailing off during the later thirteenth and fourteenth centuries (Figure 4.1). When looked at in detail, there are three important factors influencing this trend in town foundation (or, to be more precise, town *chartering*): the date *when* a town was founded; the status of the lord *who* founded it; and the location *where* the town was founded. These three factors influenced both the geography and timing of medieval town foundation, not only in England and Wales but in other parts of Europe, too. What we find is that the greater the lord, the more likely he was to possess the sort of ancient central places at which urban activity was already taking place.

What town charters often tend to obscure is the possibility that a town already existed. Because 'charters and constitutions are characteristic only of some towns at certain periods', many towns in the Middle Ages lacked 'confirmation' charters and few had a foundation charter.[16] Yet such 'unchartered' towns still functioned as urban centres (see Chapter 6), which is rather worrying if we are to use charters to map the historical geography of town foundation. Unchartered towns (Birmingham is a good example) thus need to be borne in mind, particularly so since they did not feature in the calculations of some leading historians (Beresford included) whose works we now rely on, and their attempts to understand the process of medieval 'town foundation'.[17]

There was, without doubt, a great proliferation of borough charters during the twelfth and thirteenth centuries in England and Wales.[18] The charters represent a move towards a greater level of bureaucratisation. This period was characterised by an increase in the use of documentation, especially in royal administration.[19] In this context, the proliferation of borough charters that took place towards the end of the twelfth century partly reflects attempts by the English royal household to bring urbanisation under closer control (as well as a broader shift towards putting things down in writing). It might be, therefore, that the rise in the number of borough charters exaggerates the rate of town foundation and urban growth in the latter half of the twelfth century in England. In parts of Wales colonised by the English, however, the grant of a borough charter often was contemporary with a town's foundation, though again we should always consider the possibility that some places were functioning as towns before they received a borough charter.[20]

Despite the potential obstacles to using borough charters to chart the tempo of medieval town foundation, certain observations are possible, particularly with regard to the social status and background of lords who were granting charters to establish new towns (or to be more precise, new *boroughs*) (see Table 4.1). Again, this was something that interested Beresford.[21] He found that in the years immediately following the Norman Conquest a large number of towns were founded by monarchs, though their role as town founders subsequently diminished (except for a flurry of activity in Edward I's reign). As royal town foundations started to tail off, during the latter part of the twelfth century, it seems that bishops became more involved in chartering new towns, especially during the thirteenth century. The chartering of new 'monastic towns', towns created by abbots and priors, also followed this pattern, though they peaked rather earlier than the episcopal foundations, in the reign of Henry III.

Table 4.1   *The pattern of chartering new towns in England, 1086–1350*[22]
            (per cent)

Period	Kings	Bishops	Monasteries	Laymen
1086–1100	32	4	20	40
1101–1188	19	10	11	60
1189–1215	6	9	18	67
1216–1230	0	30	35	35
1231–1300	14	14	11	61
1301–1350	9	33	33	25

Note: The periods of most active foundation are italicised.

By far the largest group of lords chartering towns were those sort that Beresford rather loosely termed 'laymen'. In fact, within this broad group he included lay lords from across a wide social spectrum; from the highest ranking nobles of the land, right down to the most minor lords. For example, men like William Marshall, with their vast estates stretching across large parts of England and Wales, were included with lords of a lesser sort, such as Jean de Gisors, whose small estate in south-east Hampshire formed the site for his new town of Portsmouth (see above, Chapter 2). To understand the fluctuating pattern of town chartering and founding in medieval England and Wales, and the role that these different groups of lords played in urbanising lordships, it is necessary for us to take a close look at some of the towns that were founded, and to enquire whether their urban ventures failed or succeeded.

Royal town foundations

Some royal towns in England, such as Liverpool (chartered in 1208) and Newcastle upon Tyne (founded in *c.*1070), were established by royal charter right from the start. Others, such as Portsmouth (1194) and Kingston upon Hull (1293), had already been established before they received their borough charters from the king.[23] In either case, it is clear that the English monarchy placed an emphasis on the control of coastal towns, and sought to acquire maritime ports. If a coastal town belonging to another lord was showing some sign of growing in its prosperity or strategic value, then the town soon became absorbed into the chain of English royal boroughs.

Royal boroughs existed in England before the arrival of the Normans in 1066. During the Anglo-Saxon and Anglo-Scandinavian periods boroughs belonged to the Crown, which is why in the Domesday Book (1086) they are usually entered under the words *Terra Regis*. Some of these boroughs (*burhs*), for example Oxford, had been deliberately created by the English monarchy in the ninth and tenth centuries and were founded as wholly new towns to combine commercial needs with defensive ones.[24] In southern England these defensible *burhs* were established by Alfred of Wessex and Æthelflæd of Mercia to create a network of strongholds capable of withstanding Danish advances in the late ninth and early tenth centuries.[25] The Danes, too, had *burhs*, collectively called the 'Five Boroughs', at Lincoln, Leicester, Derby, Nottingham and Stamford.[26] However, not all pre-Conquest towns in England were *burhs*, and neither were all towns under royal control. By the eve of the Norman Conquest, some boroughs lay entirely in the hands of Anglo-Saxon earls (Leicester, for example), while some ecclesiastical lords had established new towns on their lordships purely for commercial purposes, as at St Albans (see below).[27]

Both before and after the Norman Conquest, towns founded by royal lords were generally successful in the long term. Indeed, the most successful 'new towns' were the *burhs* established during the tenth and eleventh centuries, particularly the county towns. Towns founded later by the Norman kings were also largely successful. In general, new towns chartered by the king soon rivalled more long-established towns, in terms of both wealth and population.[28] This success was in large part due to the early foundation of royal towns, but royal chartered towns did fail, particularly if they were founded late on in the Middle Ages. In the 1280s, for example, King Edward I issued charters to Newton in Dorset and Bere in Merionydd (Wales). Although he had successfully founded new towns elsewhere on his dominions, and although Newton and Bere were both given the favourable borough customs, neither thrived commercially.[29]

Episcopal and monastic (ecclesiastical) town foundations

According to Beresford's statistics, it was the two decades either side of 1200 that saw the main surge of episcopal and monastic town chartering in England and Wales (Table 4.1). In contrast to newly founded royal towns, however, relatively few of the new towns founded on episcopal and monastic lordships developed into major urban centres. Even those monastic towns founded early on by abbeys did not rise up to occupy particularly high positions in the medieval English urban hierarchy. Of the new monastic towns founded before 1100, which includes Battle in Sussex, St Albans in Hertfordshire, and Bury St Edmunds in Suffolk, only the latter really achieved a reasonably prominent urban status.[30] The reason for the apparent lack of major success in monastic town foundation might have less to do with when they were founded and more to do with the functions that they were created for.

Many of the new towns founded on monastic lordships were intended to serve as local trading centres to feed produce from the monastery's rural estates into the markets of larger urban centres. Rather than trying to found major new towns on their rural estates, what we see instead during the twelfth and thirteenth centuries is monastic lords developing their existing urban estates and land-holdings, particularly if the monastery stood in a well-established town (see Chapter 6).[31] This tended to produce new towns that were rather small and unambitious, such as Evesham abbey's two new towns of Stow-on-the-Wold and Pershore.[32] It also meant that the new towns did not become important places in their own right: their secondary status was maintained by their monastic lord. The same was also true for many of the new towns founded on episcopal lordships. Bishops co-ordinated the foundation of new towns from long-standing pre-Conquest cathedral cities, such as Worcester and Wells, and urbanised their rural estates with towns that were generally quite small but moderately successful.[33]

One of most well-known and successful episcopal towns to have been founded in England is Salisbury. The town of 'New Sarum' lay in low-lying meadows along the river Avon in Wiltshire, and Richard Poore, Bishop of Salisbury, issued a charter to it in 1225.[34] The success of Richard's new town was helped by the fact that New Salisbury was a deliberate replacement for Old Sarum, an earlier hilltop city of pre-Norman origin situated a few miles to the north. In the first quarter of the twelfth century, one of Poore's predecessors, Bishop Roger, had also been busy founding new towns, one at Devizes (again in Wiltshire), and another at Kidwelly, on episcopal lands in south Wales.[35] Later on in the twelfth century, the bishops of Worcester were engaged in founding new towns on their lordships in the fertile Midlands (Stratford-upon-Avon, for example), while further south, during the first half of the thirteenth century, the bishops of Winchester created six new towns on their estates in Hampshire and the Isle of Wight.[36] None of these episcopal *novi burgi* became as important as Bishop Poore's New Sarum, but in fairness his new town took over the role of an existing cathedral city.

Of the new monastic orders that were gaining popularity in England during the twelfth century, the Cistercians seem to have been particularly successful founders of new towns. This may seem surprising, as their order is associated with rather remote places and is assumed to have been removed from the medieval world of commerce. In fact, Cistercian abbeys were responsible for founding two particular towns which subsequently became sufficiently important to be acquired by the king. The first of these two towns is now known simply as Hull, though its full name is Kingston upon Hull. Within 30 years of receiving land in east Yorkshire in 1160, the Cistercian abbey of Meaux had developed a port town on the Humber estuary known then as Wyke. Just over a century later, by 1293, Edward I had gained possession of the abbot's town, and Wyke had become 'Kingston', the king's town.[37] A second Cistercian town which proved attractive to Edward I was Aberconwy, situated on the north coast of Wales. Edward acquired and chartered the town in 1277, and although the Cistercians were relocated their large abbey church still dominates the townscape today.[38]

Not all of the 'new' monastic orders were as concerned with town founding as the Cistercians. For example, the military religious orders of the Knights Templars and the Knights Hospitallers seem not to have been especially keen to promote new towns on their lordships. Although they received much of their land (as gifts) at about the same time as the Cistercians, from the mid-twelfth century onwards, these two orders of 'fighting monks' founded only a few new towns in England, a number of which turned out to be unsuccessful ventures. The Templars in particular gained many rural estates that when taken together amounted to a large swathe of eastern England.[39] On one of these estates, the Templars established Baldock, one of their more successful towns. The borough of Baldock was created *de novo* on land that had been gifted to the Templars by Gilbert de Clare, first Earl of Pembroke, sometime between 1138 and 1148. From a survey of Templar property undertaken in 1185 it is clear that Baldock was prospering, and though it was no more than a small market town the people living there were engaged in a wide variety of economic activities.[40] It has been suggested that the Templars named the town Baldock in imitation of Baghdad, though whether they were expecting their new town to achieve the status of that great Islamic centre is debatable.[41]

Apart from planting new towns on their rural lordships, there were other ways in which ecclesiastical lords profited from trade and commerce in the countryside. Well before the Norman Conquest, settlements with important churches ('minsters') acted as foci for local trade as well as administration.[42] These 'proto-towns' were often subsequently chartered as boroughs, even though they had perhaps been performing urban functions for a long time. Also, apart from granting borough privileges to create chartered towns, many monastic lords issued market charters to rural settlements. The intention was not to make these places into towns as such, but rather to institute regular weekly markets. Some of these villages may already have been holding markets on an unofficial basis, and so the charters simply 'legalised' an existing arrangement. Such charters typically appear in the thirteenth century, and were given to the smallest of settlements, for example Temple Bruer in Lincolnshire.[43] They were markets where local rural people could exchange goods, and perhaps pass on their produce to more important regional markets held in nearby towns.[44] Many such 'market vills' lost their commercial functions during the later Middle Ages (after the Black Death of 1348–49), and the markets ceased.

The new towns chartered by ecclesiastical lords were all the more successful if they were established early on, as was the case with royal town foundations. Those which were established in the late thirteenth and early fourteenth centuries were the least successful enterprises, especially those that lay within close proximity of well-established market centres. One such example of failure is Newtown on the Isle of Wight, a town founded *de novo* on the shores of the Solent by Aymer, Bishop of Winchester, in 1256. By the middle of the thirteenth century, this part of southern England was thickly populated by similar enfranchised towns, all of which were competing for local trade and commerce. Newtown eventually lost out altogether, and the town gradually withered away to such an extent that now the place is but a small hamlet, with only grass-grown streets and empty house plots to show that it was at one time a reasonably sizeable and populated settlement.[45]

Seigneurial (secular) town foundations

By far the most active medieval town founders and charterers was the group of lords which Beresford called 'laymen'. In his reckoning, 67 per cent of the towns founded in the period 1189–1215 were founded by lay lords (see above). The term 'laymen' is rather too broad, however. As I suggested above, it encompasses a range of secular lords of various rank and standing. To this end, a distinction is drawn here between those towns founded by magnate lords (the king's vassals) and those that were created by minor aristocratic lords (the lesser nobility).

The status and wealth of secular (or lay) lords could practically change overnight. In the Middle Ages, social standing among the aristocracy depended on whether a person was in or out of favour with his or her monarch. William fitz Osbern and William Marshall were two great Norman magnate lords who both founded new towns on their lands, and who subsequently had their lands and titles taken from them by royal command. In these cases, lordships and estates might remain in the hands of the king, otherwise they could be allocated by the king to another lord. As estates were passed on, towns could quite quickly change hands between different lords. Conversely, however, some lordships remained with the same family over many generations. In these cases, members of each generation would often establish new towns to supplement those created by their predecessors.

The estates of magnate lords usually encompassed thousands of acres of land, and were often made up of scattered landholdings. To oversee the running of these vast areas magnates had a 'head manor', or *caput*, which invariably was either a castle or manorial hall. The scattered estates made up a lord's fief, and if a title was attached to this fief it was known as an 'honour'. In some cases, a *caput* itself was a newly founded town, created at the same time as the honour.

In the first few decades after the Norman Conquest, many of William's magnate lords established new towns to function as central places from which to organise and co-ordinate the vast estates they had received from the king. Count Alan, a Breton noble who had accompanied William over from Normandy in 1066, was given a large and important honour soon after the Norman Conquest. The new honour was centred on Richmond, in Yorkshire, where the count established a new town, adjacent to his castle, overlooking the river Swale.[46] There were other Norman magnates doing the same thing during the 1070s and 1080s, as the Domesday Book records. For example, the de Ferrers' honour was centred on a new castle at Tutbury in Staffordshire, which also had a new borough attached where there were 'forty-two men living from their merchandise only, yielding with the market place £4 10s' in dues to the lord, in 1086.[47] Other Norman magnate families who at this time were also placing towns at the seats of their honours were the de Clares, whose seat was Tonbridge, in Kent, and the de Lacys, whose towns of Weobley and Pontefract ('the broken bridge') were the administrative centres for their extensive estates in Herefordshire and Yorkshire.[48]

Towns that were created by wealthy magnate families as administrative estate centres were further supplemented by other new towns located on their outlying estates. The honour of the Earl of Chester, for example, comprised a number of rural estates which were scattered across large parts of western England, from Cheshire to Gloucestershire. By 1200, the earls had set about creating new chartered towns on a number of these estates, while at the same time they also promoted existing towns in their possession by granting them borough charters, too.[49]

One aristocratic family who pursued a particularly spirited programme of town founding on their estates was the de Redvers family. They were of Norman origin and received lands during the early twelfth century in Devon, Hampshire and the Isle of Wight. Like many similar families, they were busily involved with founding new towns on their estates. They appear to have been particularly enthusiastic in this respect. During the latter half of the twelfth century, in particular, successive family members issued borough charters to promote urban development. Within only a matter of a few years, three new towns had been established within a radius of ten miles. Two of the towns were on the Isle of Wight, and one of these, Newport (*Novus Burgus de Medina*), was placed not too far from the de Redvers' castle at Carisbrooke. The second, Yarmouth, was situated at the western end of the island, and faced across the Solent towards the third of these three towns, Lymington.[50] The de Redvers were therefore 'particularly enterprising' in respect of their policy of 'borough plantation'.[51] By being sited on the busy Solent estuary, close to the important maritime ports of Southampton and Portsmouth, each of their new towns was well positioned in commercial terms.

Although the de Redvers' three new towns did not achieve a particularly high level of prosperity during the Middle Ages, they nevertheless retained their urban functions, and today Newport is still a thriving market town. New towns were also created on lordships that had been subinfeudated to minor noble lords.

Compared with those towns that were founded by the magnates, new towns founded by lesser lords often arrived quite late on the medieval urban scene and so consequently they tended not to fare too well. Some such towns dropped out of the medieval urban hierarchy altogether. By the end of the thirteenth century, when many minor noble lords were still busily chartering new towns, the English landscape had become so saturated with market towns and villages that most subsequently foundered and failed as commercial enterprises. Even a seemingly attractive location for a new town might not be enough to make the venture viable if it was a late addition. At Bretford, in Warwickshire, for example, where the Fosse Way Roman road crosses the river Avon, Theobald de Vernon established a new borough, probably sometime before 1279.[52] His new town did not prove commercially tenable, however, because very close near by there were a host of market villages, and not much further were the two important towns of Coventry and Rugby, both well-established urban centres by this time.

Similar stories of economic stagnation and failure can be told of many of the new towns that were founded and chartered by lesser lords in England after c.1250. In fact, this trend was the same right across medieval Europe. In Pomerania, for example, out of 54 towns founded in the period from 1234 to 1500, nearly one-quarter came to lose their urban functions. As Kuhn has pointed out, of the 14 town foundations that were led by 'aristocratic' lords, three eventually 'reverted to villages', and 'all of them latecomers' to the urban scene.[53] In contrast, the failure rate was 'lowest with the ducal foundations', that is among those towns created by high-status secular lords, as was the case in England.

Briefly, in conclusion, two clear patterns have so far emerged from looking at the interrelationship between lordship and urbanisation in medieval England. Firstly, in the period 1050–1350, lords of higher social status, particularly kings, bishops and magnate nobles, tended to charter and found their new towns earlier rather than later. On the whole, the long-term commercial success of their new towns was relatively sound. Secondly, founding a town late in the Middle Ages, after about 1270, meant that it had much less chance of succeeding. This was true whatever the lord's social status, though new towns that were latecomers were all the more likely to fail if they had been founded by lesser lords, particularly the minor nobility.

Paréage and the Foundation of Bastides in Gascony

What is missing from the discussion so far is the possibility that new towns were founded not just by a single lord acting alone on his lordship, but rather by a collective process of decision-making involving a range of other people, including local lords of differing social status. In the twelfth and thirteenth centuries, such collaboration certainly occurred in Gascony in south-west France with the foundation of chartered new towns known as *bastides*. This part of the chapter addresses how and why lords in Gascony collaborated over town foundation, and offers the view that this process of collaborative urbanisation took place on lordships in other regions of medieval Europe. First, some consideration of the political context of Gascony is required.

Gascony became a wealthy region during the twelfth and thirteenth centuries as a result of the high demand for its wines. However, the region was subject to rival claims by both the English and French Crown. In 1153, following the accession of Henry II to the English throne, Gascony formed part of the vast Angevin 'empire', but this had changed by 1259. Following the Treaty of Paris, the English held the area from the French Crown as a fief. During the reign of Edward I (1272–1307), parts of Gascony which were under French lordship were ceded to the English. One area where this happened was the Haut Agenais, between Bergerac and Cahors. Between 1249 and 1271 this area was held by the Count of Toulouse, Alphonse of Poitiers. However, it was subsequently acquired by the English Crown and fell under the overlordship of Edward I.[54]

Urbanisation and English and French Gascony

Prior to the thirteenth century, Gascony was a part of France that was not highly urbanised. After 1200, the region became the focus of co-ordinated and intensive programmes of urbanisation, first under the initiative of Alphonse and then Edward I. The foundation of new towns in Gascony frequently took place by means of partnerships between different lords. Through the thirteenth century in particular both English and French lords created bastides for both political as well as economic reasons. It is now generally accepted that the bastide towns of south-west France were founded primarily for commercial rather than military reasons.[55] According to the dates provided by town charters, the foundation of bastide towns in English Gascony peaked in the later thirteenth century, whereas the peak of French bastide-founding was slightly earlier, in the middle decades of the century.[56]

Although not all of the bastide towns were fortified, the towns offered lords a chance to make their presence felt, as they did in the case of frontier parts of the early Norman kingdom of England (see Chapter 3). The actions of the Counts of Toulouse, for example, were instrumental in the creation of French bastides in the 1200s. Two noble lords who took this title, Raimond VII (1229–49) and his successor, Alphonse, both used bastides to populate and colonise their *comté*. The activities of these men reveal the complex nature of administrative arrangements that led to the foundation of bastides.

The temporal and spatial distribution of the bastides in south-west France has been mapped by Lauret, Malebranche and Seraphin in their book, *Bastides: villes nouvelles au Moyen Âge*.[57] The maps produced by them show very clearly how much more widespread and dramatic the policies of Alphonse were compared to Raimond (Figure 4.2). Raimond's bastide-founding was concentrated more in the region just to the north of Toulouse, between the rivers Tarn and Garonne; while Alphonse's bastides were established in a much broader area stretching from the Comté de Foix in the south, in the Pyrenean foothills, to the Dordogne river in the north, encompassing the Agenais. In just over 20 years, nearly 50 bastides were founded under the initiative of Alphonse, a scale of foundation that surpassed his predecessor who established 23 bastides in all. Not all the Alphonsian bastides remained in French hands,

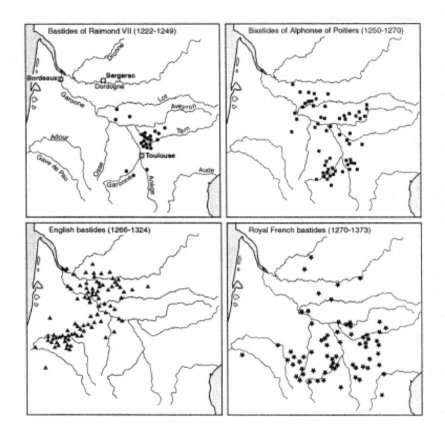

Figure 4.2   *English and French bastides in Gascony*

however – some of those in the Haut Agenais fell to the English in 1279, as did those in Quercy in 1286.

One of the principal characteristics of Raimond's and Alphonse's programme of creating bastide towns was the use of partnerships between different individual lords at the local level. Although the idea of such partnerships, or *paréage* (*pareagium*), pre-dated by two centuries the main phase of bastide foundations, it was widely adopted by overlords during the thirteenth century as a means of securing support for creating new towns on the estates of lesser lords. *Paréage* was a contract between a seigneurial overlord and one or more local lords. In simple terms it meant that lesser lords could establish a bastide on their land with royal or suzerain protection. This offered lesser lords the advantage of having legal support from their social superiors, while at the local level it gave them authority to find land and people to create their bastide.

Whether a bastide was being created *de novo*, on a greenfield site, or whether it was being created by adopting some existing settlement, the partnership contract offered by *paréage* normally represented the first stage in the foundation of a bastide town. The grant of legal and economic borough privileges usually followed in a separate town charter. To show how the *paréage* idea worked in practice, the bastide-founding activities of lords such as Alphonse de Poitiers will now be examined.

Paréage *and bastides in the Agenais*

During the later thirteenth century, Alphonse put the *paréage* principle to good use in his bid to found bastides in the Agenais region, south of the Dordogne river. In 1269, for example, Alphonse collaborated with the lord of Durfort to establish Dunes, while two years earlier both he and the abbot of Clairac granted *paréage* and customs to create a bastide called Laparade. In that same year, he also founded the bastide of Villereal by partnering with the abbot of Aurillac and the lord of Biron, and in 1254, at Villeneuve-sur-Lot, Alphonse set up one bastide on one side of the river (with the abbot of Eysses), and another town on the opposite bank (again with the abbot but also in association with a lay lord). Similarly, Alphonse's contemporaries used this same approach to establish bastides on their lands. In Ariege, for example, Mazères sur L'Hers was created by a partnership between the Count of Foix and the abbot of Boulbonne in 1253, and in Gers at a place called Masseube, meaning 'woodhouse' (*mansio silvae*) the Count of Armagnac and the abbot of Lescaladieu granted *paréage* in 1274 and borough customs in 1276.[58]

Typically, *paréage* represented the initial stage of bastide foundation. It was when the site for the bastide was chosen within a particular lordship and the time when new inhabitants were being attracted to take up residence there. Subsequently the bastide was given a charter containing urban privileges, liberties and customs. The *paréage* also typically involved collaboration between secular lords (for example, the counts), at the regional level, and local ecclesiastical lords, particularly those at the head of monasteries who were keen to make their lands more profitable. The abbots of Cistercian abbeys were especially active founders of bastides, for example, and frequently went into partnership with lay lords.[59] In this sense, the creation of bastide towns was a complex process. A web of local and regional social relations were involved in structuring the process of urbanisation on Gascon lordships. We can see this clearly in the activities of Edward I in Gascony.

Bastides of Edward I

As a largely absent overlord, King Edward I chiefly relied on his local seneschals to control Gascony and to take care of his affairs there. Initially, following his coronation, Edward showed particular interest in Gascon affairs, not least because it was an area of his dominions that was being claimed by the French as their own (a situation that started Edward's wrangle with the French that ultimately led to the Hundred Years War in the following century).[60] However, although periodically during the 1280s the king did visit the region, by and large he had little direct personal involvement in its everyday administration.

It was Edward's policy during the 1280s to continue the process of founding and chartering bastide towns in the Agenais. Following the acquisition of this area, and with it a number of bastides that had been founded by the French, Edward's seneschals established new bastides, not just in the Agenais but elsewhere in Gascony too, largely by continuing to use the *paréage* system that the Counts of Toulouse had used. Founding new bastides was thus a deliberate policy under English rule as it had been under the French. The new towns provided the remote English Crown with economic control over a subject population, as well as the profits of commercialism.

In addition to the bastides that he had gained from Alphonse, Edward and his seneschals created a denser network of chartered towns through the *paréage* system (Figure 4.2). In 1272, for example, close to the main artery into English Gascony, the Dordogne river, a new bastide was founded called Beaumont du Périgord. It was founded not by Edward himself, but on his behalf by his seneschal of Guyenne, Lucas de Thanay. Beaumont was created in partnership with three other lords, the prior of St Avit Seigneur, whose hilltop priory was situated three miles from the new town, the lay lord of Biron, and the abbot of Cadouin.[61] At the local level, these three lords were acting through the regional authority of the seneschal, while he, in turn, was acting on behalf of the king.

As was usual, the *paréage* document for Beaumont was drawn up before the town received its charter of liberties and customs, which came in 1286. This latter charter, as we might expect, confirmed that the townspeople would be free from obligations to these lords, while the lords' officials had to swear before the town court that they would themselves abide by these customs and allow the towns-people to live in peace.[62] In response to such grants of privileges it was not unknown for a neighbouring lord, who had no bastide on his lands, to complain that his rural tenants were fleeing from their obligations to him because a nearby bastide was offering them better personal and material prospects.[63]

The well-documented early history of Edward's bastides provides some interesting insight into the foundation process itself. In 1274, at Pugpito, Peter de Marchinson and his brother gave to the king a hilltop site on their land in order to 'make a bastide and enpeople' the site. As a result they themselves were to have two building plots within the new town. Similarly, at Sainte Eulalie in 1265 local landholders offered land to the English providing that they agreed to build a bastide there, the terms of which were accepted by one of Edward's seneschals, Jean de Grailly. De Grailly was an especially busy bastidor in the 1280s. He was appointed first seneschal of the Agenais in 1279, with a specific order from the king to engage in bastide-founding.[64]

In November 1274, Edward had sent letters to his seneschals in Gascony ordering them to acquire sites for bastides and to endow the new towns with customs and liberties. Following this order, de Grailly founded bastides at Beauregard (a name meaning 'good prospect') in 1286, Molières in 1278–84, Monpazier in 1285 (in partnership with Pierre de Gontaud, lord of Biron), Cadillac in 1280, Polinges in 1281, La Bastide D'Armagnac in 1283–91, Vianne in 1284 and Corneillas in 1280 – a list that clearly reflects the concentrated efforts of de Grailly and the intensity of English bastide-founding in the region of the Agenais. Another royal clerk who had orders from Edward was the abbot of Sainte-Ferme. He was instructed to build a bastide at Lados in 1281 on a suitable place, 'whether on royal land or the land of vassals'. Whatever land the abbot had acquired to fulfil this duty, it was clearly not sufficient for the purpose as the king himself had to buy more land from a lord called Raymond Guillane de la Dos – hence the name for the bastide, Lados.[65]

The bastides were not only wanted by the English overlords but by the Gascons themselves. At Sainte Quitterie, for example, in 1289, the old town was burned and local people petitioned for a bastide to be built for their protection. Here, *paréage* was called upon as a means of offering political protection to the townspeople. The charter setting out the partnership included the king, Bishop Peter and the Chapter of Sainte Quitterie. This was not always a straightforward process, however. In the case of the foundation of Lacenne 'there was a considerable delay between the original *paréage* and the erection of the town' caused by complaints received from the townspeople of nearby Agen. Their hostility to the scheme at Lacenne meant that although *paréage* was drawn up in 1283, the bastide was not developed until 1320.[66] Similar delays were also experienced in other cases, for example in the foundation of Miramont and Hastingues. In these instances the value of *paréage* becomes clear, for it provided a means by which disputes could be resolved between different parties affected by the town-founding process, with the added bonus that higher authorities could be brought into the litigation procedure. In this context, the system of *paréage* tied together the interests of local people (lords and townspeople) with those of their overlords.

To commemorate a lord's involvement with the foundation of a bastide it was common for the town to take the lord's title or name. Consequently the role of Edward's English overlordship is still inscribed on the landscape of Gascony. The bastide of Hastingues, for example, commemorated the name of its founding lord, John Hastings, lord of Abergavenny, who was seneschal of Gascony for 1302–4 and 1309–10. His bastide 'was a product of an agreement between the king and a monastic house possessing land at a place which seemed to have urban potential', on the banks of the Pau river.[67] Other English bastides which were named after their lords include Baa (1286–87), close to Bordeaux, named after Robert Barnell, Bishop of Bath; Créon named after seneschal Amaury de Créon in 1315; Libourne named after Roger de Leybourne in 1268;

Lalinde, on the banks of the Dordogne, named after Jean de la
Linde, a royal official; Toulouzette, founded in 1321 and named
after William de Toulouse, the king's seneschal of Landes, and
Valence d'Agen named after William de Valence, Edward's uncle,
soon after the English acquisition of the Agenais.[68]

As symbolic as the naming process of the bastides was the act of
reading charters of *paréage* and town customs at the construction
sites. At Toulouzette, for example, the formal act of foundation is
described in a contemporary account. It included raising a pole
(*palum*) by William de Toulouse himself (perhaps with his colours
painted on a flag flying from it), as well as a grant of the liberties
that the chartered town would receive if people came to live there.
Such proclamations were clearly intended to be visible signs of
the lord's intent and a symbol of his honour.[69] Of course, ultimately the foundation of a bastide favoured the Crown. An
agreement between the seneschal of Gascony and the men of
Bayonne was recalled by Edward III in 1331 which set out how the
bastide of Port de Lanre was founded 'for the mutual profit of the
king and his subjects'.[70]

It was an unusual occurrence for the king to be present at the
foundation of a bastide. Rather, the creation of a new town was left
to the men on the spot. However, in spring 1287 Edward I did
visit the bastide of Baa, six months after the site had been obtained for him for the purposes of founding a new town. We know
of his visit to Baa because the royal exchequer accounts actually
record that Edward had 'stood the men eight shillings worth of
drinks' while he was staying on the site, a gesture of goodwill
perhaps.[71] Once established, the king was able to profit from the
building of bastides by farming them out at fixed fees, as he did
in the case of the bastides of Beaumont de Perigord, Beaulieu,
Fonroque, la Bastide Monestier and Sainte Eulalie when he granted
them all to Henry le Waleys for periods of up to 20 years.[72]

Social relations and town foundation

Looking at the ways in which the bastide towns of south-west France
were founded reveals how interconnections between different levels of feudal lordship were implicated in the process of urbanisation.
In this context five important issues stand out: first, that town foundations relied on overlordship that was mediated through partnering

with local lords, both lay and ecclesiastical; second, that absenteeism was no barrier to urban foundation on 'remote' lordships; third, that the founding of new towns was encouraged by local people, as a means of gaining the political weight of overlords to mediate in disputes and providing them with relative personal freedom; fourth, that where *paréage* was used it invariably pre-dated the grant of customs and privileges contained within a town's charter; and finally, that lords of different status imitated one another's practices, and sometimes, where their interests clashed, petitions might be raised against them.

Although we meet with the principle of *paréage* most explicitly in records relating to the foundation of bastides in Gascony, it seems unlikely that only lords in south-west France used it. Indeed, there is evidence that partnerships were used to create new towns elsewhere in Europe in the twelfth and thirteenth centuries. In England, for example, in the 1280s and 1290s, Edward I used colloquia and commissions to establish new towns. The two well-known examples of this concern the rebuilding of Berwick-upon-Tweed and the foundation of New Winchelsea (to replace the existing town that the sea had claimed during storms that hit the south coast of England in 1282).[73] In each case Edward brought together individuals who shared an interest in urbanism and commerce to discuss the suitability of sites for creating new towns, as well as the legal and institutional frameworks that would govern them. At Winchelsea this involved three men: Stephen de Pencester, Henry le Waleys and Gregory de Rokesle.[74] Together they negotiated with local landholders and considered the needs of local townspeople, as if they were dealing with the foundation of a bastide in Gascony. In fact, le Waleys was 'a trusted administrator and diplomat in Edward's service', and had worked on the king's behalf in Gascony where he was mayor of Bordeaux.[75]

Whether such partnerships lay behind the creation of new towns in England *before* Edward's reign is difficult to determine in the absence of the sort of specific documentation that accompanies bastide foundation in Gascony. However, we may postulate that partnerships did occur in twelfth-century England between lords who wished to create new towns. One instance where partnership might have been used is Portsmouth. Here, it seems that Jean de Gisors established the new town on a previously empty site with the co-operation, and perhaps encouragement, of a nearby local ecclesiastical lord, the prior of Southwick. From early property records dating from about the time of the foundation of Portsmouth, both de Gisors and the prior are seen to be in possession of a number of properties within the town. Also, the prior and his clergy were to hold divine service in the new chapel of St Thomas in the town.[76] Partnership between these two local lords is suggested by their large stake in urban property-holding in Portsmouth. Having a new town was an investment, providing a good long-term return, and as we have already seen in the context of *paréage* in Gascony, profit from urban properties was a strong motive for the formation of partnerships between local lords.

Investment and financial return were also a significant motive to those who were involved in the foundation of towns in central and eastern Europe at this time. There the profits of urbanisation went to specially employed 'agents', or middlemen, who were acting on behalf of entrepreneurially minded lords. The activities of these middlemen, called 'locators' (*locatores*) by contemporaries, deserves close attention, for it further demonstrates the social complexity of town foundation on medieval lordships.

Locatores: Urbanisation and Lordship in East-central Europe

The chartering of towns in east-central Europe was introduced in Chapter 3. Here, the intricate relationship between lord, lordship and urbanisation is the focus of the discussion, looking at how lords and their *locatores* were jointly implicated in the promotion of new towns on lordships in areas that today form parts of Germany and Poland. The locators are mentioned specifically in contemporary accounts of town foundation in these two countries. Indeed, in Poland, such is the importance of the activity of locators in medieval town foundation that Polish historians refer to the twelfth and thirteenth centuries as the 'period of location'.[77]

The activities of Archbishop Wichmann of Magdeburg provide a good point from which to start looking at how medieval lords made use of locators. Wichmann has already been mentioned for the way that he used German urban laws to urbanise and colonise an area between the rivers Elbe and Oder in the middle decades of the twelfth century. To help in this process the archbishop appointed locators, as Quirin explains: 'Wichmann used rich locators, and it was they who attracted the settlers, who organised the settlements and, in return, received special privileges to compensate (in advance) for their activities, expenses and risks.'[78] Of course, these risks and expenses faced the founders of new towns all over medieval Europe, but by employing locators a lord could avoid having to do the local groundwork themselves. In this context, it is perhaps surprising that contemporaries outside Germany and Poland only occasionally mention 'locators'. However, just as partnerships were widely used by medieval lords seeking to found new towns on their lordships, so too can a case be made for a wider use of locators (see below).

Locatores *and their lords*

With their large and extensive lordships, influential and wealthy German lords like Wichmann would have found it difficult to settle new people and establish chartered towns without having locators. The lords themselves were prepared to underwrite a locator's expenditure and let them deal with the task of actually founding a town. It was this policy that Archbishop Wichmann was using when he established Jüterbog and its ring of dependent market settlements. To help colonise this land, his locators were founding new rural settlements as well as new towns. In 1159, for example, Wichmann granted the village of Pechau to a locator named Herbert 'to settle and make fruitful' the land. Meanwhile, at Poppordorf, two of Wichmann's other locators, Werner of Paderborn and Gottfried, were given lands which Wichmann had obtained by buying out local lords.[79]

Their lords often saw the locators as reliable and trustworthy men. Most were already wealthy and respected before they became involved with founding new towns. In Silesia, for example, locators were sometimes of knightly origin, while in Bohemia, Conrad of Lowendorf was granted a new settlement by King Przemysl Ottokar II on the basis that 'he is the right man for such things and is experienced'.[80] Locators were primarily responsible for overseeing the practicalities of establishing a new town, for ensuring that settlers came to live there and that the town became profitable for the lord. Although a locator was given power to act at the local level, really he was putting into place a programme of settlement that had much broader political and economic intent.

The incentive that led a locator to enter into a contractual agreement with a lord was financial, the promise of a rich return. As Quirin puts it, the locators 'received everything as an hereditary fief [meaning no one could take it away from them], and only the ultimate ownership remained with the lord of the town. In general, they took over the office of the Schultheiss [from the Latin *scultetus* meaning 'headman'], and the legal obligations connected with it, which included part of the profits of justice. The lord of the town, who was also the lord of the district, gave the locator the office of *advocatus* in the Weichbild.'[81] Lords thus saw locators as agents responsible not only for the creation of a new town but advisories who would carry out civic duties too, carrying through the lord's wishes and ensuring that the newly founded town had a sound political organisation. In return the lord placed the locator in a high position in the town's administration. As well as these legal privileges,

> A locator received a considerable number of hufen, free of dues or tithes: in towns one in every six hufen, in villages as many as fifty hufen. Consequently some *locatores* had income from between forty and fifty hufen – an estate larger than that of many nobles. Plainly a locator could not work all of this land himself, nor consume all that it yielded. He had to employ others to work for him and to bring the produce to market. As every charter given to a locator shows us, in the town he received income from stalls that sold foodstuffs and from bath-houses.[82]

Locators were thus used by aristocratic lords to colonise their lands in order to make them more remunerative. The locator consequently assumed great local importance and in the years following a town's creation could expect to play a role in the government of a town. Initially, locators acted as representatives for the town's overlord, promoting a new town on behalf of its absentee lord and operating as a sort of 'intermediary between town and lord'.[83] However, not all locators made easy money from founding new towns on behalf of their commissioning lords. Some ventures failed and did not pay.

By entering into contracts with overlords the locators were taking a risk and a return on their investment was not always forthcoming for a variety of reasons. It could be that the town was 'badly situated in relation to the communications system and there might be a lack of settlers, poor harvests or external enemies ... there are several charters that show *locatores* or their heirs selling properties that did not live up to their expectations'.[84] In the thirteenth century, for example, a Polish count called Bronisz had invited a German called Franco to settle Germans on the edge of his estate, but it is recalled that this venture failed to succeed 'because of poverty'. Similarly, in Silesia in 1250, an urban foundation failed because 'dissension arose among the *locatores*, some died, some were oppressed by poverty and sold their share in the *locatio* for cash'.[85] For this reason lords sometimes wrote penalty clauses into their contracts with locators.

Town foundation by 'locators'

Although town founding by locators is specifically referred to only in central and eastern European contexts, it is clear that 'middlemen' were being used elsewhere for the same purpose. In these cases, contemporaries did not always use the term *locatore*. In Pomerania, for instance, Barnim I imitated Wichmann in his use of middlemen to found the town of Prenzlau in 1234. His foundation charter records eight contractors, actually termed *fundators*, whom he had commissioned to establish the town. In return, these eight men each received ten parcels of land ('Hufen'), and were each given the right to set up mills of their own (a source of private revenue for them). The *fundators* were thus acting as locators, and effectively they became minor lords in their own right. One of the 'locators' at Prenzlau became the town's administrator, while all, like the settlers that they were commissioned to find, were exempt from paying tax for their first three years there. Along with their burgages in the town, the locators held their Hufen in free hereditary possession.[86]

While contemporaries might not always use the term *locatore* to refer to a lord's locator, it is also evident that the Latin word from which 'locator' is derived (*locatio*, 'location') came to have a broader significance. In the context of medieval Poland, for example, *locatio* referred more generally to the process of colonisation and urbanisation, as Zientara has shown. He outlines three meanings attached to the term 'location' in Poland.[87] First, it refers to the 'founding of a new settlement', where a lord transferred land to a locator by charter. For instance, in the document issued by Bishop Thomas I of Wrocław to Peter of Nysa in 1237, for 'the location of several new villages in the northern part of the Nysa region'. In its second meaning, 'location designated the transformation of the spatial layout of an existing settlement', as seen in the case of a charter of 1261 granted by Henry III to Wrocław, where an area of the town was referred to as '*inter fossata prime locacionis*'. Thirdly, in Polish historiography, 'the term "location" deals with . . . political structure and law' of new settlements, and 'in this sense, location was a legal act performed either by the insurance of a document or by public declaration at a public meeting'.[88]

The three meanings of the term 'location' found in Poland all derive from the locators' role in settlement foundation, planning and law. Locators in other parts of east-central Europe, such as Silesia, Bohemia and Pomerania, were also performing these roles. Some parallels between the process of location and town founding are evident in Western Europe, too. For example, just as Wichmann bought out local lordships to give to locators to create Popperdorf in east Germany (see above), so too did Edward I purchase lordships to found his bastides in Gascony. What is more, to all intents and purposes the seneschals to whom Edward delegated town-founding responsibilities were acting on his behalf just as locators would. In southern England, Edward's new towns of Winchelsea and Newton were founded by 'commissioners' appointed by him. Although these commissioners were not responsible for the failure of the towns, which in the case of Newton was probably as well (see above), their role was in many ways remarkably similar to that of the east European locators employed by Wichmann and Barnim. Perhaps, then, the role of the 'locator' was widely used by lords throughout medieval Europe, even though they might not always be specifically called *locatore*.

For the most part 'locators' are rather shadowy characters. Even in Poland there are 'no accounts of the operations of locators'.[89] Nevertheless, some general points can be made about locators and their role in founding towns on lordships. In east-central Europe in particular, 'he was an entrepreneur who acted as a middle man between the lord eager to develop his land and new settlers', and as such 'the locator was responsible for the mechanics of settlement, such as the recruitment of colonists and the division of land, and received in return a substantial landed estate in the new settlement with hereditary privileges'.[90] Through the act of 'location', locators founded new urban settlements, and lordships were urbanised. Those locators who were more successful found themselves in a reasonably strong economic and political position.

Conclusion

This chapter has shown that the founding of new towns on medieval lordships was a complex and intricate social process. Clearly, lordship and urbanisation were intimately linked in the Middle Ages, but rather than being simply a case of a lord issuing a borough charter to establish a town, urbanisation required lords to work alongside other individuals and groups – it required co-operation.

Three broad observations may be made on the basis of the preceding discussion:

1. Medieval social hierarchies, represented by different levels of lordship, were reflected in the process of urbanisation. That is to say, the successful urbanisation of a lordship depended upon the timing and location of a town, both of which were factors that were largely determined by the status of the town-founding lord. The chronology of medieval town foundation was thus a corollary of the founder's social status. Put simply, the greater the lord the more likely it was that he possessed the sort of place that would make the most successful towns, particularly in cases where there was already some nascent urban activity.

2. Although individual lords granted charters to found new towns, these charters often conceal a complex web of social relations underpinning the urbanisation process. Fortunately, in the context of the foundation of bastide towns in south-west France, charters reveal the presence of partnerships (*paréage*) between different lords, and thus reveal how local, or neighbouring, lords could act together in order to establish a new town. Elsewhere, too, it is also likely that these sorts of partnerships were forged, especially in cases where a magnate overlord wished to establish a town on distant lordships.

3. While the foundation of a new town might stem from the mind of an individual lord, the task of actually creating a new chartered town could be delegated to specially appointed agents.

In parts of east-central Europe, the activities of these agents, or 'locators' as they were known, are documented. The locators were entrepreneurial middlemen acting at the local level to mediate between lords and townspeople, while at the same time seeking personal financial and political reward. The locators helped absentee lords to urbanise their lordships, and again, as with that of *paréage*, the principle of using locators to found new towns was probably one that many lords put into practice. The problem here, however, is knowing who these people were and how they operated in areas outside east-central Europe.

Overall in this chapter, my main concern has been with how new towns were established on rural lordships, with how lords influenced the life of towns. A related issue, of course, is how lords used the same methods to develop their urban estates and landholdings, but this is something I wish to consider in the context of urban landholding more generally (see Chapter 6). Before doing so, it is also important that urbanisation is examined from the point of view of the physical changes taking place in towns and cities in the Middle Ages, and the processes which shaped urban landscapes.

5

URBAN LANDSCAPES

> To lay out with sufficient streets and lanes, adequate sites for
> a market and church, plots for merchants and others in a new
> town with a harbour in a place called Gotowre super Mare in
> Studland parish [Dorset].
>
> *Calendar of Patent Rolls,* 1281[1]

Much has yet to be learned about how urban landscapes were formed
in the Middle Ages. Urban design and planning is only occasionally referred to in medieval sources, for although contemporary
records sometimes reveal that a certain town or part of a town was
established at a particular time, it is extremely rare for them to
point out how a new urban landscape had been designed and
planned. The case of Gotowre super Mare (Newton) cited above is
a good example of this. The extract itself comes from statutory
records, and it refers to an order made by King Edward I to men
whom he had commissioned to lay out a new town in Dorset. His
order was carried out, but the ideas and skills of those appointed
by Edward I are no longer known to us, simply because they were
not recorded at the time.[2] Furthermore, because Newton no longer
exists as a settlement, it is not even possible to examine the form
that Edward's new town took.

The previous three chapters have looked at how urbanisation in
the Middle Ages was a product of legal and economic conditions
which principally worked in favour of feudal lords. The purpose
of this chapter is to consider what processes were involved in making
the landscapes of medieval towns and cities. The aim is to look at
how urban landscapes were created, and how they were subsequently

altered during the course of the Middle Ages. To do this it is necessary to consider the layouts of medieval towns and cities alongside surviving historical records. In this respect, the case of Newton's 'lost' townscape is relatively unusual, for the physical layouts of medieval urban landscapes were often long-lasting, and still remain visible in towns and cities today (see Chapter 1). It is also necessary to draw upon some of the material presented earlier, on lordship and urban institutions, for this is helpful in interpreting how and why medieval urban landscapes took the forms that they did – and it will also help explain why it was that urban landscapes often had broadly similar characteristics in the Middle Ages.

If they are examined closely, the layouts of medieval urban landscapes reveal patterns of expansion and growth, as towns and cities grew in response to changing political, economic and social needs. The first part of the chapter examines these patterns, and focuses on the formative and transformative changes that shaped urban landscapes between the eleventh and fifteenth centuries. The second part of the chapter then looks more specifically at how new urban landscapes were designed and planned, and explores who was responsible for actually doing the work. Some of the designs chosen for new urban landscapes deliberately conveyed aspects of Christian cosmology, while others were intended to help improve and 'modernise' the physical appearance of cities. Either way, in the Middle Ages urban design and planning was an attempt to make urban landscapes both beautiful and practical.

The Formation and Transformation of Urban Landscapes

Two processes shaped medieval urban landscapes: *formation* and *transformation*. To show these two processes at work it will be useful to take examples of each, starting first with a look at 'accretive growth', which is where towns expanded outwards. Following on from this, I turn to consider the role that redevelopment played in transforming urban landscapes to show that medieval urban growth also proceeded by a process of 'superimposition', where townscapes were cleared and new ones put in their place. I will focus on evidence from England; partly because recently a lot of new work has been done on the changing forms of English medieval urban landscapes, and partly because I wish to show that townscape formation and transformation (accretion and superimposition) occurred simultaneously within medieval towns and cities.

Townscape formation and accretive urban growth

In the new towns that were being founded along the northern and western frontiers of Norman England it is common to find evidence for three phases of accretive growth. Each phase in the formation of these townscapes added a distinct urban landscape with its own particular morphological characteristics. These characteristics will first be described here by looking at how the landscape of a small new Norman town evolved between the late eleventh and early thirteenth centuries.

It was a Norman lord called Robert de Belleme who took the initiative of removing the people of Quatford, on the river Severn in Shropshire, to a new site in a more commanding position overlooking the river and the bridge that gave the new town its name – Bridgnorth.[3] The earliest phase in the development of Bridgnorth's urban landscape is associated with Belleme's castle, which we know was under construction in the 1080s. Belleme's castle was attached to a small town which comprised a small area of the promontory site and included streets fronted by rows of plots (Figure 5.1).[4] These plots were the parcels of land where Bridgnorth's townspeople lived and worked, while the open space of the street in front of their properties provided the little town with room for its market.

Sometime soon after 1100, after Henry I had seized the castle and town from Belleme, a second stage took place in the development of Norman Bridgnorth with the creation of a new larger market place stretching away from the gates of the castle town. Fronting the new street were larger plots than those to be found in Belleme's earlier town. Rather later again, a third phase of urban development added yet another area to Bridgnorth's twelfth-century townscape. Some time towards the end of the twelfth century, or perhaps early in the thirteenth, a regular-looking layout of streets and plots was set out just to the west of the plots fronting onto the High Street market place (Figure 5.1). The regularity of this third phase of development gives the area an overall look of formality. Compared with those areas that preceded it, this later addition consisted of a denser arrangement of plots and streets.

What the example of Bridgnorth shows is a series of stages of accretive urban growth, starting with Belleme's castle town of the 1080s, and followed by the market-place 'extension' of Henry I's reign, and the 'formal' area of the later twelfth century. As new urban landscapes superseded earlier ones, so Bridgnorth gradually grew in size. This pattern is not peculiar to Bridgnorth, however, for it can be found in other new towns in England, particularly those along the western and northern edges of the Norman kingdom. In the following discussion the three phases of development evident at Bridgnorth will be examined further, firstly by looking at 'institutional urban landscapes' (castle and abbey towns), then 'commercial urban landscapes' (street markets), and finally 'formal urban landscapes' (regular 'grids'). The sequence of the discussion thus follows the chronological sequence of development represented by these three forms of urban landscapes.

Institutional urban landscapes: castle towns and abbey towns

In those parts of medieval Europe where castle building was an important institutional element in the control of land and people, as it was especially in those areas that were being colonised by aristocratic lords, castles were often closely associated with the formation of a new town. Regardless of whether they were added to an existing urban nucleus, as was often the case, or planted *de novo* on a 'greenfield' site, the landscapes of medieval 'castle towns' show certain common morphological characteristics.

The symmetry between the form of a castle and its adjacent town reflects the level of codependence that existed between them: both town and castle complemented one another. In the case of castles established during the early twelfth century, for example by the Dukes of Zähringen along the Rhine, small and self-contained towns were laid out immediately outside their gates. These usually took the form, as at Berne, of a single main street (itself communicating directly with the castle entrance and wide enough for trading to take place), fronted on each side by plots. Within these plots stood the buildings of the burgesses enfranchised by the town's charter.[5] The duke's castle town of Berne shared the same form and function of those small new castle towns being created by Norman aristocrats in England during the later eleventh century. Belleme's Bridgnorth fits this mould, for example, as do other

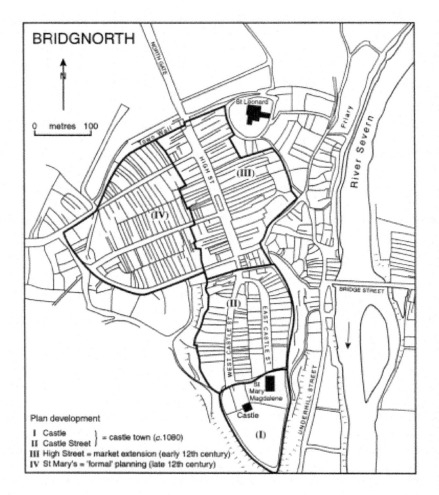

Figure 5.1   *The formation of medieval Bridgnorth and Ludlow*

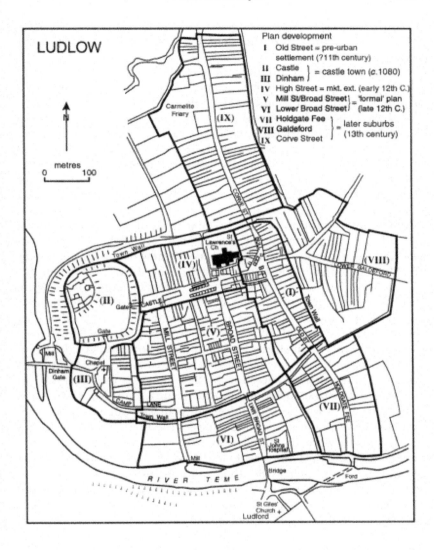

LUDLOW

N

metres
0   100

Plan development

I   Old Street = pre-urban
     settlement (?11th century)
II   Castle ⎫
III Dinham ⎬ = castle town (c.1080)
IV   High Street = mkt. ext. (early 12th C.)
V   Mill St/Broad Street ⎫ = 'formal' plan
VI   Lower Broad Street ⎭   (late 12th C.)
VII Holdgate Fee ⎫
VIII Galdeford   ⎬ = later suburbs
IX   Corve Street ⎭   (13th century)

Carmelite Friary

(IX)

Town Wall

St Lawrence's Ch

(IV)

(VIII)

(II)

Gate

CASTLE

(I)

LOWER GALDEFORD

Town Wall

Gate

Mill

Chapel

Dinham Gate

(III)

MILL STREET

(V)

BROAD STREET

Town Wall

CAMP LANE

LWR BROAD ST

HOLDGATE FEE

(VII)

(VI)

St John's Hospital

Mill

Bridge

Ford

RIVER TEME

St Giles' Church
Ludford

castle towns of this period, such as the de Vesci's at Alnwick (Northumberland) and the de Lacy's at Ludlow (Shropshire) (Figure 5.1).[6]

The practice of combining their castles with towns was widely employed by medieval lords, especially (but not exclusively) in frontier regions. The motive for this probably lay in the lords' need to impose their authority. The castle gave them a strong-hold, while the town with its market and burgages encouraged new settlers to take up residence there (see Chapter 3). The lords that followed this approach often did so having employed it else-where. In the eleventh century, the same Norman lords who were creating castle towns on their estates in Normandy were soon doing the same thing in England having acquired lands from William the Conqueror following the Norman Conquest. For example, a decade or two before Roger de Belleme established Bridgnorth he had been combining new castles with new towns on his estates in Maine, along the southern frontier of the duchy of Normandy.[7] The reason for doing so was the same: to invite settlers to colonise a frontier area, and to provide Belleme with a military foothold.

Looking at the typical form of a 'castle town' it is clear that they were usually arranged on an axis. The castle gates were aligned with the town's main street, while at one or both ends of the street stood a church to provide for the spiritual needs of the town's people. This castle–street–church alignment was used not only in *de novo* towns (like Bridgnorth and Berne), but also when lords added castle towns to already existing urban nuclei. Soon after the Norman Conquest, the townscapes of the more important Anglo-Saxon towns were extended outwards with the addition of new castle towns. Thus, the castle–market–church alignment can be found in towns such as Southampton, Bristol and Nottingham.[8] This form of urban expansion also went hand in hand with the Normans' use of new urban laws (to marginalise the English bur-gesses, as outlined in Chapter 3).

Somewhat analogous to the deliberate creation of towns outside the gates of secular (and episcopal) castles, was the formation of new urban landscapes outside religious institutions such as abbeys and priories. In this sense, ecclesiastical lords were following a similar practice to their secular counterparts. The urban landscapes of these 'abbey towns' were in many ways similar in form to the castle towns, in that they usually occupied a rather small area out-

side the institution's main gates, and comprised a widened street
with plots fronting onto it and a nearby church or chapel for the
welfare of the town's inhabitants.

Many 'abbey' or 'monastic' towns were founded in Europe during
the Middle Ages. One in particular which is well documented at
an early date is Battle in Sussex. Here a new town had been created by the abbot and monks of the abbey that William the
Conqueror had ordered to be built to commemorate where King
Harold had fallen in the Battle of Hastings. While the brethren
were building the abbey they were also engaged with laying out a
new town outside the abbey gates, using part of their estate which
William I had granted to them in 1066.[9] In Capetian France, too,
many similar monastic towns were established outside the important abbey churches that surrounded Paris.[10] While in Normandy,
abbey towns of the eleventh and twelfth centuries were being established with very similar urban forms to those that were to be
found in Norman England, as at Cormeilles and Le Bec-Hellouin.[11]
Abbeys laying out new urban landscapes in England were often
themselves Norman foundations, as was the case with Battle Abbey,
for example. Therefore, just as Norman aristocrats created castle
towns on their estates on both sides of the Channel, the religious
institutions of Normandy looked to establish towns on the lands
that they had been granted in England.

Some historians would have us believe that the formation of new
urban landscapes outside castles and abbeys was a 'spontaneous'
process. In reality, however, these institutional urban landscapes
were a product of careful, controlled development overseen by
local lords such as Belleme and the abbot of Battle Abbey. The
landscapes of these new towns were designed so as to reinforce
the political and economic position of the town's lord (just as
urban laws did), hence the close juxtaposition between the town
and its host institution. The institutional urban landscapes of the
'castle town' and the 'abbey town' are still often the commercial
hearts of European towns and cities. Although in recent years these
urban landscapes have become better studied by geographers and
historians, especially in France and Germany, and England and
Wales, their political and ideological dimensions (as products of
domination and conquest) have been rather overlooked.[12]

Commercial urban landscapes: street markets

The second phase in the development of Bridgnorth's urban land-scape, the creation of a new large market place outside the castle town, is also one that is commonly identifiable in European medieval towns and cities. New urban landscapes arranged around large and spacious market places extended the commercial capacity of the medieval townscape and reflected the economic objectives of urban lords. In the case of Bridgnorth, the area of the town associated with Henry I's High Street market place is typical of this form of urban landscape.

The creation of new, commercially centred urban landscapes became especially common during the twelfth and thirteenth centuries. As with castle towns, street markets were either tacked onto the edges of existing urban landscapes, or used to form the 'kernel' of a new-founded town. Examples of both are easy to find. Their characteristic form is a large, often lozenge- or cigar-shaped street; wide enough to accommodate traders and their wares, and lined along both sides by deep and spacious plots which often extended up to a narrow lane behind (for giving rear access to the plots). In the Cotswolds, for instance, the picturesque towns of Moreton-in-Marsh, Chipping Campden, Broadway and Northleach, all have street-market plans and were chartered with borough privileges during the twelfth and thirteenth centuries (Plate 5.1).[13]

Outside England, street markets are also common urban forms, especially for new towns established between 1100 and 1300. Examples of towns with street markets like the one identified at Bridgnorth are widely found in Germany. At Kenzingen, for instance, the town founded by Rudolph II of Üsenberg in 1249 is based on a 'High Street' market place of similar shape and appearance to Bridgnorth's (Figure 5.1).[14] In the frontier lands of eastern Germany, too, where colonising lords were actively founding new towns, the long street market was typically the first stage in a town's development, as at Brandenburg.[15] The highly acclaimed German Historic Towns Atlas series contains a number of further examples of towns, of twelfth- and thirteenth-century date, which have a street market at their core.[16]

The purpose behind creating street markets was of course to encourage and facilitate commercial development. By relying on the supervisory qualities of urban laws, lords could keep an eye

Plate 5.1 *Aerial view of Chipping Campden*

on commercial activities within a town without necessarily having their residence close to the market place. In many cases, such as the Cotswold towns mentioned above, these new commercial urban landscapes were created some distance from the direct view of a lord's castle or abbey, but of course with borough laws and customs the street markets and the properties of burgesses were all kept within the lord's sight, albeit indirectly (see Chapter 3).

At the same time as commercial urban landscapes were being created and used to form wholly new towns, it was also common for new suburbs with street markets to be added to older, more established towns and cities. During the twelfth century, for example, the Earls of Chester were extending the built-up area of Coventry by adding new, commercially oriented urban landscapes to the existing urban fringe, the result of which was a sort of medieval 'ribbon development' along approach roads.[17] The earls used existing roads to accommodate specialised markets (see Chapter 7 below), and lined these with new plots for townspeople to build upon. The land for these new plots was carved from agricultural fields lying around the town, and because the plots were derived from arable field-strips they also took on the characteristic reverse-S shape of the strips themselves.

To encourage people to take up places in the new suburbs, lords used grants of borough privileges which favoured newcomers. At Coventry, again, a new borough charter granted by Earl Ranulf II in the 1150s included a clause which specifically gave newcomers freedom from paying tax during their first year in the town, with the stipulation that they were to build houses there.[18] Special privileges and the newly established building plots generated accretive ribbon development along suburban streets in other towns and cities, too. At Bristol, the urban landscape was rapidly expanding outwards during the twelfth century, particularly to the south of the river Avon in the suburb of Redcliffe. It is not so surprising to find, therefore, that in his charter to Bristol in 1188, John, Count of Mortain, endorsed those who were 'making buildings everywhere', while in the meantime neighbouring secular and ecclesiastical lords had been busy setting out new suburbs on their lands with the familiar pattern of long market streets and reasonably sized adjoining building plots.[19]

Elsewhere across medieval Europe, field-lands were being turned over to urban use. The period between 1100 and 1250 saw most, if not all, major towns and cities undergoing some sort of suburban expansion, often at a fast rate of growth, as new, commercially focused urban landscapes were added to existing built-up areas. Such accretive growth occurred dramatically at Paris, Bruges and Prague, for example, and it took a similar form to the new suburban landscapes that were being created at the edges of English cities at the same time, such as those outlined above at Coventry and Bristol.[20]

'Formal' urban landscapes: regular 'grids'

A third common form of medieval urban landscape, identified earlier in Bridgnorth's town plan, is characterised by formal and regular-looking street patterns, and a relatively dense layout of smallish plots. With this sort of urban landscape, it looks as if an effort was being made to provide optimum living space within a relatively limited area to make more efficient use of land. The denser a plot layout, the greater the potential to accommodate high numbers of rent-paying property-holders. With this in mind, it is not too difficult to imagine that one of the motives for creat-

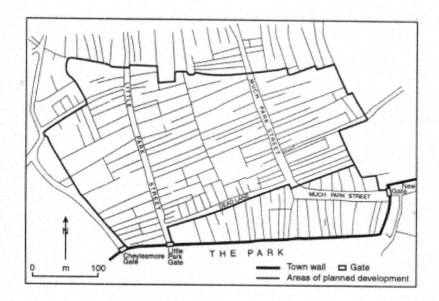

Figure 5.2 *The 'formal' layout of Much and Little Park Streets, Coventry*

ing such 'formal' urban landscapes was economic; for the more people who paid property rents, the more money there was going to the town's lord.

In the case of Bridgnorth, the area to the west of the High Street, with its regular layout of streets and dense arrangement of plots, is a form of medieval urban landscape that has parallels elsewhere. For instance, a similar pattern of street and plots can be seen at Coventry in an area of the town where the Earls of Chester had used part of their large deer-park to create a new suburb in the later twelfth century.[21] The form of this suburb is once again characterised by relatively narrow streets, laid out in parallel, with a regular pattern of comparatively small plots set out between them (Figure 5.2). This new development was a means of providing properties for rent close to the main commercial focus of the town, and in view of the earls' charter encouraging new-comers to Coventry (see above), it was clearly an area intended to accommodate the rising number of new people coming to the town in the later 1100s.

An urban landscape with parallel streets specifically favoured the urban property-holder, especially where they provided two street frontages. This is evident in the layout of Ludlow, a Shropshire town held by the de Lacy family for most of the twelfth century.[22] As at Coventry, during the time of the de Lacy's lordship, sometime in the later twelfth century, two new streets were laid out, both parallel (Figure 5.1). These streets extended the built-up area of Ludlow away from the main commercial area of the High Street in a manner bearing close resemblance to Bridgnorth. At Ludlow, however, a narrow access lane partitioned the block of land between the two new streets. This gave each property two frontages, one facing the main street, and the other facing onto the back lane. By having two frontages it was easier for the property-holders to subdivide their plots (and by doing so enable them to sublet portions of them and collect rents for themselves), while the back lanes helped to ease congestion in the main streets (see Chapter 6). The layout of this part of Ludlow was thus a very clever piece of planning, for it not only gave property-holders more scope for raising their income from rents, it also, ultimately, made Ludlow an attractive town for people to take up properties in.

During the latter part of the twelfth century, and into the thirteenth, new urban landscapes were often set out to what appear to be more 'formal' layouts, with streets arranged in parallel and sometimes as a grid, and regular patterns of plots. However, the degree of regularity varied, and not all such layouts were so highly formal and regular in form as that of Ludlow. The customary way of explaining why differences exist in the regularity of medieval urban landscapes is to argue that the more 'distorted' sorts of 'formal' town plans were the product of having to adapt an 'ideal' plan to fit local, topographical conditions.[23] This orthodoxy is beginning to be challenged, however. Other, less pragmatic reasons why some formal urban landscapes were laid out to highly regular patterns (while others were not), are considered later.

'Design contexts' and townscape formation

Looking broadly across the changing urban landscapes of the towns outlined above, it is possible to identify not only common forms but also associated periods of townscape formation.[24] For example, in the context of those towns that were taking shape during the

Table 5.1 *Three characteristic urban forms found in English medieval towns, and their design contexts for the period 1066–1215*

Urban form	Design context	*Morphological period
Castle town	Military conquest	1066–1100
Street market	Political consolidation	1100–1153
Regular 'grid'	Demographic colonisation	1153–

*A period characterised by a particular urban form.

late eleventh century in England, townscape formation was largely dominated by new Norman institutions, especially castles. Thus, at Ludlow and at Bridgnorth, two different lords created new castle towns at more or less the same time, but for more or less the same reasons – to dominate and control land and people in a period of political volatility. In this sense, these two Shropshire castle towns belong to a particular 'design context', that of military conquest. Indeed, throughout the Middle Ages, castle towns were character-istic townscapes formed during periods of conquest. Sometimes these institutional urban landscapes were added onto existing townscapes, while in other cases they were *de novo* towns in them-selves – either way, they served a common purpose.

As well as 'castle towns' and institutional urban landscapes, the two other urban forms discussed above also belong to particular design contexts (Table 5.1). Thus, while castle towns belong to phases of conquest (especially in frontier lands), the formation of commercial urban landscapes, which in England took place from the early twelfth century, belong to a second design context characterised by political consolidation (under the Norman kings). Again, these commercial urban landscapes served a common purpose, for they unified the economic space of the market with the economic legislation of borough charters, and in so doing they cemented a bond between lord and town. 'Formal' urban landscapes are charac-teristic of a third design context, associated with colonisation. The regular arrangement of streets ordered the urban landscape and optimised the amount of space used to accommodate new towns-people. We see this process of 'interior' and 'frontier' colonisation taking place in England during the later twelfth and thirteenth centuries, as population levels generally were rising, and more rural land was being put to urban use in the form of both new towns and additions to already existing towns.

In the case of the new townscapes being formed in England between the late eleventh and early thirteenth centuries, each of the design contexts reflects a particular 'morphological period' (Table 5.1). That is, there are identifiable periods when certain urban forms became more common than others, the obvious example being the spread of castle towns during the early years following the Norman Conquest. Of course, the relationship between design contexts and morphological periods will vary from place to place, depending on local political, economic and demographic circumstances. However, the relationship between urban forms and design contexts appears to be more universal. For example, in Gascony, the most common form adopted for the bastide towns was a 'formal' layout, the idea being that this sort of urban landscape helped to foster colonisation (see Chapter 3).

Until further work has been done on the morphology of medieval urban landscapes, it is risky to generalise too much about the patterns of townscape formation across Europe. However, it is clear that whatever the form new urban landscapes took in the Middle Ages, they were a product of controlled development rather than 'spontaneous' growth. The formation of townscapes was an organised and co-ordinated process, and we can see this in the medieval towns and cities by the way that there are distinct internal differences in the form of urban landscapes. These differences in form reflect phases in the evolution of urban landscapes. Even the 'new towns', which are thought to be the product of a single phase of townscape formation (such as the bastides), often actually contain different stages of plan development.[25] All this makes it a nonsense to draw a distinction between 'planned' and 'unplanned' towns, for to some degree planning will always be required to create a new urban landscape, whatever form it takes. As with the process of founding towns (see Chapter 4), it is likely that the formation of new urban landscapes was not just driven by a town's lord, but rather, would have required the advice and co-operation of others. The second half of the chapter looks in more detail at the processes involved in medieval urban design and planning, but before turning to this it is necessary to consider briefly what happened to an urban landscape once it had been created.

Townscape transformation and modification

Once established, urban landscapes were subject to all sorts of modifications and transformation. As new needs arose, adaptations altered the patterns of plots and streets; sometimes through the actions of individual townspeople, sometimes as part of a co-ordinated programme of changes overseen by a town's lord or council (see below). It is difficult to identify patterns of townscape transformation, for to do so depends on the availability and detailed study of archaeological and documentary material (see Chapter 1). The transformation of medieval townscapes is particularly evident where new institutions, such as castles and monasteries, were inserted into already existing urban landscapes.

Important royal, secular and ecclesiastical buildings were usually placed within a walled precinct to separate them physically from the outside world of urban life. Such institutional precincts were typically large users of urban land, so when a castle or monastery was removed from the townscape, for some reason, a large area of land would become available for redevelopment. A good illustration of this again comes from Coventry (Figure 5.3).[26] By the second half of the twelfth century the Earls of Chester had decided to abandon their castle in the centre of Coventry, and move to a new manorial residence situated on the outskirts of the town. With the earl's castle now redundant, the site became available for property development, and since the castle was situated right in the heart of the town, it was an attractive site for new development. New streets were quickly inserted, so as to provide access onto the site of the castle, and meanwhile the castle's ditches were infilled and its buildings removed. However, despite what appears to have been a dramatic piece of townscape transformation, the outline of the earl's former castle actually remained fossilised in Coventry's urban landscape for centuries afterwards, largely because the redevelopment was 'adaptive' in nature, and took place within the boundaries of the castle precinct.

The transformation of townscapes in the Middle Ages was often adaptive in nature, in the sense that modifications in the built environment took place without radically altering existing street patterns. There were, of course, more 'comprehensive' redevelopments which did erase earlier townscapes more completely. The medieval urban landscape was dynamic and always subject to new

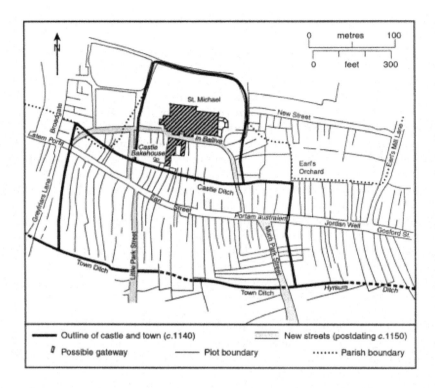

Figure 5.3   *Castle and town in twelfth-century Coventry*

demands and needs. As a result of careful archaeological and documentary study, historians have been able to piece together in detail the dramatic transformations that shaped Winchester in the four centuries which followed Alfred's foundation of the *burh* in the late ninth century. Although Alfred's Winchester initially comprised a pattern of regularly set-out streets and plots (for the most part still intact today), this layout was soon subject to varying degrees of disruption and some large-scale transformation.[27]

In the eleventh and twelfth centuries, Winchester was the royal capital of England. In this symbolic role the city was home to a host of important royal and ecclesiastical institutions. An area to the south of High Street, Winchester's main through-street, gradually saw streets and plots giving way to walled precincts for royal and religious buildings. One of the earliest transformations to affect the layout of Alfred's *burh* occurred in 903–4 with the foundation of the New Minster next to the Old Minster (an earlier church of mid-seventh-century origin). Edward the Elder founded the new church, and it occupied a large precinct which absorbed part of the town's earlier street system.[28] Despite taking up streets and plots, however, the new, larger minster precinct was arranged in such a way as to leave the commercial frontage along High Street intact. Just to the east of the New Minster, another monastic precinct was established, for Nunnaminster, 'the nun's minster', which Queen Eahlswith had founded sometime before 902–3. Later, the bishop's palace was also located in this part of the city, and enclosed in the precinct close by the abbey and the cathedral.[29]

By the time of the Norman Conquest, a swathe of precincts belonging to religious institutions had transformed the south-eastern part of Alfred's walled city of Winchester. Townscape transformation in Winchester continued to take place after the Norman Conquest, too.[30] Two major changes in particular were directly associated with the needs of the new Norman kingship – the building of a new palace and the creation of a castle. At the order of William the Conqueror, a new royal palace was built on a site within the precinct of the New Minster. The palace occupied the western part of the precinct and its construction proceeded at the same time as the rebuilding of the adjacent cathedral. By the thirteenth century, Winchester was no longer such an important royal centre, and the city began to lose out more to London. During this time, William's new royal palace was removed and the precinct transformed into a residential area and a site for one of the city's markets. The cycle of townscape transformation had thus turned full circle, from streetscape to precinct to streetscape, in no more than 200 years.

On the whole, royal palaces were few and far between in English medieval cities. In comparison, the second major transformation to have affected Winchester's townscape soon after the Norman Conquest was a much more common occurrence. This was the construction of a castle, which in Winchester was the responsibility of William fitz Osbern, one of the king's key vassals. With the construction of the new Norman castle, fitz Osbern made use of existing Roman town walls and located his castle in the south-east corner of the circuit. It meant taking up an area of the city that beforehand had consisted of plots and streets dating back to Alfred's time.[31] This sort of transformation occurred widely throughout England in the 1060s as the Normans took over English towns and planted their castles within them. Many of the new castles were built over existing streets and invariably involved some demolition of houses, and occasionally churches (as at Norwich) (Figure 3.4).[32] The Domesday Book records how English burgesses in Shrewsbury complained because Roger de Montgomery's castle caused them the loss of their houses and rents, while in Bristol, at about the same time, a new castle for the Earl of Gloucester had destroyed a part of the Anglo-Saxon town.[33]

From the evidence that we have, townscapes in the Middle Ages were subject to both minor and major modifications; some transformations were comprehensive in nature and involved radical alterations to a town's street patterns, while others were less dramatic and involved adapting existing townscapes to suit new needs. Those changes that are the most obvious are those associated with ecclesiastical and royal institutions, particularly where new precincts were carved out of areas of streets and houses. Apart from these sorts of changes, there were also many minor modifications taking place in the medieval townscape, as individual townspeople sought to make alterations to their houses, and plots and gardens (see Chapter 6).

The formation of new urban landscapes and the transformation of townscapes were processes that were usually at work at the same time in any one town or city. As new urban areas were added to the edges of towns and cities, townscapes grew outwards across fields and meadows. Meanwhile, as redevelopment took place within towns and cities, new townscapes were fashioned on the sites of older ones. In this sense, morphological processes which are still affecting urban landscapes today physically shaped urban landscapes in the Middle Ages. Moreover, not only were urban landscapes formed and transformed by common processes, their physical shape and appearance also often shared similarities. Common characteristics in medieval urban landscapes are recognisable in the layouts of streets and plots. In cases where townscapes were established for the same purpose, at about the same point in time, we find similar patterns of urban form. If we were to map the formation and transformation of urban landscapes across Europe for the entire Middle Ages then we would have a kaleidoscope of changing urban forms, some emerging time and time again (such as castle towns and street markets), and others appearing perhaps only once or twice. So far in this chapter, the changing nature of urban landscapes has been looked at in terms of the morphological processes which shaped them. What remains to be considered is the role that people played in these processes, particularly in terms of urban design and town planning.

The Design and Planning of New Urban Landscapes

In this part of the chapter the focus is on what role design and planning played in shaping new urban landscapes in the Middle Ages. More often than not, textbooks regard medieval town planning as a rather rare occurrence, and usually suggest that the 'planned' towns were those which had 'regular' layouts. In fact, to some extent all urban landscapes in the Middle Ages were 'planned', but unfortunately in most cases we do not know much about how this planning took place.

Generally speaking, 'planning' operates at different levels; it will include deciding where a new urban landscape should be put, and considerations about what form it should take and how it should be laid out on the ground. All these were important constituents of medieval urban planning. The scale and nature of this planning process would have differed from place to place and person to person (as it does today), but at the same time certain common principles would have been followed, including initial survey work, the drawing of designs, and consultation between interested parties, for example landholders. So although an ambitious exercise like the planning of a whole new town would require a rather more sophisticated and protracted approach than, say, a local property-holder's plan to build a block of new houses, in effect both would require survey, design and consultation.

In reality, urban planning in the Middle Ages produced townscapes of many different forms and even the so-called 'irregular' towns were 'planned' at one level or another. Urban planning, therefore, was about more than just laying out new towns with regular plans – it was about designing, planning and building new townscapes.

Urban design, surveying and practical geometry

To try and move away from the idea that only towns with regular urban forms were 'planned', the first thing I want to do is to address the issue of plan regularity. The formation of urban landscapes with 'formal', gridded layouts has already been introduced in the preceding section. My aim here is to look at these sorts of urban landscapes in more detail, and examine why some towns, or parts of towns, had more regular layouts than others.

Comparing those towns that are said to be 'regular' in form (for example the Gascony bastides), it soon becomes apparent that some are strictly *orthogonal* and geometrical in form while others are not. Why should such variations in regularity exist? This is a difficult though important matter. To some, a medieval town which has a distorted but broadly regular-looking 'grid' plan represents an attempt to mould an 'ideal' plan to the natural contours of the local landscape.[34] While this may have been so, it would be odd if it were the only reason for variations in regularity. There are other factors which would have influenced the regularity of medieval urban landscapes, and in this respect the most obvious (but curiously overlooked) is that new urban landscapes were designed and planned according to a range of different ideals and principles, not least in terms of the way that land was measured out and surveyed.

During the twelfth and thirteenth centuries, a period when new urban landscapes were being laid out to increasingly regular plans, scholars in universities all across Europe were busy teaching students about geometry. An understanding of geometry was fundamental to medieval science and engineering, and along with arithmetic, music and astronomy, it was one of the seven 'liberal arts' and formed part of the *quadrivium*.[35] In the 1140s and 1150s, in particular, geometry was assuming special importance among some scholars, not least Adelard of Bath, whose translation of Euclid's *Elements* from an Arabic copy into a Latin text greatly extended European understanding of 'theoretical' principles of geometry.[36] The geometry taught in universities had a practical importance, too, as it became the basis for solving geometrical 'problems' through what contemporaries called 'Practical Geometry' (*practica geometria*). This development in geometrical knowledge was just one aspect of what historians refer to as the 'Twelfth Century Renaissance':

in the context of the design and planning of new urban landscapes it also provided surveyors with new, more accurate ways of
measuring the land.[37]

Medieval surveying and town planning

It is always going to be difficult to determine how the specialised,
abstract theoretical geometry of Euclid filtered into the widely cir-
culated 'practical geometries' of the late Middle Ages. The influential
'practical geometries' written in the early thirteenth century deal
both with complex abstract geometrical problems, such as how to
define chords (straight lines connecting two points on a curve),
and how to solve practical surveying and engineering problems,
such as measuring the height of a building. In his 'Practical Geometry' of the mid-thirteenth century, Villard de Honnecourt used
diagrams to support his expositions on these sorts of surveying
problems.[38] And then there is the question of who these books
were written for.

In the introduction to his *Practica Geometria*, Leonardo Fibonacci
defines his audience in terms of two sorts of land measurer, or
surveyor (*mensore*): he distinguished between 'those who "would
work following geometric demonstrations, and those who would
proceed following common usage, or, as it were, lay custom"'.[39]
Fibonacci thus reveals to us that measuring the land was undertaken by surveyors of whom only some had an understanding of
how to use geometry for the purpose of laying out new landscapes.
In contrast, others used what, in his view, were less sophisticated
techniques to set out ground plans. This distinction between the
two sorts of surveyor is also made in a much later German text
called the *Geometria Culmensis* (*c*.1400). This practical geometry refers to surveyors as *mensores layci* ('lay' measurers) and *mensores literati*
('literate', learned measurers).[40] These 'literate measurers' were
presumably those who, as Fibonacci had put it, were 'following
geometric demonstrations'; while the lay measurers were those that
used only 'lay custom'. Evidently, then, men like Fibonacci, with
their 'practical geometries', were trying to enlighten the latter
with the knowledge and expertise of the former, with the result
that by the end of the thirteenth century surveyors had access to
methods of accurate ground measurement techniques informed
by abstract geometrical principles.

One reason why urban landscapes in the Middle Ages were laid out with plans which vary in regularity could be to do with the expertise of the surveyor employed to do the work. Although relatively little is known about who surveyed new urban landscapes in the Middle Ages, it does not seem too unlikely that the towns with streets and plots laid out to a strictly orthogonal layout were those which had been planned and surveyed by 'literate surveyors', while urban landscapes with less than perfect regularity were perhaps set out by the adept 'lay measurers'.

There were certainly professional surveyors working in the twelfth century whose duties could well have involved laying out new urban landscapes. For example, in Rome and Pisa surveyors were employed by the city authorities to measure the dimensions of properties, as there were in San Gimignano, too, in 1255.[41] In England, too, in the late thirteenth century, King Edward I could call upon men to 'devise, order and array' a new town, as was the case when he made the order to refound the border town of Berwick in 1297. The men the king summoned to do this were more likely to have been his 'government officials and businessmen', overseeing the work of others, rather than engaged in the design and planning themselves. When Edward I ordered surveys to be made for creating new towns at Winchelsea (Sussex) and Newton (Dorset), he appointed men 'to plan and give directions for streets and lanes', suggesting that those on the ground were overseeing the work of others on Edward's behalf.[42] Unfortunately, what is not recorded in these cases is how the plans for the towns were arrived at, and what geometrical knowledge and surveying expertise underpinned them. Indeed, only 'in very few cases . . . can one point with any certainty to the identity or even the professional character of the men who prepared the designs' of new urban landscapes.[43]

Geometry, architecture and urban design

There is evidence that urban design in the Middle Ages was closely connected with the work of architects. Careful study of the configuration of urban forms has shown that there was a link between medieval architectural design and urban design. This connection is apparent because from the late twelfth century onwards architectural and urban design both share common geometrical

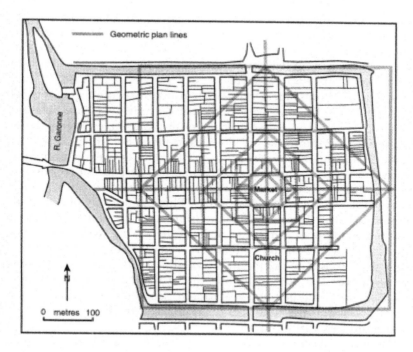

Figure 5.4 *The ground plan of Grenade-sur-Garonne*

underpinnings. One town that exemplifies this is Grenade-sur-Garonne, a bastide in south-west France founded by Eustache de Beaumarchais in 1290–91 (Figure 5.4).

It is clear that Grenade's urban landscape was designed using a method also used by architects of the period. The relative proportions of the town's highly orthogonal street blocks were derived using the proportion $1 : \sqrt{2}$.[44] This can be seen by the way that street blocks become progressively more elongated the further away they are from middle row of square-shaped street blocks. Root two was widely used in the design and layout of 'Gothic' cathedrals and monastic buildings, particularly in the construction of the pinnacles and spires that adorned their roofs. The technique used by architects and masons to do this was based not on mathematical calculations (root two equates to the ratio of $1 : 1.414$), rather it was derived from geometry and the principle of the 'rotating square'.[45] The streets at Grenade were positioned according to this method, hence the proportional relationship between the street blocks (see Figure 5.4). This suggests that the design came from the mind of an architect, someone who was familiar with the rotating square idea, and learned enough to know how to use it to make the plan of a new town.

An urban landscape with an accurately executed geometrical design such as the one we see at Grenade must first have been set out as a drawing, on either parchment or a wax tablet, before being made into a ground plan of streets and plots. Portable wax writing tablets were in use by the early twelfth century, while from the early fourteenth century a detailed manuscript plan on parchment shows with remarkable clarity the layout of a geometrically shaped 'new town' at Talamone Harbour.[46] This manuscript plan is contemporary with Talomone's foundation, and therefore might be a unique example of a drawing made to help with laying out a new urban landscape. In the context of Grenade, what is important is that the precise, geometrically formed ground plan suggests that someone felt the need to imbue the urban landscape with a perfect, proportional geometry, a 'sacred geometry', with a symbolic form that was at the time also being used across Europe to design and build new cathedrals.[47]

Apart from Grenade, other precise, geometrical urban landscapes were laid out in Italy, in the Florentine republic that flourished in Tuscany during the thirteenth and fourteenth centuries. The ground plans of some of the 'Florentine new towns' reveal street blocks positioned according to particular proportional arrangements. For example, the designs of San Giovanni (1299), Terranuova (1337) and Giglio Fiorentino (1350), all had dimensions based on proportions.[48] Of these, the 2 : 1 plan of Giglio Fiorentino was not actually realised, but the other two were. Moreover, their layouts were based on a much more complex proportional geometry than 2 : 1, for in San Giovanni and Terranuova the street blocks can be seen to 'diminish in depth from the axis of the main street to the town wall'.[49] As Friedman ingeniously demonstrates, in the case of Terranuova the plan of the town had been derived by using 'geometric measurement of the circle', based on a table of chords as set out in Leonardo Fibonacci's *Practica Geometria* of *c*.1220.[50] The apparent familiarity of Terranuova's 'designer' with such a specialised text suggests that he was indeed a highly educated individual.

To establish the new towns, town planning committees were

appointed by the Florentine city republic. However, the individual committee members themselves 'had no professional training as builders, surveyors, or designers'.[51] Instead the design and planning work was actually carried out by salaried employees and contractors. They were the ones who had the necessary experience in architectural design and building work. In 1356 for example, Giovanni di Lapo Ghini, who worked at San Casciano, was described as *magister ordinatoris* ('master of planning'), while in the 1340s Bacino Cambiuzzi, employed at Vicchio, was described as 'the chief master and overseer of works'.[52] In the case of the unbuilt town of Giglio Fiorentino, the design was the work of an architect called Neri Fioravanti, whose approach was to adopt a more simplified form of plan than some of the previous Florentine town designers had.[53]

The unusually detailed written records of the late-thirteenth- and early-fourteenth-century Florentine new towns actually enable us to see, for a small number of cases, who was behind the designing and making of geometrically formed urban landscapes. But, although the carefully executed proportional and orthogonal urban designs of certain Florentine new towns can be matched against the names of men who knew how to use texts such as Fibonacci's *Practica Geometria*, the reasons *why* they went to such lengths to use proportions and geometry in their work is *not* recorded by contemporary sources. To understand why it was that accurately laid-out geometrical-designed urban landscapes became more widespread in Europe after 1150 it is necessary to consider the symbolic significance of geometry; placing the rise of orthogonal town design in the context of contemporary theological and philosophical ideas and beliefs of the twelfth and thirteenth centuries.

Medieval urban design and Christian cosmology

Watching surveyors going about their work was something to be marvelled at in the Middle Ages. According to an account written by Lambert of Ardres, there was a surveyor called Simon the Dyker who was 'learned in geometrical work'. In 1200, Simon was to be seen 'pacing with rod in hand . . . setting out hither and thither' the defences of the town of Ardres in Flanders.[54] As well as having marvellous practical purposes, for surveying and engineering, to the medieval architect, mason, theologian and philosopher-scientist, geometry also had symbolic importance.

In medieval Christian thought geometry was used to symbolise the divine order of things. This symbolism was visually expressed in medieval art and architecture;[55] it was also expressed in the geometrical design of medieval urban landscapes, but on the whole little has been written about this, despite the evidence that urban landscapes and Gothic cathedrals shared the same sorts of design principles and probably common architect-designers, too (see above). In this context, it seems highly likely that geometrically designed urban forms, like architectural forms, had a symbolic and cosmological role as well as a practical one.

In the Middle Ages, 'everything stood for something else, and that something else was God'.[56] This idea is illustrated by a thirteenth-century German psalter depicting God, with a set of dividers in his hand, as 'architect' of the universe, *artifex principalis* (Plate 5.2). Thus, there were strong links between medieval Christian cosmology and geometrical forms. As Eco notes, in the Middle Ages 'truth and beauty were both defined in terms of form'.[57] This 'intertextuality', between God's divine order and the material form of things, is specifically referred to by Hugh de St Victor in the mid-twelfth century. In his commentary on the 'Celestial Hierarchy' (*In Hierarchiam Coelestum*), he wrote, 'all things visible, when they obviously speak to us symbolically, that is when they are interpreted figuratively, are referable to invisible significators and statements . . . for since their beauty consists in the visible forms of things . . . visible beauty is an image of invisible beauty'.[58]

In the medieval mind, then, the form of all 'beautiful' things was both physical and transcendental: beauty was a reminder not only of God's presence in the material world but also the truth of His word. Perhaps the most telling remark in this respect is one made by Thomas Aquinas in his *Summa Theologia* of 1273:

> Beauty . . . has to do with knowledge, and we call a thing beautiful when it pleases the eye of the beholder. This is why beauty is a matter of right proportion, for the senses delight in rightly proportioned things. . . . Now since knowing proceeds by imaging, and images have to do with form, beauty involves the notion of form.[59]

Since the aesthetics of medieval architectural form were underpinned by the use of sacred geometry in Gothic design, and since

Plate 5.2   *God as* artifex principalis, *'supreme architect'*

the same aesthetic ideals were also at work in the geometrical design of urban landscapes, the perfect geometrical forms evident in the ground plans of towns such as Grenade were surely symbolising God's beauty.

The perfect geometrical forms seen in the orthogonal and geometrically derived designs of towns such as Grenade and Terranuova, with their carefully executed proportional layouts, certainly look as if they were designed to delight God. After all, only He was truly able to see from above a town's perfect geometry, to appreciate its visible beauty from the air.[60] Moreover, where the design of a town's plan is based on the same rotating square principle used by architects to create Gothic spires, as was the case at Grenade, then the possibility exists that what the town's designer was trying to do was make a two-dimensional space (the layout of the town's streets and plots) into something with three dimensions – a 'pinnacle' that pointed upwards and skywards, towards God. With Grenade, the highest point (apex) of this imagined pinnacle was the town's central market square, the symbolic centre of the new town (Figure 5.4).[61] Grenade's design thus expressed a medieval Christian cosmology, embodying the idea articulated in Hugh de St Victor's 'Celestial Hierarchy', that 'visible beauty' was 'an image of invisible beauty', the beauty of God, that is.

The 'cosmological' meaning of medieval urban forms may have been all too often overlooked by modern, secular-minded scholars, but for those who lived in the twelfth and thirteenth centuries the symbolic significance of urban landscapes was widely understood. In his description of Chester for example, a local monk called Lucian wrote in the late twelfth century how, 'there are . . . two excellent straight streets in the form of the blessed cross, which through their crossing themselves make four out of two, their heads ending in four gates'.[62] It has been suggested that this description of the city's form was used in sermons to local townspeople, bringing home to them the all-pervading presence of God as well as giving Chester's townscape a cosmological significance.[63] Members of the mendicant orders were certainly doing this sort of thing in Italian cities a century or so later.[64] Lucian's reading of Chester's cross of streets is worth taking further, too, for so many of the new urban landscapes of the twelfth and thirteenth centuries were arranged to align with the cardinal points (see Figures 5.1 and 5.4). From this appraisal of urban design in the Middle Ages it is clear that understanding the form of medieval urban landscapes requires iconographic and symbolic interpretations, as well as consideration of how designs were implemented by surveyors (using 'practical geometry'). The key to doing this is carefully studying of the physical form and layout of medieval urban landscapes, contextualising them in relation to contemporary ideas about aesthetics, beauty and cosmology, as well as texts on practical and theoretical geometry. Of course, it will always be difficult to be sure that what *we* see in the design and layout of a medieval town is actually what its designer originally saw. However, it is possible to get closer to the person who initially devised the plan, to see the design through *their* eyes as it were, by drawing, mapping and studying the forms of towns such as Grenade.

To recap: rather than judging the 'regularity' found in some urban landscapes as a sign that a town was 'planned', variations in the regularity of urban forms might more usefully be seen as a reflection of differences in surveying practice as well as ideas about the symbolic meaning which geometry had in the Middle Ages. To talk of medieval 'planned towns' poses a problem, in that urban planning in the Middle Ages operated in a variety of social and spatial scales, and did not always take a regular form in the urban landscape. The processes that shaped the design of medieval towns, that is the skills and techniques that were necessary for laying out new urban landscapes, reveal that the surveyors of medieval Europe should be granted greater credit for their ability to set out, accurately, abstract ideas on the ground. We have all too frequently been told how medieval surveyors were incapable of turning their measurements of the land into ichnographic maps and plans.[65] What appears to be the case, then, is that the medieval surveyor was learned and skilled enough to turn a 'paper plan' of a town into an accurately laid-out ground plan – the reverse process to that being used by cartographers in the Renaissance.

Urban design, townscape improvement and 'modernisation'

Urban planning and design played an important role in the modernisation and improvement of many medieval towns and cities, yet this is another matter that has not received that much attention by urban historians. Perhaps this is because civic improvement often took subtle forms in the medieval urban landscape. With the growth and development of municipal organisation and corpo-rate civic bodies in the later Middle Ages, many of the improvements that were initiated in the urban landscape were on a relatively small scale. Even so, attempts to improve and modernise townscapes required careful planning and co-ordination. Today, these schemes that were being implemented by medieval municipalities would amount to what we would regard as 'modernisation' and urban regeneration. But since this dimension to medieval urban design and planning does not take the form of identifiable highly regu-lar town plans, it has often been overlooked.[66] In cases of civic improvement, carried out in a number of cities during the later Middle Ages, the role of design and planning is known because it is recorded in city archives.

Townscape improvement in Italian cities

During the thirteenth and fourteenth centuries, well-documented schemes of townscape improvement took place in the important and wealthy Italian cities of Siena and Florence. In Siena, for example, the ruling oligarchy, 'the Nine, perfected the town's street plan and directed the construction of architectural and artistic monu-ments', they also 'ordered the building of the magnificent Palazzo Comunale in Siena's shell-shaped forum, flanked by one of the world's most elegant towers, the Torre del Mangia'. Through these significant townscape developments the Sienese municipality forged what Bowsky called 'the civic ideal'.[67]

The importance of these townscape improvements for project-ing Sienese civic pride and identity was not lost on the city's council. In 1297, for instance, just before the construction of the Palazzo Comunale, the Nine 'authorised the expenditure of up to two thousand *lire* each semester for the "construction, building, and repair of the houses and palace of the Sienese commune . . . for the honour of the Sienese commune and the beauty of the city"'.[68] The building of the Palazzo was undertaken at the same time that the Campo (the central piazza) was enlarged. For this purpose, in 1293, the council purchased houses for clearance, and four years later, in 1297, a law was passed to control the appearance of win-dows in buildings around the newly beautified square.[69] Following the demolition of the Church of St Paolo in *c.*1308, the Campo itself was paved in brick. The paving was at last finished in 1347;

'its shell-like surface was separated into nine equal parts, pointing to the Palazzo Comunale – a clear reference to the presiding
regime, as were the nine merlons on the high central battlements
set on each side of the palace in 1305'.[70]

To oversee these ambitious and costly townscape improvements
the Sienese city government appointed salaried officials. The officials were employed specifically to ensure 'that any edifices that
are to be made anew anywhere along the public thoroughfares of
the Sienese commune . . . proceed in line with the existent buildings, and one building not stand out beyond another, but shall be
disposed and arranged equally so as to be of greatest beauty for
the city'.[71] The projection of a 'civic beauty' was thus the underlying motive driving the townscape improvements in fourteenth-century
Siena.

As well as the strict laws and statutes passed by the Nine concerning the regulation of what activities could be carried on in
the streets, there was also significant 'design control' attached to
the appearance of building façades along main streets. This is
indicated by a contract of 1340, drawn up between three building
masters and a merchant called Gontiero Sansedoni.[72] The contract, though primarily a formal written document, also includes a
detailed and accurate architectural drawing of Sansedoni's proposed new palace, showing its multi-storey façade as an elevation
and thus giving the 'view from the street'. The 'officials in charge
of the beauty of the city', as these men were termed, were also
responsible for the creation of public parks. As a statute of 1309
records, these parks were created 'for the beauty of the city and . . .
for the delight and joy of citizens and foreigners'.[73]

The time and effort that the Sienese put into beautifying their
city through townscape improvements were thus significant, and
as might be expected, their enterprise in these matters did not
come cheaply. In 1309–10, 10 000 lira were spent on the palazzo
alone.[74] The reason for this major municipal investment by the
Sienese is explained, in part, by Waley in terms of their 'need to
outshine the Florentines, who were at work contemporaneously
(1299–1314) on their Palazzo Vecchio'.[75] Like Siena, Florence was
also a wealthy and important city, where, under the initiative of
the municipality, a similarly ambitious and large-scale co-ordinated
programme of townscape improvement was taking place, particularly during the thirteenth and fourteenth centuries.

The Florentine improvements encompassed the same features of the townscape as those in Siena, focusing in particular on straightening streets, opening up piazzas, and constructing new civic buildings. However, in Florence there was an additional civic undertaking: the construction of new circuits of defences around the expanding built-up area of the city. One circuit was completed in the remarkably short period between 1172 and 1175, while another, much larger circuit, was constructed periodically over a longer period, between 1284 and 1334.[76] It seems that the most important period for civic design and planning in medieval Florence was in the decade from 1250 to 1260. This period was when, under the auspices of the Primo Popolo, 'the town planning measures undertaken at the end of the thirteenth century were [first] discussed and formulated'.[77] It was during this time, too, that the first building to house the city's government was built, the Palazzo del Capitano del Popolo. Work began on the Palazzo in 1255, and a time when work also started on a road circulating around the late-twelfth-century defences, thus encompassing the whole city.[78]

Despite the ever-changing internal politics of Florentine city government, the city's officials became the key agency in overseeing the new building work that was taking place. Even in the development of new suburbs, which were being undertaken by private initiative, it is said that 'the Commune supplied technical and land-surveying help in order to measure the land and to determine infrastructures such as roads and city blocks'.[79] Medieval Florence perhaps 'reached the apex of its success in urban planning' during the period of the Duecento government, when a series of interlinked townscape improvement schemes took place within the civic heart of the city.[80]

The form that the townscape improvement schemes took in Florence included the construction of new civic buildings, the opening up of squares, and the insertion of new streets. According to contemporary accounts, new straight streets like the Via Larga were laid out in order 'to enhance the decorum of the city', and to 'increase the number of beautiful straight streets and entrance routes' in the city.[81] In 1278, on previously open land, the Florentine city government along with the friars of Ognissante established the Borgo Ognissanti. This long straight street ran close to the Arno, and an open square was left part way along it between the friars' church and the river.[82] The Florentines' eagerness for straight, uninterrupted streets affected not only the design of new streets but also the rebuilding of existing parts of the town. In the 1290s, for example, streets deemed to be 'narrow and ill formed' by the city authorities were ordered 'to be straightened and [have] the deformity eliminated'.[83] This was two centuries before Europe's Renaissance architects were advancing the same doctrine.

Townscape improvements in medieval Florence extended further beyond laying new straight streets. They included building the Palazzo dei Priori, in 1298; the demolition of buildings to open up the Piazza dei Signori; the enlargement of Piazza Santo Spirito, and the construction of a new cathedral begun in 1296; the building of a new bridge, the Ponte Vecchio, in the 1340s, as well as programmes to pave streets and remove obstructions from them.[84] These improvements were seen by the civic authorities to fulfil two purposes, one practical and the other aesthetic: 'to be useful' and 'to enhance decorum', as they put it.[85] In 1298, new streets were thus created by the city for its 'honour and beauty and fulfilment'; while in 1287, a new street along the river was considered to be 'useful and proper and beautiful'.[86] This concern with marrying both the aesthetic and pragmatic aspects of civic design is the hallmark of the Sienese and Florentine attempts to modernise and regenerate their townscapes in the later thirteenth and early fourteenth centuries.

Modernisation and townscape improvement in northern European cities

In northern and western Europe, as in the south, civic officials of large and wealthy self-governing municipalities equally saw their cities as having both 'honour and beauty'. Many medieval cities north of the Alps sought to enhance and improve their public image by undertaking 'public works' that involved townscape improvement. In Toulouse, in the late twelfth and thirteenth centuries, for example, a city consulate comprising elected representatives legislated on matters relating to drainage, acquired property on which to build a town hall, maintained the city's defences and its public streets, and declared a square to be publicly owned.[87] Meanwhile, in Cologne, during the twelfth century, 'the community government was responsible for fortification, could collect taxes to support such enterprises, and held land for common or public purposes', which included the city hall in St Lawrence's parish.[88]

In England, the municipalities of both Bristol and Norwich were involved in large-scale and expensive civic improvements. Although they lack the rigorous and detailed accounts written by contemporaries in Italian cities, townscape improvements in English medieval cities nevertheless took place, with a high level of planning and co-ordination. These improvements, initiated by the English urban municipalities, signified what they considered to be necessary modernisation of outmoded townscapes. Let us first of all take a look at what was happening in Bristol, one of England's most important provincial cities by the later Middle Ages.

At Bristol, improvements to the urban landscape were carried out in the early years of the city's mayoralty, particularly during the 1240s. The most significant and impressive of the municipality's improvements was the cutting of a 'trench' to form a new quay, together with the diversion of the river Frome away from its previous course and into the new quay (Figure 5.5).[89] This major construction work began in 1240 and was finally completed in about 1247. The work was actually part of a wider modernisation plan being undertaken by the municipality. Once the new quay was finished, and the improved facilities were ready for trading to take place, attention turned to improve Bristol's old port which lay to the south of the city, along the river Avon. A new bridge was built across the Avon to join Bristol and the suburbs to the south, and downstream of this bridge a new waterfront (with stone-lined docks) were built. All this improvement work involved draining water from the Avon, a difficult feat that was achieved by digging a new channel to temporarily divert the course of the river. As the new quay had by this time already been completed, disruption to Bristol's international trading traffic was kept to a minimum.

When the new quay was finished, and at the same time as Bristol was being joined to its southern suburbs by the new bridge over the Avon, negotiations were made in order to unify the suburb with the city of Bristol, thus making 'of two but one corporate town'.[90] This act of corporate unification was cemented, literally and metaphorically, by the bridge-building across the river. The new Avon bridge was built in stone rather than timber, and so as well as providing a more lasting crossing-point for the city's inhabitants to use, the new bridge also symbolised the intended permanence of the important new union between city and suburb. As at Florence, therefore, the townscape improvement schemes of

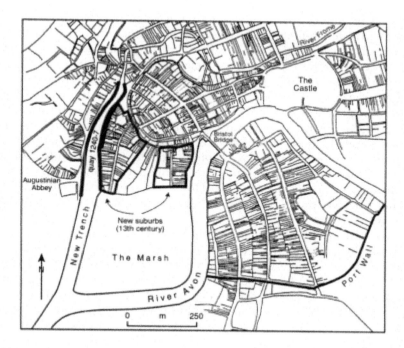

Figure 5.5 *Civic improvements in thirteenth-century Bristol*

the early mayoralty at Bristol were driven partly by practical necessity (of enhancing the harbour facilities and making a stronger bridge), and yet at the same time it was also being led by corporate and civic pride, showing the outside world, as it were, what an honourable and proud city Bristol was.

In the case of Norwich, townscape improvement and modernisation mainly involved constructing new defences and civic buildings. The city's principal civic buildings stood in the large market place that was the focus of the Norman 'new borough' created in the late eleventh century (see Chapter 3). By the fourteenth century this market place included the municipality's Toll House (where market tolls were administered), their Murage Loft (where payments for maintaining the walls were kept), and their Gild Hall (town hall and council chamber).[91] These were important buildings for the city, for they not only performed a practical role in the day-to-day affairs of the municipality, but also were the focus for civic ritual at certain times of the year. The buildings were thus a reflection of the city's status and were therefore looked after. Towards the end of the thirteenth century, having had its liberties restored by Edward I, the city spent sizeable sums of money on building the Toll House and Murage Loft. This improvement was an attempt to restore some element of civic pride in the city following on from its loss of respectability and rights due to rioting by the townspeople against the prior a few years earlier. Later still, in 1404, and following the reorganisation of the city's government structure, a mayor was appointed for the first time in Norwich (see Chapter 2). At this time more municipal money was spent, in this case to modernise the Toll House and convert it into a Gild Hall for civic functions. The building still stands today, albeit in 'restored' form.

As well as completing new civic buildings, the municipality of Norwich also turned its attention to modernising the city mills situated at the edge of Norwich on the river Wensum. The story behind the rebuilding of the city's mills provides some insight into how civic improvements were carried out in English cities in the later Middle Ages. The rebuilding was needed because the mills had been out of repair for 12 years. The process of rebuilding was recorded by the city in its treasury accounts.

Firstly, in 1398–99, municipal records describe 'one man coming from Lynn to examine the defects of the Common River', probably acting to advise the municipality on what could be done to the Wensum. Two years later this initial survey was followed up, as a William Fulkes was sent to Colchester in order 'to consult there with a man called Blaumester'.[92] Blaumester must have appeared knowledgeable (or convincing) for in the same year he was brought to Norwich 'for examining the place for the water mills to be newly built'.[93] Blaumester's repute as a surveyor must have been distinguished enough, at least in eastern England, for the municipality to have called upon him for his expertise and advice. The city's officials then proceeded by contracting a John Swanton to supervise the construction of the new mills, which were completed some 30 years later in 1429. However, soon afterwards the new mills were found to cause the river to flood upstream, involving the municipality with a lengthy legal dispute and perhaps leading them to regret what Blaumester had told them.[94]

The modernisation and improvement of the city's new mills at

Norwich serve to show how municipal authorities sought professional help in technical matters such as surveying and building construction in the later Middle Ages. Unlike Siena or Florence, the municipality of Norwich evidently could not call upon expert advice from within its own membership, but rather had to look outside. The same was also true when the city had to make other less permanent but nevertheless important 'improvements' to the townscape, especially during royal visits. In the 1440s, for example, the city's gates were 'beautified' for royal occasions, while in 1468, John Parnell, a 'devyser of storeys', was brought from Ipswich to build a stage around Westwick Gate in order to heighten the drama of Queen Elizabeth Woodville's entry into the city.[95] The planning and design of these temporary improvements also had to be carefully co-ordinated, for their success not only reflected civic pride and identity but also contributed to the material wealth of the city and its inhabitants.

Reflections on urban design and planning

In the Middle Ages, the design and planning of urban landscapes was a complex and sophisticated process. This process was far more complex than superficial studies of urban form suggest. To understand why some new urban landscapes had highly regular forms means looking at how certain medieval towns were designed and laid out according to strict geometrical and proportional rules, while others were not. It is also worth interpreting geometrically derived urban designs in the context of contemporary, medieval ideas about the symbolic meaning of geometry, and its link with Christian cosmology and teaching. Of course, there was more to medieval town planning than 'regular' patterns of streets and plots however, as is evident from the schemes carried through by municipal governments to improve the appearance and quality of their townscapes. Here we see urban design and planning operating on different social and spatial scales but nevertheless reflecting similar concerns and ideals, and requiring technical and professional expertise.

The townscape improvements considered above in this chapter were significant civic undertakings, involving co-operation between individuals and institutions, 'public–private' partnerships, negotiation between different landholders, the buying-in of skilled professionals, paying for the costs of materials and labour as well as committee meetings and officials' expenses. Put in these terms the civic improvements that took place in towns and cities across Europe in the later Middle Ages do not sound that unfamiliar and in fact have a certain resonance in our age of 'civic boosterism' and urban regeneration programmes. Indeed, the cutting of new streets and harbours, and the construction of new civic buildings, such as bridges and town halls, are all forms of 'creative destruction' – a characteristic of the 'modernisation' of cities in the last two centuries. Towards the end of the Middle Ages urban governments across Europe had a very clear vision of how they wished their city to appear: for them it had to be both beautiful and functional, at one and the same time adding to the spiritual and material wealth of the city for both its citizens and visitors alike. It is therefore more appropriate to say that each age, the Middle Ages included, invents its own sense of what it is to be 'modern'. This sense of modernity was inscribed into the medieval townscape, making it legible to those that came to the city and those who lived there.

Conclusion

This chapter has examined the medieval urban landscape in two ways. First, by revealing how urban landscapes were formed and transformed, sometimes over long periods of time and sometimes quite rapidly. Although the expansion and evolution of medieval townscapes took many different forms, at a general level it is possible to identify some common morphological characteristics. The discussion focused on three particular urban forms found in medieval towns in Anglo-Norman England and sought to place the formation of these urban landscapes in the context of contemporary political, social and economic changes. Following this the impact 'that transformations in the townscape had on the evolving physical forms of medieval towns and cities was considered, particularly changes initiated by institutional landholders during the eleventh and twelfth centuries.

Second, the chapter has examined aspects of medieval 'town planning'. Careful morphological study of medieval urban landscapes reveals how towns with strictly geometrical and orthogonal forms would seem to be the product of two processes; one connected with changes in how land was being surveyed and measured in the late twelfth and thirteenth centuries, and the other to do with how geometrical order was being viewed in this period as a reflection of God's beauty. By the end of the thirteenth century we see a coming together of the practical and cosmological dimensions of geometry in the plans of certain European new towns. This is an area of study that has to be explored still further, and so too is the subject of medieval townscape improvement and modernisation. Because medieval town planning has been viewed rather narrowly in the past, the various forms that urban design and planning took in the Middle Ages have been rather overlooked.

Having considered in this chapter how medieval urban landscapes were formed and transformed, and having looked at the processes involved in the design and planning of new urban landscapes, the following two chapters will show how these townscapes were peopled – how they were places full of life and activity, a 'stage' on which townspeople lived and worked.

6

URBAN PROPERTY AND LANDHOLDING

The king is prepared to commit the said lands and tenements [of *Nova Villa*] to merchants and others willing to take them, and to enfeoff them thereby for the purpose of building and dwelling there.

Charter of Edward I (1286)[1]

That each of them may make improvements as much as he can, in making buildings everywhere, on the river-bank and elsewhere, so that there be no damage to the borough and the township [of Bristol].

Charter of John, Count of Mortain (1188)[2]

In the Middle Ages, as now, the way that urban property was distributed within society reflected and reinforced social hierarchies and relationships. Urban landholding not only encompassed the interests and concerns of wealthier, elite elements of medieval society, it involved the great variety of people who lived and worked in the towns themselves. Merchants, burgesses, artisans and traders, all had a stake in urban property-holding, alongside kings, princes, abbots and bishops. How they organised their properties influenced the physical character of the urban landscape as well as the way people inhabited the townscape. This chapter examines how land-holding structured medieval towns and cities, both socially and spatially.

The purpose of the first part of the chapter is to show how medieval lords maintained a presence in towns and cities through

178

urban landholding. 'Feudal' landholding influenced the process of urbanisation in two ways. Firstly, the pattern of lords' landed estates in and immediately around towns had a bearing on how the urban landscape evolved. Using their land to capitalise on urbanisation, lords often created whole new towns alongside old ones. With these new towns lords created, in effect, 'towns within towns'. Secondly, at the same time as many lords were urbanising their rural landholdings (see Chapter 4), they were also maintaining and developing urban estates. Lords could retain their own private control over an urban estate, which sometimes gave rise to distinct 'feudal' jurisdictions within a town. In this way, in some towns an estate continued to be held directly under seigneurial control, rather than enjoying privileges which the rest of the town had. To explore both of these themes I will adopt Hilton's idea of 'the feudal presence in towns'.[3]

The second part of the chapter moves away from the urban landholding activities of high-status lords, and considers more the role that townspeople played in developing urban property. Patterns of urban property-holding not only structured the urban landscape, but also mirrored social structures, and thereby helped to reinforce social hierarchies. By looking at who held property, and how their property was sublet to others, we can start to understand the sorts of relationships that existed between different groups of townspeople. This means taking a look at the wide variety of property that was rented out to townspeople in the Middle Ages, looking at its relative location and status, as well as the processes that altered the character and composition of urban property during the later Middle Ages, as population levels increased and demand for urban properties rose. To do this I will look again at the urban landscape, but this time we will encounter the houses and yards that belonged to medieval townspeople, and pry a little into what sort of properties people held. Having then examined the nature and organisation of urban property, the next chapter will look at what people were actually doing in the medieval townscape.

Lordship and Patterns of Urban Landholding

The pattern of landholdings in and around medieval towns and cities was usually highly complex. Urban landholdings were often a jigsaw of interlocking lordships, each belonging to different people. These landholdings were the framework within which, and through which, urbanisation took place. Where lords held land close to an established town they sometimes used it to establish a suburban 'new town'. By doing so (and by issuing charters with defined urban privileges), they created one town next to another, the newer town having its own administration and jurisdiction that separated it from the older, adjoining town. This particular process gave rise to often large urban agglomerations, composed of a single built-up area, unified in its physical appearance but containing individual and administratively autonomous towns on separate lordships.

Urban development on adjoining and neighbouring lordships created competition, and sometimes conflict, between towns, lords and townspeople. One example of a town where 'internal' competition led to conflict is Coventry. There the town was divided between two lords, the Earls of Chester on the one hand and the priors of St Mary on the other. Both sides had been busily developing their respective landholdings in Coventry during the twelfth century, such that by the thirteenth the built-up area had expanded dramatically with new suburbs pushing out the urban fringe on three sides of the town (see Chapter 5). As a result of the division of lordship in the town, conflicts arose.

In 1307, the inhabitants of the earl's 'half' of Coventry were accused by the prior as having illegally traded in their part of the town on his market day.[4] The issue had arisen because the two lordships had created two quite distinct 'towns', both joined together as a physical entity but divided by virtue of being two separate landholdings, or 'estates', with two separate jurisdictions. The conflict that arose between Coventrians and their respective lords was not resolved until the middle of the fourteenth century, when Queen Isabella reduced the area covered by the prior's jurisdiction and made Coventry an incorporated city.[5] The conflict had been caused because of the way Coventry had evolved on two lordships, probably as a result of a decision made in the middle of the eleventh century when Earl Leofric of Mercia granted an estate on part of his land in order to found an abbey. The abbot was himself soon developing a town right alongside the part of Coventry that was still in the earl's hands, hence the confusion among townspeople two centuries later when the prior asserted that his market jurisdiction applied to all the townspeople of Coventry and not just those living in his half.[6]

Elsewhere in England, jurisdictional differences, coupled with separate urban lordships like that at Coventry, also gave rise to internal disagreements between lords and townspeople. At Norwich, for example, the city was divided into three 'fees', each separate jurisdictions of which the largest was that governed by the city itself. In 1274, the prior was besieged by those townspeople who lived outside his lordship and beyond his jurisdiction; they burned his cathedral but then subsequently suffered as their privileges were taken away from them by the king (only to have them 're-stored' a few years later).[7]

Patterns of interlocking lordships and landholdings not only structured the administrative organisation of medieval towns and cities, they also structured the process of urbanisation itself. The role that lordships and landholdings played in extending and expanding urban areas is exemplified particularly well in the case of France.

Suburban bourgs in France and Normandy

In parts of France during the late tenth and eleventh centuries, 'agglomerated' towns developed into large cities as neighbouring suburban lordships were progressively urbanised by their respective lords. This urban growth on 'suburban' lordships came about through the foundation of specially enfranchised and chartered *bourgs*. Although these new *bourgs* were established just outside existing towns, and were therefore suburbs, they became as 'urban' in character as the town onto which they had been grafted. These suburban *bourgs* were thus, in effect, 'new' towns, strategically positioned by entrepreneurial lords at the edge of 'old' towns.

By definition, a *bourg* had its own set of urban institutions and its own individual legal and economic status – it was a 'borough' in just the same way as other new boroughs were (see Chapters 2 and 4). So, institutionally, the suburban *bourgs* shared the same sort of privileges as those boroughs that were being founded on lordships all over Europe at this time, and likewise the *bourg's* privileges were set out in charters which covered a specific area within the lord's jurisdiction. The founding of the new suburban *bourgs* created clusters of distinct, self-governing 'towns', and formed an urban agglomeration.

For the most part, as was the case with Coventry, these agglomerated towns comprised just two estates divided between two lords, with each half of the town having its own set of urban institutions and jurisdiction. For example, this was the arrangement in Narbonne in Languedoc.[8] However, other agglomerated towns in France comprised more than just two *bourgs*. Poitiers was home to five suburban *bourgs*; while in and around Paris there were seven, on both sides of the Seine, surrounding the island Cité. The *bourgs* in Paris were situated on lands which belonged to the abbeys of Saint Germain, Sainte Geneviève and Saint Marcel, and (perhaps most famously of all), St Denis.[9] These abbeys saw their suburban estates as an ideal opportunity to establish new and potentially profitable towns within close proximity to the royal Cité. Elsewhere, for example at Rheims, the town was divided into three separate lordships, one belonging to the archbishop, one to the cathedral chapter, and one to the abbot of St Remi. Marseilles similarly had three separate lordships, one each held by the bishops, the cathedral chapters and the viscounts, while Tours had six, the most important being an ecclesiastical *bourg*.[10]

It was the proximal and agglomerated nature of these suburban lordships which gave lords the incentive to use their lands to stimulate further urban development. It seems likely that they were inspired to do so by having seen how their neighbours had founded *bourgs* on their estates, and because they too wished to make profits in the same way. Such was the incentive to create suburban *bourgs* that in the case of the abbey of St Martin, just outside Paris, the abbot employed a 'locator' to reclaim the low-lying land on his lordship in order to make it suitable for new urban development.[11]

The creation of the French suburban *bourgs* was an especially ecclesiastical phenomenon; as Musset has noted, the promoters were generally monastic lords.[12] This is also evident in the duchy of Normandy, notably in the period before Normandy became a fief of the French Crown.

In Normandy, suburban *bourgs* were commonly founded during the eleventh and twelfth centuries outside existing towns on estates which had been granted by the Norman dukes to religious institutions, a case in point being Caen. Although according to Beresford, Duke William 'himself had planted two *bourgs*' at Caen, 'alongside and beneath the old ducal *bourg*... after negotiations very like those of a *paréage*' (see Chapter 4); to be more exact, the two *bourgs*, the Bourg l'Abbé and the Bourg l'Abbesse, were in fact both established next to two new abbeys founded by the duke.[13] Caen is first mentioned in 1025, while the two abbeys were founded in *c.*1059 and *c.*1063 respectively, on low-lying land adjacent to the ducal residence. Two charters of 1082 and 1083 'show clearly not only the effects of an expanding population but also the endeavours of the great landholders to regulate and control its growth'.[14] The two charters refer to the construction of two new parish churches, St Gilles and St Nicholas, to serve the new urban communities around the religious houses of La Trinité and St Etienne.[15] The chance survival of a list of parishioners at the Bourg l'Abbé reveals that, in 1083, perhaps 20 years since the *bourg* was established, 78 named individuals were living there (which in reality was probably a population of over 300 people).[16]

The pattern of urbanisation on suburban lordships in Normandy is further revealed in the development of other of towns in the duchy, for example at Rouen and Bayeux. Writing at the start of the twelfth century, the Norman historian Orderic Vitalis recalled the greatness of Rouen and its ancient origins. By the mid-eleventh century Rouen was a thriving port on the Seine. On one side its urban core was bounded by a suburban *bourg* which belonged to the abbey of St Ouen. The *bourg* prospered and so, at the end of the twelfth century, it was made part of the city proper.[17] Meanwhile, along the coast at the important episcopal city of Bayeux, five new *bourgs* had been founded during the course of the eleventh century. This dramatic level of expansion has been described as 'a kind of urban overspill', carefully controlled and encouraged by Norman lords, of course.[18] However, whether these new suburban *bourgs* should be seen as a kind of deliberate form of medieval 'decentralisation' is debatable. It would seem more likely that the new *bourgs* were intended, first and foremost, to act *centripetally* rather than centrifugally, attracting newcomers and promoting trade by riding on the success of an already existing urban centre.

'Suburban bourgs*' outside France: Durham and Westminster*

The Norman and French *bourgs* of the eleventh and twelfth centuries have parallels in other parts of Europe, too. Coventry has already been noted as a case where urbanisation proceeded to take place on two separate but adjoining lordships. Although the 'halves' of

Coventry were not called *bourgs* by contemporaries, to all intents and purposes that is what they were, at least in principle. Elsewhere in England, a number of growing towns were composed of these 'pseudo-*bourgs*', although the proliferation of such *bourgs* was by no means on the scale as that in France.

In northern England, one city which had a number of distinct suburban *bourgs*, or rather 'boroughs', was Durham. Here, three new boroughs are mentioned in the late twelfth century, in charters conferring grants of urban privileges. The charters concern new suburban development on land below the bishop's ancient cathedral city. The three suburban *bourgs*, the 'Old Borough' (or Crossgate), Elvet and St Giles, were each separate jurisdictions in their own right. Also, each was established on land belonging to an ecclesiastical lord. In the case of Elvet, for example, a charter given by Prior Bertram and his convent granted privileges to his burgesses in 'the new borough', sometime after 1188. The borough of St Giles, near by, received its charter from Bishop Hugh du Puiset in *c.*1180, granting free burgage to the master and brethren of the hospital of Kepyer.[19]

On each of the three ecclesiastical lordships adjoining Durham, urbanisation was taking place at about the same time. Although the Old Borough was so called in 1242–43, it was really only 'old' in relation to the two adjacent 'new' boroughs of Elvet and St Giles, from which it had to be distinguished. The content of the prior's borough charter for Elvet follows the usual, familiar formula (see Chapter 2). As far as the legal rubric of borough chartering was concerned, it mattered not that the prior was founding his new borough in close proximity to an existing town, under the shadow of a bishop's *cathedra*, instead of on some distant part of a rural estate:

Bertram the Prior, and the Convent of the Church of Durham to all who see or hear these letters, health. Be it known to you all that we have granted and confirmed to our faithful burgesses of our new borough in *Elvethalch*, that is, from the way which lies near the house of the Abbot of the new monastery on the northern side towards *Scaltoc*, that they shall be free and quit from customs and exactions and all aids, except that we retain our court and our please in our own hand.[20]

The examples considered here concern the creation of suburban *bourgs*, by means of enfranchisement set out in a borough charter, on sites alongside but outside existing towns. Many, but by no means all, suburban lordships were urbanised by lords using the legal paraphernalia of borough charters and burghal privileges. Some lords held onto their suburban landholdings, and saw them prosper with urban development, yet kept them under their control as distinct *manorial* jurisdictions. An example of this sort of urbanisation on a suburban lordship is Westminster, now a built-up part of London but in the Middle Ages an independent and separate settlement situated outside the city's walls.

Westminster's origin and status as a 'town' was unusual, even by medieval standards. Following an initial grant made by King Edgar in *c.*960, a large estate to the west of London came under the single lordship of the abbot of St Peter's.[21] In terms of its location and subsequent urban development, the abbot's estate of Westminster 'resembled an extra-mural [i.e. suburban] *bourg* under the seigneurial control of a wealthy religious house'.[22] Yet, no borough charter was issued to found a *bourg* at Westminster. Urban activity on the estate took place under the manorial supervision of the abbot of Westminster, who continued to maintain a strong hand in the government of the 'vill' throughout the Middle Ages. Nevertheless, although the abbot of Westminster did not create a legally defined 'borough', and although 'the neighbourhood possessed no jurisdictional rights of its own', the secular inhabitants of the area managed to develop 'a large measure of corporate self-determination' through 'the manorial system of local government and the parish'.[23] In this case, the 'jurisdiction' of urban Westminster was not defined in terms of a borough administration put in place by a foundation charter, but rather it came about organically, through the vill's inhabitants who had 'partially adapted the manor court to serve their own public ends'.[24]

Despite the absence of burgage tenure and borough courts at Westminster, the abbot's 'vill' became prosperous and populous during the thirteenth century. Like the French *bourgs*, the 'vill' of Westminster functioned and developed as an urban estate, riding high on the success and prominence of the nearby City of London and feeding off the role that the abbey played in English royal administration. Of course, in reality, a marked legal and institutional divide separated the inhabitants of Westminster from the inhabitants of an enfranchised suburban *bourg* like Elvet at Durham, or Bourg l'Abbé at Caen. However, whether or not they enfranchised them as *bourgs*, the 'new towns' established by lords on their suburban estates were still serving the same purpose: they greatly extended the urban area of a town or city; they attracted newcomers to come and settle, and they put into place a framework of urban landholding which, by acting on a town's spatial and social organisation, came to exert a presence for years afterwards.

Urban estates: lordship and landholding within towns

While urbanisation was taking place on suburban lordships, lords were also developing their estates *within* towns. A lord's relationship with such 'intra-urban' estates was largely an economic one, for not all urban landholdings belonging to a lord were independent jurisdictions. A lord's urban inhabitants usually shared the same privileges as other townspeople residing on estates elsewhere in the town. Even so, such urban landholdings enabled lords to maintain a 'feudal presence' within a town, and at the same time provided them with a means of supplementing revenues raised from their rural landholdings. This close relationship, between lordship and urban landholding, is apparent in the context of late-eleventh-century towns in England, as well as cities in Italy during the thirteenth and fourteenth centuries.

In Anglo-Norman England, the same lords who were responsible for founding chartered towns in the countryside were also holding profitable urban estates within long-established boroughs. This is known from the Domesday Book (1086), which makes it abundantly clear that both Norman and English magnate lords had strong interests in urban landholding. The lords articulated their presence within the 'Domesday boroughs' by holding discrete blocks of land, which made the tenurial geography of most towns in eleventh-century England a complex mosaic of urban estates. To describe the composite nature of urban landholding in these towns, and to express the varied multiplicity of the lordships and urban estates, Ballard (following on from earlier work done by Maitland) formulated the term 'tenurial heterogeneity'.[25] By this Ballard simply meant that the land within a Domesday borough was held by different lords. These lords viewed their urban estates like their rural manors, vills and farms – they were all landholdings helping to support the lord's household.

Urban estates in the 'Domesday boroughs' of Norman England

The integrated nature of rural and urban landholding in Anglo-Saxon and Norman England is known because the Domesday Book assessors recorded it (see Chapter 3). They did so in two ways. Sometimes, a lord's *urban* landholding was itemised separately within the entry for a particular borough, but recorded in connection with an outlying *rural* manor. In the Domesday entry for the borough of Leicester, for example, Hugh de Grandmesnil's urban estate was recorded in terms of houses connected with outlying rural manors that were scattered across the surrounding county (Leicestershire). Thus, ten houses belonging to the earl in Leicester pertained to his rural manor of Belgrave, while seven others belonged as part of his manor and vill of Arnesby.[26] A similar situation existed in the adjacent county, at Warwick. In this case, as Hilton points out, those properties situated *in* the borough, and belonging to lords 'such as the count of Meulan, Earl Aubrey of Northumbria and Hugh of Grandmesnil', were 'appurtenant to the lands which they held *outside* the borough'.[27] Hilton further suggests 'that the burgesses contributory to manors, occupied borough houses as much as agents of the lord on the borough market as for military duty'.[28] That is, the burgesses living in houses belonging to these lords engaged in trade and thereby contributed to the economy of the lords' manorial estates.

Domesday assessors were also accustomed to recording a lord's urban landholding, not under the particular entry for an appropriate borough, but under the heading of a rural manor instead. This is an idiosyncratic feature of the Domesday Book, which in the past has generated confusion, as it led some to believe that the burgesses or houses recorded under an entry for a rural manor were situated there rather than on the lord's urban landholding. Ballard was keen to avoid such oversights and in his *Domesday Boroughs* he properly pointed out that, although 'Domesday Book records the existence of forty-six burgesses belonging to the property of Westminster Abbey at Staines, the Domesday entry relates to burgesses living in London but [who were] *appurtenant* to the manor of Staines'.[29]

According to Ballard, it does not really matter whether 'the contributed houses were entered under the various rural properties to which they were appurtenant', or whether instead 'they were entered in the boroughs in which they were situate, and stated to belong to the owners of the rural property to which they were appurtenant'; for in the final analysis, he contends, the more important issue is to recognise that 'there was a certain connection between some of the rural properties in the county and certain houses within [the] borough, in such manner that those houses . . . were valued as integral parts of the properties'.[30] The urban estates held by magnate lords in the 'Domesday boroughs' were thus part of a manorial economy as much as an urban one. At one level, the inhabitants of properties situated on a lord's urban estate were, like their rural counterparts, subject to *his* authority, but at the same time they also came under the legal umbrella of the borough jurisdiction.

That urban estates formed discrete and defined units of land is also supported by much earlier documentary evidence than the Domesday Book. In 857, in London, a 'profitable little estate' called *Ceolmundinghaga* was granted to the Bishop of Worcester.[31] This estate was a block of land situated at the east end of the Strand, not far from other early documented urban estates one of which, *Hwaetmundes stan*, has been located by Dyson.[32] The term *haga* means 'enclosure' in Old English. Over two centuries later, the Domesday assessors were still using this term when they described urban properties belonging to 'contributory manors' of magnate lords (for example, see the entries for Canterbury and Chichester).[33] Archaeology has shown on these 'urban estates' there were houses and gardens, the properties where the lord's tenants lived.

The Domesday boroughs of late-eleventh-century England provide a good example of how medieval towns were divided into a number of small estates, each belonging to lords of varying rank and status as part of a broader pattern of interconnected rural and urban landholding. It is this interconnectedness, linking urban and rural lordship, and urban and rural landholding, which Hilton refers to when he writes of the 'feudal presence in towns'.[34] What subsequently happened to these urban estates of English and Norman lords after the late eleventh century is considered further in the second part of this chapter. To conclude this particular section, I shall examine how lordship was also important in structuring the organisation (and development) of landholding in towns and cities in thirteenth-century Italy, for this provides yet further evidence to support Hilton's view that having urban estates helped lords to maintain a 'feudal presence' in towns – not only in northern European towns, but in the south, too.

Urban estates of the Florentine magnates

In her book on the noble magnate lords of thirteenth-century Florence, Lansing (like Hilton), puts forward the view that 'the model ... of the city as a "non-feudal island in a feudal sea" has not held up'.[35] Her evidence for this comes from having looked in detail at the activities of a 'prosperous castellan class' living in Florence, which 'characteristically kept their ties to the country and their urban property'.[36] In Italian cities such as Florence, Pisa and Siena, the nobility of the surrounding countryside (*contado*) held properties in compact blocks within the confines of the city itself.

In Florence, magnate lords and their 'noble families dominated the countryside'; while at the same time they 'based their identity on urban rather than rural holdings, on palaces and towers rather than country estates'.[37] Such a system of landholding was also to be found in other of the Italian city republics at this time.[38] In the city itself, nobles' landholdings were organised through a system of patrilineage, where families secured their political and social strength by ensuring that their urban properties were not divided.

Magnate properties in thirteenth-century Florence were held jointly among members of the same family. In the countryside, however, it was more common for rural estates to be divided and held by individual family members. One example of this sort of arrangement concerns the Amidei family and their estates encompassing urban and rural property in and around Florence. In the city itself, their urban estate consisted of 'collections of towers, houses and palaces, with shops below ... clustered in a single neighbourhood'. Within this neighbourhood 'the Amidei urban property was kept intact', but while 'a few pieces of rural land may also have been shared' between members of the Amedei family, the properties that were located in the countryside were 'gradually broken up' after 1250 by a 'few individuals buying the rest out'.[39] The cohesion of a magnate family's urban landholdings was based upon the premise of defence within the city, with a view to dominate their neighbours by constructing towers and palaces (a characteristic feature of many other cities in Italy at this time).[40]

A magnate's urban properties were important for their family's identity, but of course they were also important for contributing to their material wealth. The urban estates formed a basis from which revenues could be derived through commercial and business activity; though as Lansing notes, 'property that served primarily to generate income typically was not held as joint lineage property'.[41] A number of privileges and rights accompanied joint-lineage property-holding, including patronage rights over churches, something which tended to forge greater lineage solidarity.[42]

The development of popular opposition against the wealth, status and influence of the magnates in Florence took place in the later thirteenth century, at a time when the city's government was undergoing a series of important transformations (see Chapter 2). This was also when many of the magnates' urban properties held by joint lineage were being broken up into smaller units (by statutes defined by the established government) in order to restrict the power of the urban nobility.[43] Despite this process of fragmentation, magnates' urban estates sometimes proved remarkably durable. This is evident from a map drawn earlier this century which shows the organisation of property held by noble families in central Florence in 1427 (Figure 6.1). As Renaissance Florence flourished, land-holding in the city still remained based on those blocks of land originally formed in the later twelfth and thirteenth centuries by the noble Florentine magnates. The della Tosa family, for example, held land in unified blocks in the city in 1427, despite having lost 'substantial chunks of property in three parishes just to the north of the market' in the middle of the thirteenth century.[44]

In terms of their spatial organisation, and also in terms of their tenurial organisation, the pattern of landholding in late-medieval Florence was not so very different from the urban estates of 'tenants in chief' in eleventh-century England. In both cases, noble lords retained a mutual interest in their rural and urban properties, and in the process of so doing they were able to articulate their 'feudal presence' in the town as well as the countryside. By holding property and developing estates in towns, seigneurial lords exercised their authority and control. In doing that they were also structuring property-holding activities of townspeople. The property-holding relationship that existed between urban lords and their townspeople will be considered next.

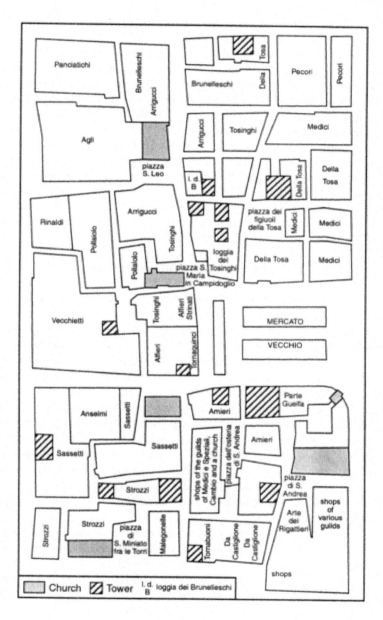

Figure 6.1 *Parcels of properties in Florence, 1427*

Urban Property and Social Order

There was a wide range of property to be found in medieval towns and cities, and there was also great variety in how urban property was organised socially. However, despite the variations, urban property-holding ubiquitously served to tie townspeople to the townscape. Through a hierarchical system of property-holding and tenure, urban lords regulated and controlled the activities of a town's inhabitants in their dwellings and workplaces. In this part of the chapter I shall examine some of the different types of property which were available to townspeople. I will then go on to look at how urban property was organised as a hierarchical tenurial system based on wealth and status. Finally, I will consider the role that property development and speculation played in driving spatial and temporal changes in urban property-holding.

Types and patterns of urban property

Where it has been possible to map in detail the distribution and topography of property patterns for a particular medieval town or city for a particular time, the picture that emerges is one of great diversity. We find units of property of all sizes and shapes, some very small indeed, and crowded into restricted spaces, and others more spacious, occupying large areas of a town. In the Middle Ages, as now, variations in property *size* related largely to differences in property *value*. On the whole, area for area, the smaller units of property in a medieval town, shops and stalls for example, had generally high rents, and thus a comparatively high land value, while the more extensive sorts of property unit, particularly gardens and crofts in outlying fields, had lower land values. Of course, the relative land (rental) value of a property unit depended not only on its dimensions but also on its location within the townscape, as well as its occupation and usage.

The variety of urban property which existed in the Middle Ages is known to us because urban lords and townspeople documented changes in tenure and rents in various written charters and accounts. Before thinking about property in terms of its relative value, I will take a look at how properties were categorised, starting with the smallest, the stall (*seld*) and shop (*shoppa*).

Shops and stalls could measure as little as five feet in width and ten in depth. A *seld* was usually located in a market area and was used to display and sell wares, whereas a *shoppa* was often more substantial in nature and typically formed part of a larger building. In thirteenth-century York, for example, shops were located beneath and at the front of multi-occupied buildings, and thus lined the street at ground-floor level.[45] Similarly, shops formed an integral part of properties belonging to noble families in Florence. They were built on the ground floors of their tall stone towers.[46] Shops and stalls also stood on road bridges over rivers, as was the case in Paris with the Grand Pont. In the later twelfth century, this important bridge over the Seine had a 'roadway down the middle . . . lined on both sides by small houses'; these were 'little more than booths and stalls', and 'each little house had a counter open to the roadway and a steep ladder or stair mounting to a *solar*, or upstairs room'.[47] Other small units of urban property were ovens (*furni*), workshops and cellars (*cellari*), more for commercial and industrial use, as were stables and warehouses.

Properties for private dwellings comprised either a whole building or just a part. A range of terms were employed by contemporary scribes when they were describing properties used for dwellings, the choice depending variously on the property's location within a town, the type of tenure associated with it, the whim of the scribe, and the date at which the property was recorded. Dwellings were termed *messuagium* ('messuage'), *tenementum* ('tenement'), *burgagium* ('burgage'), each potentially reflecting some difference in the property's (and tenant's) status. A dwelling might simply be described as a 'house' (*mansa* or *domus*), a 'hall' (*aulem*), or a 'cottage' (*cotagium*), while occasionally an adjective provided a clearer description of the building, as in *mansa lapida*, 'stone house'.[48] Parts of buildings were also used for private dwellings, including individual rooms, cellars and garrets, as well as gatehouses in town defences. In the late twelfth century, for example, Alexander Neckam rented just a bedchamber and a kitchen within a much larger building while he was studying in Paris.[49] Although urban dwellings in the Middle Ages were often described using different terms, the rents that people were paying for them might not be so very different, so that a messuage (for example) could cost no more in rent than a burgage. Property value actually depended more on a property's location than its size, and of course varied from town to town according to local demand for land.

Urban property comprised more than just buildings for commercial, industrial and domestic purposes. There were, in addition, a number of open lands available for rent, even within the built-up area of a town or city. There were gardens (*gardinium*), orchards, meadows, crofts, closes, riversides and yards, as well as rights of way, arable lands and fields of pasture.[50] All these frequently appear in written accounts relating to urban property, as well as in contemporary descriptions of towns and cities. For instance, William fitz Stephen's well-known description of London in the late twelfth century refers to the open spaces of the town, 'the spacious and beautiful gardens of the citizens . . . planted with trees'.[51] In the thirteenth century, in nearby Westminster, orchards and fields lay behind the built-up frontages of streets on the abbey's estate.[52]

The medieval townscape was thus a mosaic of different sorts of property – some large, some small, some expensive to rent, some less so. There was hardly a piece of land within any medieval town or city that did not have some claim made upon it by one person or another. However, picturing urban property using the Latin terminology of legal documents presents a rather too 'clinical' view of the sorts of properties that medieval townspeople occupied. To bring to life their houses and yards, the shops and the stalls, to find out what the physical appearance of medieval urban properties was like, it is necessary to consider the evidence that comes from the archaeological record.

The physical appearance of urban properties

In towns and cities in the Middle Ages, property parcels were typically demarcated on the ground by a physical boundary. In the centre of towns, property boundaries were more likely to be marked by stone walls or by timber fences, but on the urban fringe, in suburban areas, hedges and ditches usually sufficed. Physical property boundaries were an important expression of privacy and rights of ownership for medieval townspeople, and once in place the position of boundaries might remain unchanged for many centuries, as excavations in British cities have shown.[53] The 'proper' placing of physical property boundaries was of such importance that in twelfth-century Italian cities surveyors were employed to measure the frontages of properties. Records of the measurements

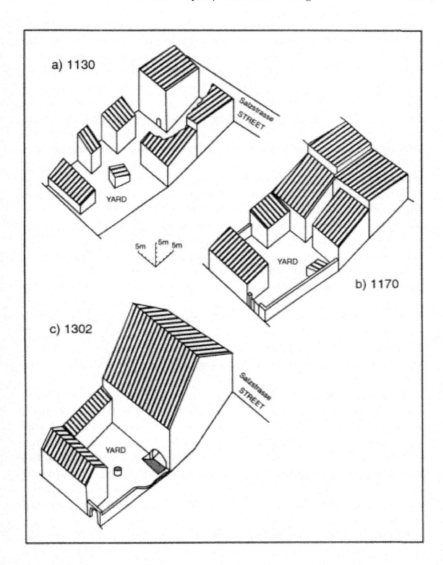

Figure 6.2 *The development of properties in Salzstrasse, Freiburg im Breisgau*

were kept by civic authorities, as was the case in Pisa and Siena.[54]

Close to market places, and along principal streets where demand for property was highest, there were quite dense patterns of property. Typically, by 1300, streets in the core of towns and cities across medieval Europe were fronted by rows of tightly packed buildings, usually of substantial construction whether of timber or stone. Behind the buildings along the street frontages, in a rear plot, or yard, there were often other, less substantial, timber-built structures, functioning often as storage spaces, workshops and stables. This sort of physical arrangement was widespread in towns and cities both north and south of the Alps.

Taking northern Europe first, at Lübeck, excavations have shown that by the end of the twelfth century even along the minor streets, away from the town centre, the street frontages were almost continuously built-up, and in the plots that lay behind the principal buildings were a host of ancillary structures.[55] Potentially, all such structures represent individual property units, each providing someone with a living or working space. The same sort of property arrangements have also been found in towns elsewhere in Germany, for example at Freiburg im Breisgau (Figure 6.2), as well as in the towns and cities of east-central Europe, such as Prague.[56] Further west, too, in France, in the Low Countries and in Britain and Ireland, comparable urban property patterns existed during the high Middle Ages.

Turning to southern Europe, in some Italian cities, buildings have survived through to the present day from the twelfth century, thus providing a valuable opportunity to see how buildings and properties were arranged in the Middle Ages. In the Chinzica quarter of Pisa, for example, one twelfth-century street block between the Vicolo Lanfranchi and the Vicolo da Scorno comprised a mosaic of individual properties (Figure 6.3).[57] Here, the property units were made up of multi-floor buildings fronting onto the two main streets, north and south. Access to the rear of the properties was gained from behind, from the two narrower side-streets, through gates, passages and yards, while within the buildings themselves stairways led up to the upper floors. The spatial organisation of the properties within this particular street block in Pisa reveals the same sort of dense but clearly defined arrangement of buildings and plots that also characterised medieval towns and cities north of the Alps.

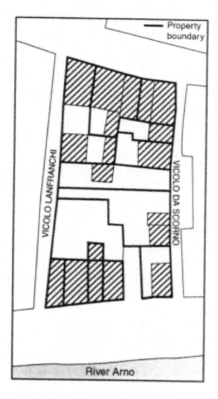

Figure 6.3 *Twelfth-century properties in the Chinzica quarter, Pisa*

Archaeology, in combination with the study of contemporary written records, allows us to recreate the physical appearance of medieval urban property in three dimensions, which not only helps us to understand more fully what the built-up townscape looked like, but also provides us with a picture of how built-up urban properties, particularly private dwellings, were arranged 'volumetrically'. Of course, this is often difficult to achieve, especially for the earlier medieval period where the foundations of a building might be the only part of it to have survived. Even so, there are cases where large parts of medieval buildings have remained relatively undisturbed, either above or below ground, and from these it is possible to view medieval buildings in three dimensions rather than just two.

Even today, many European towns still contain at least some stone buildings dating back to before the thirteenth century. Such examples of still standing medieval buildings provide an opportunity to examine their internal character and organisation. Even if from the outside a building looks to be post-medieval in date, it may well be containing a building of much earlier origin. At Southampton, for example, the remains of a twelfth-century stone-built merchant's house was discovered 'inside' a visibly much later building.[58] Sometimes, more unusually, domestic stone-built structures survived through from the Middle Ages without undergoing major exterior changes. In Italian cities, medieval stone buildings sometimes formed a terrace rising to a height of up to four storeys, as was the case in the Via Mazzini in Pisa.[59] In Britain, the so-called Jew's House at Lincoln had two floors (Plate 6.1). Detailed architectural study of this twelfth-century building has shown how it originally comprised a row of shops on the ground floor, fronting directly onto the street, with a hall situated above. The shops were physically self-contained from the rest of the building, showing that they formed distinctly separate units of property, while the upper floor was accessed from the outside by an exterior staircase.[60]

Stone buildings generally stand a greater chance of survival than timber-built structures. Nevertheless, medieval timber structures do survive and below ground are well preserved in waterlogged and anaerobic conditions. In London, for example, timber buildings dating from the tenth century onwards are now known to have been quite elaborate in their design. Some were also substantial in size and rose to more than one storey in height, with complex arcading inside. Equally, though, many medieval urban timber buildings were small, single-storey structures of a relatively simple construction.[61] In Kiev, from the late ninth through to the thirteenth century, timber rather than stone was used for the entire construction of properties. In the suburb of Podol, for example, single-storey cabin-like buildings were built of logs, with access to them provided by means of a ramp that led up to a covered porch.[62] Similar wooden buildings are known from other medieval towns in the Baltic coast area, for example, at Riga, where timber-built houses dating from the thirteenth century were enclosed by palisaded fences (along with their yards and outbuildings), each interconnected by timber-surfaced walkways.[63]

Plate 6.1   *The Jew's House, Lincoln*

Urban property and social hierarchies

Diversity in the size and appearance of urban properties was one of the hallmarks of European medieval towns and cities. The wide range of property made available to townspeople provided them with both living and working spaces (see below, Chapter 7). Furthermore, property-holding embraced all levels of urban society (except for the very poor, the destitute and homeless), and the size and value of an urban property, or collection of properties, was some indication of the wealth and social status of the property-holders themselves. Thus, the hierarchy of urban property-holding mirrored urban social hierarchies. Indeed, personal wealth and status were not only reflected in the amount of property an individual held; the sort of property it was, as well as where it was situated and what kind of tenure it represented, all helped to reinforce an individual's place in the medieval urban social hierarchy.

Where particular individuals or groups of people acquired a number of properties within a town urban 'estates' emerged, where either the properties formed one contiguous block or were scattered across the town. The size and extent of these estates were in constant flux during the Middle Ages, as properties were amalgamated and also fragmented. At the same time as certain entrepreneurial, property-minded individuals, such as merchants, were acquiring properties and amalgamating them to form 'estates', the large urban landholdings of secular and ecclesiastical lords were being broken up into smaller units of urban property. One example of this comes from Coventry, where during the thirteenth and fourteenth centuries members of the Catesby family started acquiring properties across the town, gathering revenue from properties and at the same time gaining greater local importance in local urban affairs.[64]

The dynamic nature of urban property markets in the Middle Ages should not be underestimated, therefore. As the medieval urban property market became more complex and legalistic in nature, particularly during the thirteenth century and afterwards, more detailed and precise written accounts of property transfers and agreements were made. No doubt the urban property market was also active prior to 1200, it is just that after this date the transfer of properties becomes more 'visible' in written records. In southern England, we know that urban properties were being both accumulated and sublet from at least the middle of the ninth century.[65] As a result of successive property transfers over lengthy periods of time, complex tenurial structures emerged. Where a single property was held by one person it could (and usually did) accommodate a large number of other people, 'subtenants'. At the same time, this multi-occupied property might be just one part of a much more extensive 'estate' of similar urban properties, all under the possession of one individual or institution. Such private 'estates', made up of accumulated individual properties, could either be administered at a distance, perhaps from a place just outside the town, or from a 'capital messuage' within the town, as was the case with the Catesbys.[66]

The socially extended patterns of property tenure that characterised landholding in medieval towns and cities have been termed 'tenurial ladders' by historians. The reason for this is that urban property-holding operated though interrelationships between different property-holders, whose social status was defined by their place in the 'ladder'. These tenurial and social relationships were thus hierarchical, with property-holders of higher social status having more urban property than those who occupied positions lower down the hierarchy. Tenurial ladders can only be reliably reconstructed from property records where written accounts of who held what land are sufficiently detailed and numerous. These preconditions are only rarely met in the early medieval period, but from the twelfth century onwards, when the volume of written records relating to urban property increases, 'tenurial ladders' become more visible. One such example comes from work carried out by Keene on a survey of property undertaken in 1148 for the city of Winchester (Figure 6.4).[67]

In the mid-twelfth century, Winchester was still the royal 'capital' of the kingdom of England, even though it was gradually losing this function to London. The detailed survey of urban property compiled in 1148 is sufficient to enable historians to piece together a tenurial ladder for one particular property situated in the High Street, the commercial core of Winchester.[68] The following hierarchical arrangement of property-holding can be worked out.

From one single property situated in the centre of Winchester, the king acquired six pence (6d.) a year in rent, paid to him by Herbert the Chamberlain.[69] The abbot of Tewkesbury also received rent from the property, a sum of twelve pence (12d.) a year

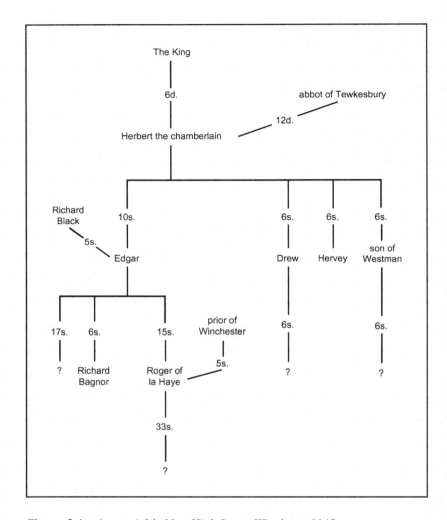

Figure 6.4 *A tenurial ladder: High Street, Wincheter, 1148*

(Figure 6.4). The king and the abbot were thus at the top of the ladder for this particular property, followed by Herbert, but of course, neither the king nor the abbot would have occupied the property themselves; rather, they sublet it to Herbert, and expected rent from him in return. On the ladder below Herbert were a number

of tenants who were, in turn, paying rent to Herbert. The total
18d. that the king and abbot collected from their High Street
property looks very measly in comparison to the amount of money
that the property was generating for the subtenants. In 1110, the
property had been worth a total of 109 shillings and 6 pence in
rents, rising to a total of 122 shillings and 6 pence at the time of
the survey in 1148. The main earners who were benefiting most
from these sums were the subtenants, like Herbert the Chamberlain. Indeed, Herbert himself was collecting 28 shillings a year
from four tenants occupying lower positions in the tenurial ladder. Bearing in mind that Herbert was paying out only a shilling
and a half to his two landlords he was making a tidy profit every
year. Of Herbert's four tenants, three were themselves collecting
rents from others, who were positioned yet further down the tenurial ladder. One of these, Edgar, was paying Herbert 10 shillings
while a further 5 shillings went to a Richard Black. However, Edgar
was not down on the deal, for he in turn was collecting a sum of
38 shillings from *his* subtenants. It seems that for this particular
property, the 'middlemen' were reaping the highest returns.

This particular example of a tenurial ladder reveals a lot about
the complexity of urban property-holding in the Middle Ages. For
this one property, 'nine people of institutions were receiving
rents . . . and there were at least five successive rungs in the ladder of tenure'.[70] Furthermore, 'of the eleven people named, probably
only two occupied parts of the property, which seems to have been
divided physically into at least six parts'.[71] What we are seeing, of
course, are only those individuals whose activities in the property
market are well documented. Missing from the tenurial ladder are
those who were further down it, and hence further down the social
hierarchy. The social status of tenants becomes so low at the bottom
of the ladder, that the poorest of the tenants are rendered 'invisible'.
The poor must have been there, of course, for it was their rent
payments that Edgar and his fellow subtenants were collecting.
Roger of la Haye was taking 33 shillings annually from the High
Street property from unnamed tenants beneath him, most probably
from those who were more likely to move on. But the presumably
small rooms being rented to the poorest tenants for a few pence
are not detailed at this early date. All that is clear from the accounts
is that there were some individuals making high returns by subletting
to less wealthy tenants.

The mid-twelfth-century 'tenurial ladder' from Winchester provides a rare opportunity to see how the social organisation of medieval urban property-holding worked at the micro-scale. The tenurial ladder is in fact a microcosm of medieval urban society, with overlords sitting at the top, entrepreneurial rentiers in the middle (creaming off the most profit), and a large group of less well-off people lower down the hierarchy. If we were to map this social hierarchy onto the internal structure of the property itself, the more wealthy tenants, paying the higher rents, would be seen to have the principal rooms, probably on the first and second floors. Meanwhile, tucked away in smaller rooms, perhaps in the roof-space or at the back of the building, were the poorer tenants, perhaps living in just one single room (see Chapter 7). This was the pattern of property-holding to be found in London during the fourteenth century, and it was not unusual for tenants to fall into the street from their upstairs rooms, sometimes with fatal consequences.[72]

It should by now be clear that 'tenurial ladders' and 'tenurial geographies' were closely interlinked in medieval towns and cities. The hierarchy of social relations created by ladders of urban property-holding was thus also embedded, in a physical sense, in the location, layout and structure of the properties themselves. Those people with the most property tended to live in more privacy, away from multi-occupied properties, while within the multi-occupied properties, a person's place in society was clearly reflected by where they lived within the property. It is clear, therefore, that within any single property, there could exist a 'nested hierarchy' of smaller units of property. For this reason it is perhaps as well to differentiate between a physically demarcated property unit – a 'plot' – and an individually tenanted unit of property – a property 'parcel'. What now needs some consideration is how these urban plots and property parcels changed as property markets within towns and cities waxed and waned.

Property markets and transformations in urban property

Urban property was by no means a static entity. Properties changed hands, as well as value and use, during the course of the Middle Ages. Properties were often amalgamated to form larger units, or subdivided to form smaller ones; it became built-up as demand for urban land increased, and it became derelict if it was not occupied. These changes were largely driven by the vicissitudes of the local, urban property market, which could vary from town to town, and also between different areas of the same town. Here, I will focus on the sorts of changes that took place as demand for urban properties increased as a result of demographic and economic changes in the high and later Middle Ages. In essence, this was a period that saw urban property patterns become densely built-up, and although the timing of this 'densification' varied from place to place, it was generally commonplace right across medieval Europe.

First, let us consider some aspects of changing urban property values. The higher demand for property in central locations within towns has already been remarked upon, but in its details the inter-relationship between property size and value was a complicated one in the Middle Ages. Having looked in detail at changes in urban property in Winchester using the 1148 survey, Keene remarks that

> We can contrast the densely built-up, high value properties of the commercial district in High Street, with an area that was almost equally densely built-up but contained low value properties (presumably dwellings of the poor), with [yet] another street where low values reflected the sparsity of settlement, and [yet] another area where the large high value properties were clearly residences of the elite.[73]

What is interesting here is how the size of an urban property can be *inversely* related to its value, and vice versa. The reasons for this have much to do with how property size and value related to spatial and social factors operating within medieval towns, particularly the circumstances of the local urban property market and patterns of urban land-use.

Urban properties changed value as demand for land increased or decreased. Changes in demand would vary as a response to both exogenous and indigenous forces. For example, Winchester's property market fluctuated as the city's role in English political administration changed during the twelfth century.[74] While Winchester was the 'capital' for the English and Norman kings, the city had a buoyant and prosperous property market, but when this royal interest switched to London and Westminster, in the later twelfth century, the demand for urban property in Winchester dropped off. Conversely, at Westminster, the period between $c.$1200 and $c.$1300 saw 'furious activity, and consequently rising land values, in the market for land in the neighbourhood' of the royal abbey.[75] In this period, too, private urban property records begin to proliferate, itself an indication that urban property was more in demand and thus of more importance to townspeople.

We know patterns of urban property were changing during the Middle Ages because of archaeological work and because of detailed studies of property records. In recent excavations undertaken in Freiburg im Breisgau in Germany, for example, it has been possible for archaeologists to reconstruct a sequence of property development, starting in the early twelfth century and running through to the fourteenth (Figure 6.2).[76]

Herzog Bertold II founded Freiburg in the late eleventh century, and it seems that not long after the town's creation the first properties were being built up, even in minor streets. The earliest development of these properties took place along the street frontages, at the 'plot head', though there were also smaller ancillary structures behind, in the 'plot tail'. In one particular side street in the town, called Salzstrasse, the earliest buildings dated to about 1130.[77] At this stage, buildings (of wood and stone construction) stood only at the plot head, and the frontage along the street was discontinuous, being disrupted by narrow lanes which provided access to the plot tail where the outbuildings were. However, within 50 years this arrangement had changed: the buildings along the street at the plot head now formed a continuous frontage, and access to the rear of the plot had been altered. The building-up of the street frontage testifies to a growth in demand for property in Freiburg, during the later twelfth century. At the same time, buildings at the plot head were rebuilt to form more substantial structures, thus raising the density of occupation on the plot, especially towards the front. Meanwhile the perimeter of the plot had acquired a stout boundary wall, marking the property out as a physical and distinct landholding, separate from its adjoining neighbours.

By the end of the twelfth century, the Salzstrasse property had developed into a clearly defined plot, containing a group of buildings. A little over a century later, by the start of the fourteenth century, this group of buildings had been entirely rebuilt, so as to form a single structure containing at least five floors (including a cellar). This new building took up the whole front half of the plot, while in the yard at the rear, outbuildings had also been changed to more substantial structures.

The sequence of property redevelopment taking place between the twelfth and fifteenth centuries in Freiburg's Salzstrasse was also typical in many other European medieval towns. For example, a similar pattern of redevelopment affected buildings on medieval properties in Alms Lane in Norwich.[78] Like the Salzstrasse in Breisgau, Alms Lane was a relatively unimportant street, a factor that could explain why the earliest structures dated only from the late thirteenth century, and not before. The site became progressively built-up with substantial structures, such that by the fifteenth century it comprised three property parcels, each having a clay-walled house. Further north, at Hull, development of properties along Blackfriargate likewise saw a closing-up of the street frontage during the later Middle Ages. During the fourteenth century, entryways separating buildings were closed and infilled with new timber buildings – a clear sign that there was increasing pressure for building along the street – and similar to the sequence of property development along Salzstrasse in Breisgau.[79]

As urban property became more densely built-up during the high and later Middle Ages, so a greater number of properties became available for multi-occupation. The buildings themselves also became more durable and longer-lasting. During the twelfth and thirteenth centuries in Cheapside, in London, a transition took place towards more durable buildings. Initially, structures of timber with wattle walls predominantly occupied properties in Cheapside, but with time, new buildings were more commonly of stone and timber construction, while later still, more and more structures were wholly built of stone or brick.[80] This transition in building fabric not only made urban buildings more durable, it also made buildings larger and higher, thus opening up new opportunities for property-holders to house more tenants on their properties.

A transition towards buildings of more permanent nature also made it possible for landholders to start redefining the sorts of properties they were leasing. Thus, rather than simply leasing pieces of land, more specific leases were made, described in terms of individual buildings, or parts of buildings. In England at least, this transition in the nature of urban property is reflected in the way that properties were described in private property deeds and charters during the twelfth and thirteenth centuries. If we examine the changing usage of Latin terms in property charters during the course of the later Middle Ages, an interesting sequence emerges, with particular terms becoming popular at particular times.

The earliest property deeds and charters for Gosford Street in Coventry date from the start of the thirteenth century. At this period, properties were commonly referred to simply as *terre* ('land'). Before too long this was superseded by a different legal term, 'messuage'. This again soon changed. Towards the end of the thirteenth century, deeds begin to refer to properties as 'tenements', and then, by the early 1300s, they were described as 'houses'.[81] This transition, from 'land' to 'house', suggests as dwellings became more solidly and permanently built during the thirteenth century, property-holders sought to redefine property leases. Rather than leasing to a tenant the land on which a building stood, as was the case at the start of the century, by 1300 it was more common for tenants to be leased an individual building. This reflected a trend towards smaller units of property, as demand for urban property increased. Towards the end of the Middle Ages, Coventry's property market was buoyant, and in Gosford Street, as in Cheapside in London, properties were becoming more built-up, with longer-lasting dwellings.

A further indication of the growing intensity of property development in medieval towns and cities is to be found in written agreements concerning disputes between adjoining property-holders. Living in close proximity to others in properties where land was at a premium, it is no surprise to find squabbles between neighbours. Litigation was usually required in order to resolve such disputes, the outcome of which was written down for future reference (should there be a need to go back to see what was agreed).[82]

Cases of disagreement between property-holders provide a fascinating insight into the social implications of living in a closely packed medieval townscape, revealing the zealously guarded property rights of townspeople in the high and later Middle Ages. In Bristol, a covenant was agreed in 1344 between John Pridye and William atte fford ('at Ford') concerning the maintenance of a gutter on the wall which divided their two 'tenements' in Redcliffe Street.

Rather earlier, in 1308, a 'moiety of a wall' between two other properties in the same street was granted by Ralph atte Slope to John de Garmestone, while John was to 'make all easements in the way of gutters, etc'.[83] Such was the concern to define urban property boundaries and maintain them. In Coventry, an extraordinary private agreement between two neighbouring townspeople points to a similarly dense townscape, and equally possessive tenants. This concerned a property situated right in the heart of the town, in the principal market place, and a man called John de Chiltone who in 1301 granted to Robert Fraunceys 'all the water dripping and falling from gutters and roofs of their buildings'![84]

With the high demand for urban property in the high and later Middle Ages, it is not surprising to find property speculators at work, developing land by putting up new buildings for rent. For those able and willing to involve themselves in the urban property market it provided a potentially rich return. Urban property provided a 'convenient way of employing capital not immediately required for trade', and during hard times properties could be disposed of to free up personal funds.[85]

Examples of new buildings being put up with the express purpose of leasing them to new tenants can be found in many important cities in medieval England. At York, for instance, blocks of commercial property were built in the early fourteenth century in order to accommodate retail activity and to provide tenants with some limited living space above the shop. These 'rows', as they were termed, were two-storey buildings, built under the direction of religious institutions as well as private individuals.[86] In other important provincial English cities there were similar sorts of speculation. In the centre of Coventry's market place, the prior of St Mary's possessed what were described in 1410 as 'newly built' tenements and shops, though at the time it is evident that he was still actually looking for tenants to occupy them. Similarly, in London, contracts dating to the period 1369–73 relate to the construction of long rows, or shops, with living accommodation above, 'erected by, or in the ownership of single landlords'.[87]

Speculative urban property development not only involved building commercial properties. Residential buildings were also purpose-built by speculators in order to provide more living space for townspeople and more revenue from rent. The type of structure constructed for this purpose sometimes consisted of a 'terrace' of individual dwellings contained within a single building. In Spon Street, in Coventry, a timber-framed building of early-fifteenth-century date was put together using 'pre-fabricated' timbers. The whole structure was adapted to fit an unusually shaped plot, and it replaced earlier buildings on the site.[88] This new terrace was built as a type of building known to architectural historians as a 'Wealden house'. It fronted onto one of the main roads entering the city from the north, and this position would no doubt have made the property a worthwhile investment by someone willing to speculate.

Examples of medieval speculative property development that have so far come to light in England largely date to the fourteenth and fifteenth centuries. It may be that earlier examples are yet to be found, as it seems likely that like-minded entrepreneurs existed in previous centuries, too. Those willing to take up properties and 'speculate' in urban real estate, developed and transformed the physical character of the medieval townscape, such that in the period between the eleventh and fourteenth centuries most large towns saw urban landholdings progressively become more densely built-up and occupied by buildings which provided townspeople with their living and working spaces.

Conclusion

The purpose of this chapter has been to show how urban landholding played an important role in the process of urbanisation during the Middle Ages. The first half of the chapter showed how urban landholdings shaped the development of towns and cities, and how lords held land both inside and outside towns. Sometimes a lord's urban landholdings were often part of a larger 'estate' that included rural property. It is important to remember, therefore, that there was no inseparable gulf between town and country in the Middle Ages, but rather a close relationship between the two, forged through joint urban and rural landholding. This interconnectedness is what Hilton calls the 'feudal presence in towns'.[89] The feudal presence was also important in the way that some lords used their landholdings as a basis to foster urban development around existing towns and cities. By creating a suburban *bourg* just outside a town, for example, lords created what were in effect, 'towns within towns', the result of which were towns and cities made up of an agglomeration of urban landholdings (sometimes retained by a lord as a private jurisdiction).

In the second part of the chapter, attention turned more towards the role that townspeople played in developing urban property, and the processes that were instrumental in changing the physical appearance of the medieval townscape. Here again, it is necessary to consider how a 'feudal presence' structured the organisation of urban property-holding. The wide variety of urban property available to medieval townspeople ultimately belonged to someone, and that 'someone' was usually a major landholder, who might or might not live in the town where the property was situated. All sorts of people had a stake in holding urban property, for the property market provided a good source of revenue and capital. Within any one single property, there would usually be a range of buildings, some used for private dwellings, some as workshops and some as storage spaces. Most urban properties in the Middle Ages were multi-occupied. Those who lived in a particular building might share it with a host of other people, some poor, some not so poor. Such properties were usually sublet, allowing 'middle men' rentiers to profit by charging amounts that added up to more than the rents they were paying to landlords. Such 'tenurial ladders' served to create and reinforce social hierarchies. Indeed, the social organisation of medieval urban property was a microcosm of medieval urban society. What people did in and around their properties is the focus of the next chapter.

7

TOWNSPEOPLE AND TOWNSCAPES

A poon [poor] pedlar, who carries nothing but soap and needles, shouteth and calleth out clamourously what he beareth; and a rich mercer goeth along quite silently.[1]

It is a common saying, 'from mill and from market, from smithy and from nunnery, men bring tidings'.[2]

Previous chapters have viewed urban life in the Middle Ages through the activities of town founders, borough officials, surveyors and architects, property-holders and speculators. It is time now to consider more specifically the activities of 'ordinary' townspeople, and look at the sorts of things they did on a day-to-day basis. The medieval townscape was the setting, or stage, on which and through which everyday social interactions were performed. As such, townscapes came to symbolise social relations, and particular sorts of townscape acquired distinct cultural meanings and values, depending on what kind of social activity took place there.

While townscapes shaped the everyday lives of townspeople, people's activities shaped the townscapes they lived and worked in. In this chapter, I consider how townscapes were mutually constituted by, and constitutive of, everyday life. This means taking a look at the home and domestic life of townspeople, as well as the places they worked in, and what they did to make their money. To establish where people were living and working, and how they interacted with one another, I will look at townspeople's homes and workplaces; their domestic arrangements and occupations; and their social and cultural values. The latter involves taking a look at how certain groups of townspeople became associated with particular areas of a town, because of who they were; and how the medieval townscape had the capacity to project an image of a person's 'place' in medieval urban society.

In the first part of the chapter I deal specifically with people's home and domestic life, and take a close look at what was going on inside townspeople's houses and households. I aim to portray the sort of rooms people inhabited, the kind of foods they would have eaten, and some of the social etiquette that was expected. Of course, it is impossible to do all this in detail, but an attempt is nevertheless made to show how townspeople of differing social and economic status would have lived their public and private lives, in particular across the twelfth to the fourteenth centuries. The second part of the chapter presents the spectacle of work in the medieval townscape: the markets, the hostelries, the quaysides where goods and services were exchanged and the workshops, backyards and open spaces where craftspeople and artisans manufactured objects from raw materials. Finally, the chapter concludes with some discussion of social behaviour, and how this was reflected in, and reinforced by, the spaces people occupied in the townscape. In just a single chapter, all I can hope to do is provide an impression of everyday urban life in the Middle Ages, as seen and heard through the eyes and ears of those people who made up the bulk of the medieval urban population.

Home and Domestic Life

Over the last few years, social historians of the Middle Ages have increasingly concerned themselves with matters of 'everyday life'. Two important books, by Dyer and Hanawalt, provide vivid and lucid accounts of many aspects of medieval everyday life, such as diet and health, the working day, poverty and charity, as well as the routines associated with particular stages in a person's life, the cycle of birth, childhood, adolescence, marriage, old age and death.[3]

On the whole, the everyday and the mundane were not widely recorded by contemporaries in the Middle Ages, which means that a variety of sources have to be used to help reveal what 'ordinary' people did and what they thought when dealing with domestic issues, such as burial customs, childbirth, table etiquette and kitchen contents, and so on. Since late-medieval documentary records are much more informative about the 'ordinary' and 'everyday' than earlier records, historical studies of urban social life tend to be more concerned with the later Middle Ages rather than the earlier part of the period. Here, it will be useful to start with a brief look at how wealth and poverty were affected by a person's financial status, for personal wealth had an important bearing on many aspects of townspeople's home and domestic life.

Social status, wealth and lifestyle

Some Marxist historians of the Middle Ages have used notions of 'class' and 'class struggle' to examine and conceptualise the socio-economic structure of medieval towns and cities, particularly in Britain and France.[4] Of them, Dyer's model of medieval urban social hierarchy, although it is based on a specific, situated historical context (England in the later Middle Ages), nevertheless provides a useful starting point for discussing lifestyle issues related to personal wealth.[5] He broadly differentiates medieval urban society as follows. Throughout medieval Europe, merchants invariably occupied the highest levels of urban society, followed by master craftsmen, journeymen and apprentices. Towards the lower echelons of society were labourers and servants, and finally, at the lowest level, were what some historians now term 'marginals', that is those who were seen to be marginal within medieval urban society, particularly beggars, vagrants and prostitutes. Taking these groupings in turn, let us consider how a person's home and domestic life reflected wealth and social status.

Merchants were preoccupied with 'trade on a large scale, over long distances, sometimes involving highly valued commodities like wine and cloth', particularly in larger urban centres.[6] They also held power through their role as buyers of products made by craftsmen and their journeymen and apprentices, and because they usually occupied a place in urban government they could influence the regulatory controls that governed the activities of others working and living in the town, such as craftsmen, or 'artisans'. Craftsmen were also relatively wealthy themselves. They were employers of apprentices, usually young men over the age of about 14. They were also employers of 'journeymen', men who had already served their apprenticeship, and so were qualified as craftsmen, but who had no workforce and no workshop of their own (see below).[7]

The wealthier medieval households, those of merchants and craftsmen for example, employed servants who were engaged in domestic duties, such as water carrying, cooking and the like. Domestic servants would usually live in the same house as the master's family, often in a small room in the roof-space of a house, in the 'garret'. Men and women were both as likely to enter into domestic service, but either way it was typically a task undertaken by adolescents. Those who became servants were not necessarily either uneducated or from low-status families – in late-medieval London, for example, servants who were intelligent and polite were highly sought after in high-status households.[8] The number of servants a person had was a measure of personal wealth. As Hanawalt puts it, 'anyone who could afford a servant had one, and it was a matter of prestige to have as many as possible'.[9]

Labourers provided a town with a cheap workforce which carried out unskilled and semi-skilled manual tasks such as digging and carrying for building work.[10] Like other workers in the medieval town, labourers were employed on a contractual basis to work on particular tasks for specified periods, and for this reason a worker's employer could frequently change, and in between times, when an individual was without work, they would be without an income and liable to poverty.[11]

Poverty in the Middle Ages affected those who, through disease, disability or age, were unable to be wage-earners themselves but relied on the charity of others in order to survive. Equally though, poverty also affected those who did work but who were, for whatever reason, either unemployed or underemployed, or perhaps deemed to be 'marginal'. Social attitudes to the urban poor changed through the Middle Ages. As Dyer notes, the early fourteenth century saw 'harsher attitudes towards beggars' as labour was becoming more scarce and the 'bonds of society seemed to be breaking'.[12] Prior to this period – a period in which the whole of western Europe was suffering from plague epidemics and a large fall in population – the poor were generally seen by medieval society to be 'a natural part of the social scene'.[13] The Church ultimately shaped attitudes to the poor. A 'deserving poor', unlike the 'undeserving poor', would ultimately gain salvation in death, but those who were rich but did not show 'mercy and pity by their gifts' to the poor would be denied entry into Heaven.[14]

The way the 'deserving poor' were provided for by urban society altered during the course of the Middle Ages. From the eleventh century onwards, hospitals were founded by wealthy benefactors to provide for poor people in many if not most towns and cities in Europe. As Gilchrist notes, 'the medieval hospital was not a casualty ward, nor a place for the treatment of the severely diseased . . . rather, these hospitals catered for the general sick poor, and particularly for those most vulnerable groups within the life-cycle'.[15] This population included the very young, particularly orphans, as well as the aged and infirm. In York in 1370, for example, there were 23 orphans and 224 adults accommodated in St Leonard's hospital.[16] By this time, secular hospitals and almshouses were being established in a number of towns and cities, and these supplemented the earlier hospitals which had tended to be more monastic in their character.[17]

Differences in urban poverty and wealth reflected the level of income and expenditure of townspeople. Recent calculations by historians have sought to establish what sort of wage a medieval townsperson could expect to earn, and how much money they would need to live in reasonable comfort. From accounts of wages paid we often know how much certain people earned, but it is usually much more difficult to establish how much money they might have *spent*. As Dyer points out, in Florence in 1290, at a time when a labourer earned about 52 shillings and 6d. a month, and a skilled worker earned 96 shillings a month, some 43 shillings and 3d. was actually needed for a person to be housed and clothed, and to eat sufficiently well.[18] In England, in the fifteenth century, the relative wealth of artisans living in York has been cautiously calculated by Swanson using the evidence of wills as well as taxation records.[19] She suggests that tanners and butchers seem to have been particularly well off, with plasterers, tilers, carpenters, and textile piece-workers being the least prosperous (though even within a single craft there was sometimes a large gap between rich and poor).

Inside the medieval home

Perhaps the most visible outward reflection of a person's wealth and social status was the home they lived in, the lifestyle they followed, and the clothes they wore. The nature of domestic furnishings and belongings that were used to decorate and embellish the medieval home clearly would have depended upon the financial status of the householder, which was largely determined by their occupational position. From a late-fifteenth-century probate inventory, Hanawalt offers this description of a hall in a property belonging to a reasonably 'middling' sort of craftsman called Richard Bele, living in London:

> The walls were hung with cloth painted with designs and, as was typical in these halls, with old weaponry. Furniture was sparse, consisting of a few chairs and stools and a folding table made in London. A container for holy water hung by the door. A fireplace, burning either wood or coal, heated the room . . . the buttery and the kitchen contained such luxuries as candlesticks, pewter pots and a chafing dish. Most of the valuables . . . were kept in the chief chamber [*solar* – 'a private room on an upper floor and for many households the only withdrawing room or bedchamber'][20] in chests and cupboards. The house also included a sparsely furnished room for a maid and, finally, the garret, where the apprentice might sleep and which was also sparsely furnished, with old and broken furnishings.[21]

This description presents a rather homely idea of Bele's household. Earlier, contemporary written accounts also reveal a tolerable level of home comfort, at least for some.

Surviving from the last quarter of the twelfth century are a series of remarkable descriptions of domestic rooms written by Alexander Neckam, a travelling scholar who spent time studying in Paris. His observations provide vivid views of the sorts of interior furnishings and daily domestic practices that he was familiar with in the 1170s.[22] In his *De nominibus utensilium*, Neckam paints a colourful image of a bedchamber, a kitchen, a pantry and a latrine, aspects of which are worth repeating here.

First of all, 'in the bed chamber', Neckam declares,

> Let a curtain go around the walls decently, or a scenic canopy, for the avoiding of spiders and flies . . . near the bed let there be placed a chair to which a stool may be added, and a bench nearby the bed. On the bed itself should be placed a feather mattress . . . a quilted pad of striped cloth should cover this on which a cushion for the head can be placed. Then sheets of

cotton, or at least pure linen, should be laid. . . . A perch should be nearby on which can rest a hawk . . . from another pole let there hang clothing.[23]

The image that this depiction presents to us is rather serene and restful. Of course, it may be that what Neckam is trying to do here is set out how a bedchamber *ought* to be, rather than what it actually was like. On the other hand, twelfth-century manuscript illustrations showing bed-scenes corroborate Neckam's description, while his eye for the details suggests that he was commenting faithfully on the fashionable room furnishings of the time.

In the more well-to-do medieval home, the bedchamber was altogether separate from the part of the house used for more 'public' functions, such as entertaining guests. The place for this was the hall (*aulem*). In 'an affluent household' of the later twelfth century, the hall would have had 'a raised floor, or *dais*, at the fireplace end, where those who were of higher rank sat and ate', while the cooked 'food was carried up from the kitchen without much respect for distance'.[24] Eating was a less formal occasion in the homes of lower-status people, as the *Roman de Renart* records; 'for a poor man who has no money does not sit by the fire, nor sit at a table, rather he eats on his lap'.[25] Social etiquette and eating habits thus clearly varied according to a person's status, and in this respect, despite the passing of eight centuries, medieval domestic 'dos' and 'don'ts' still have a rather familiar resonance.

Turning next to Neckam's description of a kitchen, he maintains that

There should be a small table on which cabbage may be minced, and also lentils, peas, shelled beans, beans in the pod, millet, onions, and other vegetables of the kind that can be cut up. There should also be pots, tripods, a mortar, a hatchet, a pestle. . . . The chief cook should have a cupboard [*capanna*] in the kitchen where he may store away aromatic spices, and bread flour sifted through a sieve. . . . Let there be also a cleaning place where the entrails and feathers of ducks and other domestic fowl can be removed and the birds cleaned . . .; in the pantry let there be shaggy towels [*gausapes*], tablecloth, and an ordinary handtowel which shall hang from a pole to avoid mice. Knives should be kept in the pantry, an engraved saucedish, a saltcellar, a cheese container, a candelabra, a lantern, a candlestick, and baskets. In the cellar or store room should be casks, tuns, wineskins, cups, cup cases [*henapiers*], spoons, skewers, basins, baskets, pure wine, cider, beer. . . .[26]

What is particularly striking about this description is how much evidence it contains for cleanliness, hygiene and order. Separating the areas used for meat and vegetable preparation, and hanging towels so that mice could not get at them, are clear demonstrations that twelfth-century townspeople understood food hygiene.

Although Neckam's account is probably of a kitchen belonging to a wealthy person's household, the domestic refuse recovered by archaeologists from rubbish pits and cess pits show that many of the items he lists (particularly the various types of cooking vessels) were in fact quite commonplace possessions among medieval householders. In any part of Europe, one only has to visit a municipal museum to see such objects, a tangible legacy of centuries of cooking and eating in medieval towns and cities. From the vast amount of medieval domestic pottery recovered by archaeologists from medieval urban sites, it has even been possible to differentiate tableware ceramics from pottery vessels that were used solely in the kitchen, and between pots that were used in cooking and those used for storage.[27]

Diet and health

Having considered some of the domestic arrangements of medieval urban households, it seems appropriate to continue the discussion by looking more at the diet and health of the householders. In the Middle Ages, as now, a person's life expectancy and health depended upon what food they ate and the quality of the water they drank. Nutrition and diet varied between individuals, and between social groups. No doubt there were differences, too, according to the status and geographical location of the town as a whole, for we might expect the inhabitants of a metropolitan city such as London to have had a different sort of diet compared to people living, for example, in a small town on the south coast of England or a hilltop bastide in south-western France.

Food for urban consumption was often produced by the townspeople themselves, in fields surrounding a town or within the gardens of their properties. For the larger towns and cities, food-stuffs would also have been brought in from the urban hinterland, or from further afield.[28] The bastide towns of south-west France, for example, were encompassed by arable fields tilled by local towns-people.[29] Meanwhile, the same was also true for English towns. As Maitland noted a century ago, 'some of the leading men of Cam-bridge were rich in arable strips' which lay around the town during the Middle Ages.[30] On the strips, vegetables and cereals would have been grown, and presumably eaten, by local inhabitants, while in the town itself most properties had some space on which house-holders could produce food for themselves. Growing a few vegetables, keeping domestic fowl and a pig or two (they were good consum-ers of waste), as well as growing fruit trees, were commonplace urban activities.[31]

As well as producing food locally, imported foodstuffs, traded in a town's market (see below), provided an urban population with an additional source of nutriment. The quantities of grain needed for bread-making, the large consumption of ale, and the young livestock brought to urban markets from rural areas, all suggested to Dyer that, on the whole, 'townsmen . . . enjoyed a better diet than their country counterparts'.[32] The quality of foodstuffs con-sumed by medieval townspeople would also vary from place to place according to factors such as the success of the year's harvest, the length of time food had to be in transit between field and market, and the methods by which food was stored. Prices paid for food reflected its quality, and urban governments frequently put various regulations into place in order to control the pricing of particular basic foodstuffs sold in markets, especially bread.[33]

It is only very recently, thanks largely to environmental archaeol-ogy, that more has become known about medieval urban diets; about what townspeople actually *consumed* as opposed to what foodstuffs they were producing and buying. There is now growing archaeo-logical evidence to show that diet among medieval townspeople was really quite varied, and typically included vegetables, cereal and meat; while from the analysis of skeletons it is also possible to establish levels of malnourishment among the urban population, as well as townspeople's physical build and life expectancy.[34]

From London, analysis of a group of 234 individuals buried in the cemetery of St Nicholas Shambles in the eleventh and twelfth centuries revealed a 'comparatively healthy' group of townspeople, with just 17 per cent of skeletons showing signs of having been affected by 'nutritional disease'.[35] Using skeletal remains from the period between the tenth and fifteenth centuries, archaeologists in Britain have also been able to calculate how tall medieval urban dwellers were. From their sample they found that men ranged between 155.1 and 177.8 cm (5 ft 1 in. – 5 ft 7 in.), while women stood between 156.2 and 165.1 cm (5 ft 1 in. – 5 ft 5 in.).[36] These heights are really not so very different from those of people who were living in Britain in the late nineteenth century.

Diet and nutrition were important factors determining a person's life expectancy, though of course mortality was not solely conditioned by what food people ate. In the Middle Ages, people tended to live shorter lives than they do now, as evidence from York shows. A study of skeletons in the cemetery of St Helen on the Walls revealed that out of 1041 individuals only 9 per cent reached an age of over 60 and 27 per cent died as children.[37] Whether medieval townswomen survived for longer than their male counterparts is open to question. Some evidence from York showed men to outnumber women in the over 35 age-group, possibly because 'females suffered poorer nourishment than males . . . as well as the special hazards of child-bearing'.[38] In Florence, documentary evidence suggests that 'some 20% of all women who died . . . in the years 1424, 1425 and 1430 died in childbirth', leaving children to be cared for either by their fathers, friends or kin.[39]

Leaving aside death due to malnourishment and childbirth, infectious diseases and congenital abnormalities were liable to lead to many an early death, particularly among the young and the old. Figures are difficult to find, but between 1309 and 1497 nearly a third out of 631 orphans in London (32 per cent) died.[40] The Black Death, which swept across Europe during the fourteenth century, dramatically increased mortality rates, but there were also many other forms of infectious disease which could strike and kill, such as influenza, lung and bronchial diseases, whooping cough, measles, smallpox and tuberculosis.[41] Medicinal plants were used to combat these and many other illnesses. Some of these plants are known because their remains have been recovered in archaeological excavations, while others are known because herbals and cures were often written down.[42] No doubt flowers and herbs for medicinal use were grown in people's own gardens, otherwise they could be bought from an apothecary whose shop typically stood within the town's market place, as was the case in Norwich in the thirteenth century.[43]

In this brief discussion of home and domestic life, it has only been possible to touch upon some facets of the everyday habits of ordinary medieval townspeople. Contemporary accounts from the Middle Ages present a picture of reasonably refined and enlightened urban standards of living. For some townspeople this may well have been the case, but of course it is impossible to be sure how those living in poorer households dealt with everyday life, quite simply because their voices are comparatively silenced by the historical record. One thing that united both rich and poor in the medieval town and city was work, for work occupied a central place in the lives of all townspeople.

The Place of Work

Work not only occupied a place in medieval townspeople's lives, it also occupied particular places within the townscape. This part of the chapter looks at how places of work were organised in medieval towns and cities, and how people worked within them. Three aspects of urban economic life are considered here: trading, production and 'servicing'. Each of these activities produced particular sorts of townscape, and within them townspeople worked according to particular codes and regulations, often endorsed by the municipality.

In looking at the place of work in medieval towns and cities, it is important not to assume that individuals had only one occupation, for it was commonplace in the Middle Ages for both men and women to have various sources of employment depending often on the time of year, or personal circumstances. By understanding the medieval townscape as a place of work we are seeing it *at* work, with townspeople negotiating busy lives in order to make ends meet. Of all the activities a working townsperson might be engaged with trading was perhaps the most visible and public.

Trading places

Trade was the lifeblood of Europe in the Middle Ages. Within towns and cities, trade converged on designated spaces within the townscape, and was closely regulated by local codes and laws. Town charters (considered earlier in Chapters 2 and 4) ensured that trading activity within towns was controlled, and that the profits from exchange and commerce went to the 'right' sort of people. To this end, a town's officials carefully administered exchange. Those involved in civic administration had to make sure that traders worked according to the rules of municipal laws and statutes, and when disputes arose, to resolve them lawfully.

Despite numerous municipal codes and statutes, the regulations concerning trading activity in medieval towns were difficult to enforce. Indeed, the regulations governing trade were probably more a statement of intent rather than a true reflection of the way people conducted themselves on a day-to-day basis. Lately, historians have recognised that trading activity could quite easily take place 'behind closed doors', away from the watchful eyes of the borough administrators and town officials. Such 'hidden trade' was in fact an important dimension of trading in medieval towns and cities, as well as in the countryside, and it usually occurred informally, in private, perhaps in quiet streets or in a noisy tavern (see below). It has also become increasingly clear that a good deal of trading happened in the countryside, too, well before goods had actually entered an urban market place.[44]

The focus of the following discussion is on the places in medieval towns where trading took place, which in essence was either at the waterfront or in a market place. I have precluded any specific discussion of fairs, for although these were an important element of the townspeople's year they usually occupied spaces outside the town, on temporary sites.[45] A good example of this comes from Winchester, where Keene has shown that the annual fair of St Giles (fairs were invariably associated with saints' feast days) was sufficiently organised by the end of the twelfth century that the field where it was held was periodically divided up to create 'streets' and *placae*.[46] Waterfronts and market places were, on the other hand, used on a daily, if not weekly basis. Both were open spaces in an altogether more urban setting, where people and goods all intermingled, and where people could keep watch over one another. Although they were open-air arenas, waterfronts and market places did not lack buildings, as trading required not only large open areas of land, but also places for storage, as well as some protection from the weather.

The waterfront

Recently, the development and role of medieval urban waterfronts have become better understood. The well-preserved state of organic materials in waterlogged, anaerobic conditions (especially timber, leather and foodstuffs) has enabled environmental archaeologists to reconstruct not only the physical setting of the medieval waterfront, but also the details of how vessels docked along the quayside and what the contents of their cargoes were. One of the striking features of medieval urban waterfronts is their long usage, often on the same site for many centuries, as well as their extensive nature along the shores of both tidal and non-tidal rivers, and along coastal inlets.

Long-distance trading in medieval Europe relied principally on maritime transport and shipping between coastal ports.[47] Much inland trade also relied upon water transport, though how far rivers were navigable to craft capable of carrying goods is a matter of some dispute for historians.[48] Nevertheless, those towns and cities situated far inland, especially on great rivers such as the Rhine, Rhône and Danube, relied on their riverside waterfronts as much as maritime ports did. Either way, the waterfront functioned primarily as a trans-shipment point, where incoming goods could be loaded onto carts and wagons for local distribution, or otherwise transferred onto smaller, lighter vessels for river transport to other market centres. The waterfront was thus an important focus for trading activity in many of the more significant medieval towns and cities, a meeting place for merchants, sailors and traders from all over Europe.

With both inland and coastal ports, urban waterfronts typically comprised quaysides and wharves held up by timber revetments to facilitate loading and unloading. In both London and Bristol, for example, such timber-built quaysides have been found to date from before 1200 (Figure 7.1).[49] In contrast, at Norwich in the tenth century, use was made of wicker mats placed along the banks of the river Wensum upon which the boats were dragged.[50] By the twelfth and thirteenth centuries, land reclamation had taken place along the waterfronts in London and Bristol. This pushed the quaysides further and further out into the river channel. Even so, the larger seagoing vessels were moored where the draught was deepest, in the centre of the river, while smaller craft were used to bring items ashore and to be unloaded at the quayside.

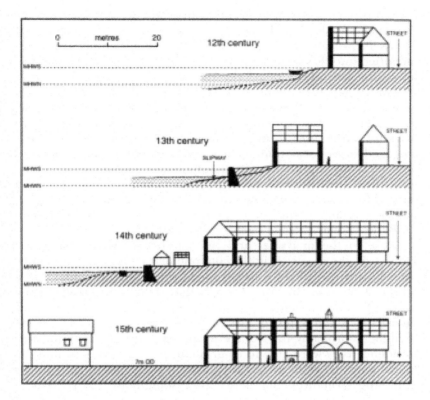

Figure 7.1 *Waterfront reclamation in medieval Bristol*

The quayside itself was festooned with all manner of winches and cranes to offload and load merchandise, while steps and slipways led directly down to the water's edge. Stone-surfaced slipways were found in excavations of waterfronts in York and Bristol, and presumably they helped to facilitate unloading and loading at low tide. On the quayside itself, goods were subject to inspection by customs officials. By 1275 customs were being exacted on goods shipped into the port of London, and in 1382 a new Customs House was built on a site next to the river close to the White Tower (the 'Tower of London').[51] Here goods brought into port had to be declared. The surviving records of taxes levied on merchandise provides a detailed picture of the variety of commodities traded by merchants in medieval towns and cities. In 1331–32, for example, silk-cloth, casks of ashes, onions and garlic, planks and stone, fish of all types, hemp and oil, were all among the items imported into Bristol and taxed by the city with the explicit purpose of raising revenue to help keep the city's quays in good repair.[52]

Storage facilities situated close to the quayside were also an important feature of the medieval waterfront. At Bergen, for example, the waterfront was divided into long narrow properties which were used for warehouses, as well as offices and living quarters for those engaged in overseas trade. The earliest of these long properties extended out onto the shore, allowing boats to be drawn up alongside them, but subsequently the properties were built up on a quay. The characteristic long and narrow form of the earlier buildings was retained, and some surviving examples can still be seen in Bergen today (having been restored after fire damage).[53]

Close to the quaysides and the warehouses were merchants' houses. In the case of Bristol again, one particular merchant family called Canynge is known to have held a substantial building on a property close to the river Avon, within sight of the river. In the fifteenth century, apart from providing the Canynge family with living space, the waterside property included a complex of stone buildings, probably for storage purposes (Figure 7.1). From this residence they were able to co-ordinate their activities in international wine and cloth trade.[54] Merchants' stone houses were typically imposing structures and hence they sometimes still survive. A merchant's house of fifteenth-century date, and now in the care of the National Trust, still occupies a prominent place in the townscape of Tenby in west Wales, while at Southampton earlier examples of merchants' houses have been identified and preserved. Under a merchant's house it was usual to find an undercroft, or cellar, which provided a space for storage and somewhere to keep goods cool and safe.[55] The impressive nature of their houses surely added weight to the merchant's image as a wealthy and trusted member of urban society, an image that endures through to the present day.

Of the towns and cities in medieval Europe, the wealthiest were undoubtedly those ports linked with long-distance, international, trading networks, the mercantile cities of Venice and Bruges, for example. The network of urban canals and waterways which characterise Bruges and Venice today represent the outcome of a medieval urge to have townscapes with as much waterfront as possible. For both Venice and Bruges took the waterfront right into the urban core, the very heart of the municipality, and thus maximised the extent of quayside available for trading activity and mercantile entrepreneurialism. In the case of Bruges, the city's canal network was developed and improved at the same time as a new waterway was being constructed to link the city with the sea, at the end of the thirteenth century, and as an added measure of defence a double line of new waterways was made to circumscribe the whole of the city, the courses of which are still very much a part of Bruges' celebrated 'medieval' townscape.[56] During the fourteenth and fifteenth centuries, these canals were fronted by brick-built houses with imposing stepped façades, the homes of mercantile families involved with long-distance textile trade.[57]

The market place

While much of the city's day-to-day trading activity occurred along its canals and waterfronts, within Bruges, there were, as was usual in medieval towns and cities, a multitude of market places where goods could be bought and sold. The principal market place of any town was its physical and symbolic heart, where townspeople could gather for local social and cultural events, as well engage in all sorts of trading activity. Many large towns and cities had more than just one market place. It was also common to have separate market places specialising in the sale of particular goods and merchandise, for example, livestock and timber. As well as selling commodities in separate markets, each market place was usually divided up into different areas, with specific parts of a market place designated for the sale of particular items, such as food-stuffs, ironmongery, pottery and so on. This sort of spatial ordering and segregation helped to ease congestion and it kept together those traders selling the same things.

Separating out particular trading activities, and placing them in markets in specified areas of a town, was commonplace across medieval Europe. In Poland, for example, towns founded in the thirteenth century, in the period of 'location', had separate market places for fish, horses, vegetables and hay.[58] Separate market places also operated in the Crusader cities of the twelfth century. Markets that had formerly sold cattle under the Muslims were used for the sale of pigs by the new Christian European settlers, for

example. More specifically, in the case of Jerusalem, while vegetables, fowl, fish, spices and textiles were all sold in what was
known as the 'tripartite bazaar', the 'larger volume products, such
as oil and grain . . . had their own, large open air market', and in
yet another market, situated outside the city in a valley between it
and Temple Mount, cattle were sold.[59] The pattern is thus one of
a hierarchy of different market spaces; smaller and often more
precious items were sold in central areas, whereas bulky and more
durable items, such as livestock, were pushed out to markets at
the edges of the city. This sort of arrangement existed in towns
and cities elsewhere in Christendom, too.

Livestock markets required a large amount of space for setting
up pens and stalls in which to keep animals, and so animals were
sold in street markets situated around the outskirts of a town in
areas where space was at less of a premium. At Southampton, the
principal market place was the High Street. This long and broad
main street ran the whole length of the town and along it there
were particular stretches dedicated to the sale of specific types of
merchandise. Parts of the street were locally named after the sorts
of activities carried on in them, the 'street of the smiths', for
example, where ironmongery was sold. In Southampton, too, the
valuable and perishable merchandise (for example, butter and eggs)
was sold in the central part of the High Street, at the town's centre, while the more bulky and durable goods were sold towards
the edge of the town.[60] Likewise, in thirteenth-century Coventry,
livestock markets were situated in outlying streets, while the town's
main market place was located centrally, with the highest and driest
part of the market designated as the 'place where bread was sold'
(Figure 7.2).[61] The pattern of markets at Southampton and Coventry
thus followed the sort of spatial organisation as the markets in
medieval Jerusalem.

In larger towns and cities, buildings were set up on the market
place to accommodate particular groups of traders. Within the large,
central market place created by the Normans in the 1070s at
Norwich, rows of shops were established, each with a specific
business. By the late thirteenth century, for example, there was an
Apothecary Market, a Cordwainer's Row, and a Spicer's Row.[62] This
sort of arrangement existed elsewhere, too. There was an Ironmonger
Row, a Potter's Row and a Butcher's Row standing in the centre of
Coventry's main market place by the 1200s (Figure 7.2).[63] Creating

Figure 7.2 *Markets in medieval Coventry*

rows of shops helped to regulate and control trading activities in market places by keeping specialised traders in specific areas. At the same time, those who held these properties, the prior of St Mary's in Coventry's case, and the town council in Norwich, were able to profit from them.

Textbooks typically state that medieval market places were gradually 'infilled' over time by a process of illegal encroachment, where temporary stalls were sooner or later converted into buildings of a more permanent sort.[64] However, such a casual process seems to conflict with the evidence that markets were highly regulated spaces in the Middle Ages. In this context, it seems likely that the rows of shops built on medieval market places were built deliberately, probably to ensure that the market continued to function in an orderly manner, as well as to secure a steady income from shop rents. Having rows of shops in a market place provided landholders with a source of dependable revenue, unlike temporary structures, such as stalls, which came and went on market days. In the case of York, it is clear that the 'rows' there were built as single, speculative developments, and this also seems to have been true for those in Coventry's market place (see Chapter 6).[65]

There were numerous rules and regulations governing market places in medieval towns and cities. Municipal ordinances frequently referred to demands that traders were to keep the market streets clean and clear of rubbish. It was invariably the responsibility of individual stallholders to ensure that their part of the street was clean after they had used it. At certain times of the day, or week, stalls had to be taken down; they were not allowed to remain standing once the market day was over. Trading in the market places was only permitted at certain times, usually certain days of the week, and if it was found to have taken place outside the limits of the market place, or at times other than those agreed in the town's laws, then a fine would be levied against the offenders. The town's court dealt with both 'forestallers', those individuals who bought goods before they reached market, and 'regrators', those 'who sold retail outside the official markets'.[66] There were also strict regulations concerning weights and measures, too, and standards of weight and quality had to be adhered to.

To sell goods of inferior quality, or to use incorrect measures, was a serious offence. Beer and bread were the foodstuffs that usually suffered from an underhand watering down.[67] At Monpazier, in Gascony, the fourteenth-century wooden market hall that stands in the market square contains stone vessels which were used to assess different measures of corn to ensure fairness (Plate 7.1).[68] As if all the rules and regulations concerning trading activity in markets were not enough, the market place was also often the site of the town's main guildhall or town hall, from where the civic officials could keep a watch over the goings on in and around the market place. At Norwich, the Toll House, and later the Gild Hall, stood at one corner of the central market place, while in Bruges, the famous early-fourteenth-century *Belfort* continues to looks down upon the 'Groote Merkt', the city's main market place.[69] Such municipal buildings, often grand and imposing in nature, served to remind those traders (and others) who congregated in the market places of towns that they were under the watchful eye of the municipality.

Although market places were where townspeople bought and sold goods, there were also shops located on streets outside market areas. Such shops were usually situated on main thoroughfares and they typically occupied a place underneath a larger building, such as the Jew's House in Lincoln (see Chapter 6). Away from

Plate 7.1 *Monpazier, grain measuring vessels in the market hall*

the main commercial core of a town, the more common use of urban properties was for industrial manufacture and the production of goods and merchandise.

Production: artisans and industry

A range of different products were made by medieval urban artisans in specialised industries and crafts. They processed raw materials and turned them into saleable items, either for local consumption or for export to other markets. Townspeople who engaged in secondary sector economies may be grouped according to the stuff they worked with; metals, textiles and livestock. Here I shall look briefly at the social organisation of those urban crafts and industries that manufactured items from these materials, and consider the spatial contexts in which the process of manufacturing and production took place within the townscape.

Hilton remarks that 'the most widespread unit of production in the medieval town was the artisan workshop'.[70] Medieval artisans 'were skilled manufacturers, processing goods for sale: some might have their own workshops, others were paid piece-rates or a daily wage'.[71] Usually, the workshop and artisan's home were both rented property, and although in some cases a high level of investment might have been needed to make a property a worthwhile unit for industrial production, for others it was possible to adapt a domestic property to form a suitable workshop.[72] Labour was supplied by a master craftsman's family, with males and females both involved in the production process. Siblings, cousins and grandparents also had a role to play. In addition, apprentices were employed. They lived with the master craftsman's family, while 'journeymen', qualified craftsmen who worked in the employment of another, commonly lived in rented accommodation elsewhere in a town.[73] The products made by artisans were often sold by them too: 'the boundary between manufacturing and retailing was a fine one'.[74] There was also a close link between the provision of goods and services (see below).

Guilds, fraternities and craft organisation

Despite the artisans' ability to turn their hand to a wide variety of tasks, groups of like artisans came together to form fraternities, or guilds, each representing a particular activity, such as glove-making or weaving. Although craft organisations varied from town to town, their role, to administer the affairs of artisans and merchants, was largely the same wherever they were. Guilds, and craft organisations more generally, were emerging as powerful, self-regulating assemblies from the thirteenth century onwards. The term 'guild' had broad usage in medieval contexts. As Swanson points out, 'it could apply at one extreme to a handful of people who clubbed together to pay for a light to burn on the altar of their parish church; [while] at the other extreme it encompassed powerful organisations of merchants who ostensibly used religious association as the basis for political power'.[75]

The origins of medieval craft organisations have long been argued over by historians. In England and France in the 1200s, it appears that journeymen specialising in particular crafts were finding it increasingly difficult to take charge of their own workshop, and as a consequence they 'began to organise in order to maintain reasonable wages and hours of work'.[76] In Italy, craft-guilds (*arti*) became powerful voices in local urban politics, sometimes aligning their interests with those of the city government, or joining together collectively to constitute an urban government. This occurred in

Padua in 1293, where 'the guilds . . . resolved to form a "single body . . . to conserve and maintain the city"' (see Chapter 2).[77] The *arte* were supposed not to fix prices, or to exclude a qualified person from becoming a member, though they could fix wages for their particular craft.[78]

Medieval craft guilds almost universally 'became organisations for the policing of craft manufacture for the urban authorities'.[79] At the same time, urban authorities also had their own role to play in controlling urban industry. By the 1260s, in Paris, for example, the rules and regulations for governing city's artisans and craft production were written down in a document known as the *Livre des métiers* ('Book of Crafts'). This covered 101 different crafts, and the *Livre* reveals clearly the extent to which urban craft production was regulated. The widespread practice of apprenticeship is evident, the length of time that apprentices served varying between one and 12 years, depending on the type of craft. The number of apprentices in each workshop was limited to just one or two, while for journeymen contracts were agreed with their masters over matters relating to the length of service, their hours of work, holidays and pay. Working at night-time was permitted only in 'special cases', and although at the death of their husband women might become the head of a workshop they were excluded from any position 'of control within the craft organisation' at the level of the town.[80]

As well as having social linkages through fraternities and guilds, artisans who were engaged in similar or related sorts of manufacture and production located themselves in groups in particular areas within towns and cities. This spatial grouping had a lot to do with minimising the inconvenience of transporting materials around the city, but it was also something which was deliberately encouraged by urban governments. Municipal ordinances governing industrial activities were drawn up to ensure that the disposal of waste from industrial processes did not interfere with the well-being of the town as whole (see below). This usually meant keeping the worse polluters away from the town centre, and this could be done by grouping industrial production. To examine how particular types of urban industry were socially and spatially organised, the following discussion looks in turn at the production of manufactured items.

Metal-based industries

Metal-based manufacturing included the production of items made from gold, silver, tin, lead and iron, as well as alloys, such as bronze and pewter. Ferrous and non-ferrous metals were invariably smelted. Items were cast and worked on the same site, in workshops which were usually sited at the rear of properties, behind built-up street frontages. The domestic and the industrial were thus closely interconnected in the medieval townscape. The craftsman and his family lived and worked on the same site, and home and workshop coexisted side by side.

Medieval metalworking shows up well in the urban archaeological record, which makes it a particularly visible form of industrial activity. Scraps of waste produced by working metal, or slag produced from smelting ore and casting, are usually to be found in large quantities where metalworking took place. At a site in Alms Lane in Norwich, archaeologists revealed evidence for ironworking from the thirteenth century onwards. The process took place in an extensive corner property, which also included a brewery, with the smelting done in a timber building. Although by 1400 this property had been built up to form three tenements, ironworking continued to take place on the same site.[81] Metalworking carried a high risk of fire, especially where buildings were predominantly of timber construction. This fire risk may account for the often suburban location of metalworking, for it seems to have been an activity associated especially with the urban fringe. This was the case in Kiev, where the suburb of Podol became large and prosperous because of the extensive ironworking industry located there.[82]

Metals were manufactured into all sorts of items, such as weapons, ploughshares, nails, hinges and keys. For the production of some household and personal items, metalworking was combined with other materials, like bone for making combs, and wood for making furniture. A suburb of Coventry, newly established by the Earls of Chester in the twelfth century, was the focus for metal and bone working in workshops that continued to be used for this purpose for two centuries, during which time the residential and industrial occupation of properties had separated.[83] Three adjoining tenements in fourteenth-century Worcester were occupied by artisans engaged in bronze and bone working, an arrangement that appears to have persisted for a century or more.[84]

In those medieval towns and cities with sites of religious pilgrimage, or with locations on pilgrim routes, metalworkers were particularly active in producing badges and tokens which were bought by pilgrims as a souvenir of their journey. While metal manufacturing might thus feed directly into local patterns of consumption, certain medieval cities became widely known for producing particular wares. In these cases, artisans fed markets that lay far beyond their immediate environment. Textiles were especially important exports in this respect.

Textile production

In the Middle Ages, textile production involved many specialised processes, not all of which were carried out by the same person on the same site. Wool in its raw state had to be combed and carded to make it usable for the manufacture of clothes and furnishings. Swanson notes that 'the preparation of woollen yarn by combing, carding and spinning was done almost exclusively by women', and was 'highly labour-intensive work'.[85] Weaving cloth, on the other hand, with the need for large and expensive looms, was a more specialised and capital-intensive activity. A weaver from York, who died in 1413, had been renting a four-roomed house in the city, using one of the rooms for his two looms; like other weavers, he 'was his own master to some extent, buying wool and supervising most of the stages of production under his roof'.[86] Once wool had been woven to form 'broadcloth' it was then fulled, ready to be made into clothes or furnishings, a process that was almost invariably carried out by other artisans on separate sites within a town.

Cloth-finishing, particularly fulling and dyeing, was an industrial-scale activity that artisans carried on principally in the suburbs of a town. Fulling and dyeing both required relatively large open spaces, and both were processes which used large quantities of water. Fulling cloth was sometimes done using watermills, which mechanised the process, or otherwise by physically treading the cloth in troughs of water and 'fuller's earth'. Fullers also used urine to soften cloth, and so it is not surprising to find that the process contaminated urban water supplies, and thus became a frequent source of complaint and conflict among townspeople.[87] Watermills were typically leased to fullers, often at quite low rents compared to water-driven corn mills.[88]

Associated with the fulling process was the need to hang cloth in order to dry and stretch it, and for this purpose tenter frames were used. 'Tenter fields' were a common sight at the edges of many towns and cities in Europe in the Middle Ages, and were frequently depicted on city plans of the sixteenth and seventeenth centuries. Like fulling, drying and stretching the cloth on tenter frames required large areas of land. They were situated close enough to be convenient to get to the fuller's workshops and troughs, but also far enough from the built-up area of a town for sufficient land to be available. Tenters were valuable pieces of property in their own right. In Exeter, for example, empty houses were demolished to make way for tenters in 1420, giving rise to one of the earliest maps of urban property in medieval England.[89]

As with fulling, dyeing was a messy business which often led to complaints from townspeople about contamination and pollution. It was also a highly skilled process, and was an industry in which 'there was a clear gulf between the independent masters and those who were obliged to work on piece-rates', such that, 'from the twelfth century onwards, the industry was dominated by dyers who were "merchants and entrepreneurs" rather than artisans'.[90] Dyers located in suburbs, too, and in some cases their large wooden vats have been unearthed by archaeologists.[91] Because dyes were liable to pollute water supplies, it might be thought that dyeing would have been confined mainly to downstream locations, but this was not always the case. For example, in Coventry and Bruges, two cities well known for their medieval cloth manufacture, dyers in the thirteenth century worked in areas that were in upstream locations! Once the cloth was dyed, it went on to be made into garments (or furnishings) by tailors, cappers, and glovers.[92] Or it was sold as broad cloth to merchants for sale in markets elsewhere.[93] Thus, 'Coventry drapers used Bristol for exporting cloth to Portugal, and the east-coast ports for the Baltic market'.[94]

Animal and livestock-based industries

As well as textile manufacture, another source of material for both clothing and furnishings came from processing products derived from livestock. All parts of a slaughtered animal, whether cattle, sheep, pig, deer or boar, were put to some use in the Middle Ages, and processed in the workshops of urban artisans. Animals of all kinds were often butchered by the same people, and the by-products that came from butchering an animal for meat were distributed locally to specialist artisans, such as horners and tanners.[95] For this reason, tanners and horners, as well as butchers, were frequently located close together, near to where the animals were being slaughtered.

Before being slaughtered, animals were typically pastured at the edges of a town, near to the suburban livestock markets (see above). In London, for example, in the fourteenth century, butchery of large beasts was deliberately confined to the suburbs of Knightsbridge, Stratford and St Leonard's Bromley, well away from the walled city itself.[96] Some butchers in the capital headed west, to the vill of Westminster, where butchery became a perpetual matter of concern among local inhabitants, particularly with regard to the disposal of offal – an unsavoury problem faced by many medieval urban authorities.[97] Apart from providing meat for eating, animal carcasses were also a source of material for a variety of purposes; bones for boiling to make glue, and horn and bone to make combs, needles, and even spectacle frames. However, it was the processing of skins and hides of the animals that dominated livestock-based industry in medieval towns and cities.[98]

Leather was one of the principal products derived from livestock, and leather-working was a major industry in most medieval towns and cities. Of the various industries in Wigford, a suburb of medieval Lincoln, those individuals with surnames associated with the leather trade made up the highest proportion of local residents.[99] Tanning leather was a large-scale production process, and like aspects of the cloth-finishing process, it sometimes proved to be rather unpopular with local townspeople. Consequently, as Keene remarks, 'attempts were sometimes made to banish noisome leather-making processes to the suburbs'.[100] The reason for the noxious nature of leather production was that hides were treated using 'woozes' of differing strengths, and then placed in pits to soak for up to nine months before being dried and curried to make the leather supple.[101] The pits used by tanners have been found by archaeologists, and sometimes waterlogged conditions preserve the timber lining of the pits, as well as pieces of oak bark which were used in the soaking process.[102] Once tanned, leather was used by other groups of artisans to make all manner of items, such as shoes, belts, scabbards, as well as saddles and girdles for horses.[103]

In all, the metal-goods manufacturers, the textile workers, and those involved in animal products, formed only a part of a wide range of the industrial activities carried on by townspeople in the Middle Ages. Although these were common industrial activities, there were of course many other sorts of urban industry. For example, there were potters, glassmakers, soap-makers and rope-makers, to name but four.[104] Industrial specialisation was practised in the smaller market towns, such as Stratford-upon-Avon, as well as in the more major cities like London.[105] To complete this brief discussion of the place of work in medieval towns and cities, some consideration needs to be given to those groups of townspeople who were involved in the 'service economy', in servicing the city.

Servicing the city: food, ale and sex

The boundary between providing goods and providing services was a blurred one in towns and cities in the Middle Ages, as Swanson has noted.[106] Although there were distinct service-providers, notably those who were involved in the victualling trade (the supply of food and drink), there was a tendency for medieval artisans to engage in both the secondary and tertiary sectors.[107] For example, artisans who had small arable plots and gardens could grow and sell produce without them going through the official market place. Here I shall focus on those people who were principally service-providers dealing in food, ale and sex.

There was always a high demand for foodstuffs in the medieval town, and this demand was met in part by food-traders known as 'hucksters'. Hucksters redistributed meat and vegetable produce locally within a town, but on a casual basis. Their activities were closely regulated. In Coventry, in 1428, the mayor's register records that, 'hucksters were not allowed to buy victuals for resale until 11.00am, that is, after the market was open to local purchasers'; while a subsequent entry, in 1431, stated that 'bakers were forbidden to sell bread to hucksters who would then re-sell retail'.[108] Hucksters were usually women 'who frequently acted illegally in by-passing the official market'.[109] For this they were severely dealt with by the town's authorities. A woman in London, in 1306, 'was found guilty of forestalling hens and capons at Southwark outside the city', for which she was imprisoned and fined 40d., a punishment that was by no means light.

Though commonplace in English towns and cities, it seems that in medieval France there was a higher proportion of foodstuffs reaching urban households directly without passing through the official market than was the case in England.[110] As well as hucksters selling food, there were also cooks processing foodstuffs, and selling pies, pasties, cakes and breads direct to the consumer. Cooks in late-medieval Coventry had their shops and stalls situated close to both the market place and the town's main street, no doubt locating there to attract passing trade and to supply hungry passers-by on market days. The cooks were to be found close to part of the market called the 'fysshebords' (the place where fishmongers sold their fish); a proximity which reflects the close connection that is known to have existed between cooks and fishmongers in the Middle Ages.[111] Near to the street where the cooks worked there was another important element of Coventry's food supply, the 'common oven'. The remains of this were uncovered in recent excavations which showed it to consist of two large bread-baking ovens, the likes of which have been found in excavations in other towns and cities, too, as have the remains of vats used for brewing.[112]

Beer was an important staple in the Middle Ages and was essential to everyday urban life. It was drunk by both adults and children, and included 'small beer', which was weak and drunk on a daily basis, and ale, which was stronger. The great scale of brewing and beer supply within medieval towns and cities has been demonstrated in urban excavations. At the Alms Lane site in Norwich, for example, brewing was one of the earliest activities to take place, though the fragmentary nature of the remains of the buildings makes it difficult to get a firm idea of what a brewery looked like in the thirteenth and fourteenth centuries.[113] Before the use of hops (which made beer), ale would have needed drinking soon after it was made. But with hops (used in beer-making in London in 1420) came the need for greater storage spaces, and consequently larger brewhouses became more common in towns and cities of the later Middle Ages. On the whole, ale production was a small-scale, female-dominated industry, while beer-brewing was a more large-scale, capital-intensive industry, carried out by men.[114]

In towns and cities throughout medieval Europe, there were numerous retail outlets selling beer (and wine) locally. Alehouses, taverns and inns were an essential part of the medieval townscape, and an integral part of urban life. The variety of medieval public houses is something that should be noted, for they each served a slightly different purpose. Taverns were situated in undercrofts and were subterranean drinking environments where deals were struck and where goods could be (illicitly) exchanged.[115] Taverns were usually smaller premises than inns, and typically formed part of larger establishments and properties. For example, the 'Peter and Paul' tavern in Paternoster Row in London 'comprised an undercroft provided with fire places . . . and drinking rooms or partitioned areas on both ground and first floors', while the 'New Inn' in Earl Street in Coventry, described in 1410 as 'one large tenement with a stone tavern', had four tenants living above it, each with their own shop, hall and chamber.[116]

Inns provided accommodation. In addition to selling food and drink to visitors and travellers, 'hostellers' would also provide overnight accommodation. Again, in London a guest could obtain a single room in an inn by 1345, and by 1380 it was noted that it was the custom of the realm to give a key to each of the guest rooms of an inn.[117] Inns were commonly concentrated along the approach roads to a town or city and able to provide stables for horses. In 1390, at St Paul's Wharf in London, one inn offered a 'suite of rooms comprising hall, chamber, buttery and kitchen'.[118] In some cases a town had its own 'official' visitors' accommodation, as at Norwich, where the municipality owned the 'common inn', which provided for civic guests from the 1380s onwards. At Coventry the 'prior's guesthouse' had long performed a similar hospitable function for those visiting the adjacent priory of St Mary's.

Not surprisingly, establishments that sold alcohol were a good source of revenue for medieval municipal authorities. As Hilton has noted, 26 per cent of municipal income in Toulouse in 1405 was derived from a 'tax on the retail sales of wine, mostly supplied to taverns'.[119] Another important and widespread medieval service activity which provided municipalities with a source of income was prostitution. Prostitution was an everyday part of medieval urban life and has recently become the subject of a number of detailed and critical studies by historians, one of most notable being Geremek's work on the margins of society in late-medieval Paris.[120]

Although extramarital sex was condemned by religious authorities in the Middle Ages, official attitudes to prostitution were ambiguous. On the one hand the role of the prostitute in medieval urban society was institutionalised. This was the case with the 'stews' in Southwark (south London), which at one and the same time provided unmarried clergymen with sexual gratification while providing the Bishop of Winchester with a source of financial income.[121] On the other hand, prostitutes were also sanctioned against in city statutes. This was especially the case with prostitutes who did not work from officially recognised brothels (often taverns and alehouses), but who instead worked the streets and lanes plying for trade (see below).[122] For example, in Perpignan in Roussillon (France), only prostitutes working in designated areas were recognised officially,[123] while in many English towns and cities street names such as Grope Lane commemorate the places where street prostitutes sought their clients. Such clients were perhaps just visitors to a town, for the streets which are named after sexual acts are usually to be found close to principal market streets where traders would have gathered.[124]

This short discussion of the place of work in medieval townscapes points to the close relationship between the social and spatial organisation of towns and cities. In the context of places of work, we have seen how certain economic activities were thought appropriate for suburban locations, particularly those that were unpleasant to the human nose or eye, while other functions, especially those of a commercial nature, were placed at the centre of the town, at its heart. Clearly, certain places in the medieval townscape were deemed more 'appropriate' than others for certain types of activity, whether selling livestock, dyeing cloth or smelting metal. The townscape was thus ordered *spatially* in as much as townspeople were regulated and controlled *socially* by civic and seigneurial authorities. To complete this chapter, the final part of the discussion continues with this theme to show how in the Middle Ages it was understood that 'where you are' stood also for 'what you are'.

Place and Identity

The medieval townscape was, at one and the same time, both constituted and constitutive; that is, it was shaped by the actions of townspeople (see Chapters 5 and 6), while it also shaped the activities of townspeople. So far I have discussed this dialectical relationship between townscape and townspeople in the context of domestic and workplaces. In the final part of this chapter I

shall look at how a people's place in the medieval townscape reflected and reinforced their 'place' in urban society. In the Middle
Ages, social identities were literally and metaphorically mapped
onto and out from the places people occupied (see Chapter 3).
This 'mapping' of social identities through urban spaces worked
because in the Middle Ages certain parts of the townscape were
deemed to be appropriate places for certain sorts of social activity,
and for certain sorts of people. In this sense, there were 'moralised
townscapes', townscapes that told people who they were because it
placed them in relation to others.

In the same way that ancient Roman cities were viewed as micro-
cosms of a wider Roman cosmology, the social and spatial ordering
of the medieval townscape acted as a mirror of a broader medieval
cosmology.[125] In particular, there was a belief that what was good in
the world was situated at the centre, while what was 'other' or
different occupied the 'edge', the spatial margins. This principle
is illustrated by medieval *mappae mundi* showing Jerusalem as the
spiritual and symbolic centre of the medieval world, with the edge
of the world, the map's margin, depicted as the home of monsters
and evil creatures.[126] This 'core–periphery'/'inside–outside' idea
is also reflected in ninth- and tenth-century depictions of the holy
Jerusalem descending from Heaven. Shown as a circle of walls,
with three gates at each of the four quarters (signifying the 12
disciples of Christ), contemporary images of the Heavenly Jerusalem convey the medieval Christian idea of a sanctuary 'within'.
Jesus is thus depicted as either the 'Lamb of God' or the 'tree of
life' at the centre of the holy city, inside its walls (see Plate 1.1).[127]

Moralised townscapes and civic ceremony

One way of moralising the medieval townscape and its occupants
was for municipalities to set out local by-laws which defined what
was considered to be appropriate and 'proper' behaviour for the
town's citizens. Already, examples of civic ordinances against antisocial activities have been mentioned in the context of rules relating
to the cleaning of streets and the regulations against throwing
rubbish into waterways and public highways (see Chapter 2 and
above). Such urban laws and codes were commonplace in the Middle
Ages, but there was another way in which people could be reminded of their civic duties. This involved using the townscape as

a 'stage' on which to enact moral stories and displays of civic ideals.

Regardless of whether a townsperson was literate or not, visual displays and enactments of biblical stories staged in the streets of a town would have been understood by all. Such storytelling, rooted within particular places within the townscape, such as market places and street corners, and performed at certain times of the year, usually in association with religious feast days, inscribed moral virtues onto the medieval townscape. An example of this sort of moralising of the townscape (and townspeople) is the procession and festival of the Assumption of the Virgin, held in Siena from the late twelfth century. The religious festival was also a civic one, a show of corporate display and civic pride as Bowsky records:

> One can imagine the festive parade that wound its way towards the cathedral, the members of the signory and other high magistrates with their foliated candles, representatives of subject towns and contado nobles with their candles and unfurled standards, and the urban Sienese parading in their military companies – all accompanied by musicians and professional entertainers, mimes, singers and jugglers.[128]

Moreover,

> The governors must have been aware of the psychological advantages of reinforcing allegiance and displaying their own rule through a combination of religious and civic display that would have had to impress the minds and feelings of even the most illiterate or recalcitrant Sienese.[129]

In the minds of those people who lived and worked in the same streets that formed the stage for such choreographed displays of civic pride or religious narrative, the symbolic meanings and associations of streets and buildings would have continued to live on, long after the parades and pageants had gone. In other words, the townscape of Siena acted as a reservoir of memories, or to use a slightly different metaphor, the townscape was inscribed with symbolic and moral meanings, and these could be reinforced (reinscribed), time and time again, by the repeated use of streets for processional routes, or as a stage for enacting religious and moral plays.

Although some medieval historians have examined the role of religious (and civic) 'spectacle' in constructing social meaning and civic identity, it has been argued that few have studied with necessary depth the textual capacity of the medieval townscape, and the 'space in which the ceremonies occurred'.[130] For instance, the symbolic use of gates for processions entering into walled cities has perhaps not had the attention it deserves, though it is well known that when important visitors arrived at a town or city the municipal authorities often went to great lengths to provide a sense of drama, usually set around a gateway. In Norwich, for example, a royal visit in 1469 entailed erecting a temporary stage at Westwick Gate and decorating it with royal colours and providing entertainment just as Queen Elizabeth Woodville arrived there.[131] Such lavish arrangements were clearly intended to reflect civic unity and pride, but the use of the gate as the stage for the display is surely also significant, for it marked the symbolic boundary of the civic space of the city. The queen's entrance through it could be seen as a mark of corporate assent. Similar grand entrances took place in other cities too in the later Middle Ages (when urban corporate bodies had attained a greater measure of strength and identity). Such urban spectacles not only 'bore witness to the prestige of the community, they expressed the power relationships of its members, and they permitted a visual reminder of the ordered and unified structure of the urban social body'.[132]

Moralised townscapes and marginal groups: prostitutes, lepers and Jews

The textual capacity of the medieval townscape, its propensity to instil both a sense of social order and identity, can be seen in other, perhaps more subtle ways than the displays and civic rituals which punctuated the Christian year. The identity and status of certain groups in medieval urban society were predicated on their place within the townscape. This was particularly the case with marginal(ised) social groups, such as prostitutes and lepers, and to some extent Jews. Once again, the Christian belief in a moral 'centre' can be seen to have been an important agent in defining social and cultural boundaries between certain urban social groups.

In the Middle Ages, the physical edge of a town or city was seen as the 'right' place for undesirable people to live, the place for 'antisocial' activities. This spatial marginalisation (of marginalised social groups) was promoted by civic, religious and royal authorities alike. In Bristol, for example, a royal charter of Edward III set out the city's liberties and customs. In it, two marginal(ised) medieval social groups, prostitutes and lepers, were placed under the same item: 'it is ordained and agreed that in future no leper reside within the precincts of the town (*infra procinctum ville*), nor any common woman dwell within the walls (*infra muros*).[133] In this case, not only were Bristol's lepers and prostitutes marked out as a social 'other', or outcast, but their marginal social position in the city was reinforced by their mutual physical exclusion from the city's walled area, the urban core. The spatial exclusion of prostitutes and lepers was widely practised in towns and cities throughout medieval Europe.

The act of social exclusion, and the displacement of 'others' from the city to the suburbs, was widely used as means of confirming a person's outsider status. The physical expulsion of prostitutes (or their containment within certain marginal areas of a city), was often 'mapped' onto their body by laws requiring them to wear special items of clothing. In Bristol, in the fourteenth century, prostitutes had to wear a striped hood, while similar marks were employed in towns and cities in France. Prostitutes at Avignon and Dijon, for example, 'were compelled to wear a white badge four fingers wide on the arm'.[134]

In Paris and in Perpignan prostitutes were allowed to work in brothels, as they were in Southwark in London (during daylight hours), but strict penalties were imposed on those prostitutes found to be working outside these designated places.[135] In court records of the later Middle Ages, prostitutes in Paris were divided between two types, those that worked in brothels ('settled prostitutes') and those that did not ('women of a "lesser sort"').[136] For those women of a 'lesser sort', sex acts took place in out of the way places, in dark lanes and around the city walls, as well as in cemeteries, the reputed places of iniquity and deviance in late-medieval Parisian society.[137] The marginalised places where illegal prostitution took place served to further reinforce the already marginal place of the prostitute in medieval urban society. The same was true for lepers, who like prostitutes were usually forced to wear particular clothes as a way of identifying themselves.

Leper hospitals were common features of medieval towns and cities, especially during the twelfth and thirteenth centuries, and were typically established by pious benefactors. The hospitals themselves were located at the very edge of a medieval town, often actually beyond the built-up area of suburbs. Two hospitals for lepers established at Bristol in the later twelfth century stood in the outer suburbs, albeit on important roads that led into the town.[138] At Berwick-upon-Tweed, the town authorities had, in their own words, 'already taken care that a proper place be kept outside the town' for lepers.[139] The 'proper place' for lepers was therefore a visible one, but at the same time it was also a peripheral one.[140] A peripheral location for leper hospitals came in part from the fear of contamination, and in part from biblical instruction. For example, Leviticus (14: 45–6) unambiguously states that 'all the days wherein the plague shall be in him he shall dwell alone; without the camp shall his habitation be'. This marginal place for the leper also acted to confirm their 'outsider' status.

The marginalisation of perceived 'deviant' social groups, particularly lepers and prostitutes, is an example of how social identities were mapped onto the medieval townscape, and how the townscape became 'moralised' in the process. The townscape thus acted as a mirror of social boundaries and boundedness. At the core of the (walled) city, the buildings of civic and religious institutions and the commercial focus of the market place provided a setting, or 'proper place', for civic and corporate displays, pageants and ceremonies; while a city's suburbs and outskirts were seen to be the proper places for social deviants and acts of deviance, which included not only illicit sexual acts but also the more antisocial forms of urban industry (such as tanning and dyeing).

The medieval townscape was thus a microcosm of a broader medieval, Christian cosmology, where walls and gateways represented symbolic boundaries of inner sanctity, and separation from 'other', less safe or desirable worlds. The placing of executed criminals on gates and entrances to the city served to reinforce this idea of the wall as a boundary between inner order and outer chaos. However, there were also 'marginal' social groups living in the heart of towns and cities, side by side with the citizenry at large, which points to a more complex (fluid) relationship between identity and place in the medieval townscape.

Much has been written of late about the place of Jews in medieval urban society. What emerges from this work is a social and spatial coexistence of Jewish and Christian townspeople, and for the most part the integration of Jews into the fabric of medieval urban society rather than outright exclusion from it. In Norwich, for example, the 'Jewish quarter' in the thirteenth century consisted of properties situated immediately around the market place, within close proximity to the synagogue.[141] This quarter has been described as 'a close-knit community, whose members lived near one another for safety, for religious observance, and for social and intellectual companionship'.[142] This location is perhaps not without significance, for Jews are first recorded in England after the Norman Conquest and the main market place in Norwich was a Norman product (see Chapter 3). In towns and cities in Normandy and France, too, Jewish streets ('rues aux Juifs') typically occupied central urban locations, as at Rouen.[143] In Paris, too, the *Juiverie* was centrally located, in the Île de la Cité, on a principal route through the city, and, as Chazan notes, the physical separatism gave medieval Jewish communities a remarkable cohesiveness that was defined not only socially but also spatially.[144]

Although social and spatial coherence is the hallmark of Jewish 'quarters' in European medieval towns and cities, we should also recognise that despite (perhaps because of) the apparent centrality of Jewish communities in medieval urban life, there was widespread intolerance directed by Christian townspeople towards their Jewish neighbours. There were frequent acts of reprisals and anti-Semitic racism against Jews throughout the Middle Ages, culminating in the expulsion of Jews by royal decrees, such as the one issued by Edward I in England in 1290, and the expulsion of French Jewry in 1306.[145] Furthermore, not all Jewish quarters were accommodated within the cores of medieval towns, for in Polish towns Jews were spatially marginalised, and in a sense ghettoised.[146] The notion of the Jewish ghetto thus precedes that of Venice, regarded by some historians as the first of its sort.[147]

In summary, I have argued here that a close relationship existed in the Middle Ages between a person's identity, or a group's identity, and the place that they occupied in the medieval townscape. The medieval townscape was not inert but was charged with all manner of social and cultural meanings. Townscapes thus functioned as 'texts', and from them a moralised social order and identity could be read by those who lived and worked within them. The placing of certain people within different parts of a townscape was carried out by secular and religious authorities, keen to impress order

onto the medieval town, and keen to keep in place those people
that were considered to pose a threat to civic order. To an extent
therefore, the social relations of medieval townspeople were mapped
onto and out from their surrounding townscapes.

Of course, it was also possible for individuals to transgress and
resist their 'proper place', for it has to be said that although rules
and regulations concerning the appropriateness of certain types
of social behaviour were a perennial issue for many municipal
authorities in medieval Europe, the fact that new penalties and
new codes of conduct had to be issued year after year suggests
that then (as now) few people kept to the rules. However, what
also has to be acknowledged is that underlying all the processions, the rituals, the rules and the regulations, is intention; and
that like the acts of exclusion and expulsion experienced by certain social groups, these practices reflect an overall fear of the
'other'. By inscribing moral, Christian beliefs into the spatial order of the medieval townscape, townspeople were put (and kept)
in their 'rightful' place, in both a literal and figurative sense. This
was true whether they were a Christian or a Jew, a leper or prostitute, or a merchant or tanner.

Conclusion

This chapter has covered three themes; domestic and home life,
the place of work, and the issue of place and identity. What emerges
from this discussion is an impression of how people lived their
lives in towns and cities in the Middle Ages. Inevitably, certain
issues are missing, such as the role that the Church played in
everyday life, in worship and in customs. Even so, something has
been said about how the medieval townspeople lived, about how
their homes looked, about how long they might expect to live for
and what they might die of. As well as looking at their homes,
something has also been said about how townspeople earned money
and made a living. Here, it is important not to compartmentalise
medieval townspeople into social groups according to their occupation, for many people had a number of jobs, as many people
still do today. There were particular spaces within the townscape
where people worked; places where trade was carried out, places
where items were manufactured, and places that provided services

to hungry, thirsty and lusty townspeople. Finally, something has been said here about the importance that townscapes had in the minds of medieval townspeople, about how the places that they lived and worked in also said things about their place in urban society and their social identity. Instrumental in shaping these placed identities was the role of religious and civic moralising, either through ceremonial practices and rituals, or through locally reinforced legal codes and laws.

CONCLUSION

Over the next century or so, many European towns and cities will be celebrating 1000 years of continuous urban life. The dates chosen for these millennial celebrations will mostly be determined by when a town or city first received its charter granting urban privileges. It might be argued by some that the date of such a charter does not truly represent the time when a place first became urban (see Chapter 2). Be that as it may, what is for sure is that the various celebrations will serve to remind us all of the thread of continuity the links urban life today with urban life in the Middle Ages.

My aim in this book was to set out how urban life evolved during the later Middle Ages. This has meant looking at the ways that towns and cities came into being and how they fared subsequently. To do this I have examined the people who were controlling urban life, questioned what their motives were and how they achieved success. During the course of the book, then, I have considered the ways in which all sorts of people, of all sorts of backgrounds and social standing, engaged with urban life in the Middle Ages, and shaped the towns and cities they inhabited. Of course, not only were people active in shaping the life of towns, urban life was simultaneously 'shaping' them. To understand the influences that urban living had on people, I have explored how the spaces of the medieval townscape ordered what people did, and how it articulated the authority of social elites. What emerges from this approach, then, is the dialectical nature of the relationship between urban space and society. This dialectic between people and place is usually explored in the context of contemporary culture, particularly by urban sociologists and geographers.[1] In contrast, surprisingly little has been done to explore the dialectics of urban life in the Middle Ages. Indeed, on the whole, medieval urban life is rarely considered using theoretical frameworks or conceptual schema.

Urban histories of the Middle Ages are invariably empirical, in both substance and outlook. This is quite contrary to the ways in which historians deal with more recent periods of history, for example the nineteenth and twentieth centuries. Here, there is a much greater consensus towards linking theoretical ideas (for example, about social authority and power relations) with empirical study. It is unfortunate to find that the medieval town and city is treated so conservatively by medievalists, when there is clearly so much potential for bringing in theoretical ideas to make sense of what the historical records tell us. The potential also exists for us to use this empirical evidence about urban life in the Middle Ages to critically review those contemporary social and cultural theories that currently dominate thinking in the arts and humanities. All too often, broader theoretical discussions about the nature of, say, social relations, sideline the Middle Ages. This is unfortunate because it reinforces the long-held idea that the Middle Ages is fundamentally different from later periods. Such skewed thinking leads some commentators to overlook the similarities that exist between how townspeople acted and thought in the Middle Ages and how people engage with urban life today.[2] Sure, there are differences between the two, but I would also urge us not to forget the dimensions of urban life that actually bind together the 'medieval' and the 'modern'.

The case can thus be made to think both critically and theoretically about medieval urbanism. It may be that the medievalists' retreat into empiricism is the consequence of past criticisms of historical theorising. Here, I am thinking particularly of Sjoberg's book, *The Pre-Industrial City*, and the criticisms it attracted from medieval historians.[3] However, over recent years attempts to theorise about the nature of past cultures have become more subtle and nuanced in their use of conceptual frameworks (not 'models'). Good examples of this sort of work are Johnson's *An Archaeology of Capitalism*, and Gilchrist's *Gender and Material Culture*.[4]

One way of theorising is to adopt a comparative, anthropological approach. In this respect an approach that may be fruitful, but to my knowledge remains yet to be explored, involves comparing the culture of the European Middle Ages with 'medieval' cultures elsewhere in the world. In 'feudal' Japan, for example, during the

Edo period (AD 1603–1868), similar sorts of castle towns were established to those created by Norman lords in England during the later eleventh century (see Chapter 5).[5] In medieval India, the physical organisation of urban landscapes laid out in the twelfth and thirteenth centuries (AD) reflected contemporary Hindu cosmology,[6] and in terms of the use that was made of proportional geometry in these towns' plans it is easy to start drawing similarities between them and European medieval urban landscapes, such as Grenade-sur-Garonne, where the use of geometry likewise performed a symbolic role. This was also a time when the Florentine city government were busy laying out new towns according to geometrical rules, and a time also when men such as Giordano da Pisa were using the form of medieval cities to articulate Christian views on order and beauty.[7]

It is probably too soon to piece together in detail aspects of urban life that were common to 'medieval' cultures inside and outside Europe, but if it were done, I would expect it to breathe some new life into how European medieval urbanism is understood and interpreted. My feeling is that it is all too easy to neglect the fact that medieval, Christian 'ways of being' played an important role in structuring not only everyday life in Europe's towns and cities, but also the social machinery that made places 'urban'. In the many studies of 'medieval cultures' in China, Japan and India, it is far more commonplace to find scholars dealing conceptually with the intimate dialectics that mutually constructed and constituted urban life.[8] So why not do the same with the study of European medieval urbanism, and in both concrete and abstract ways explore the relationships that existed between urban spaces and urban societies in the later Middle Ages?

In all, I intended this book to offer a challenging (in both senses of the word) view of urban life in the Middle Ages; to suggest some new ways of looking at the characteristics that constituted medieval urbanism. For this reason I have stressed how medieval urban landscapes determined the ways that people negotiated their lives, and how, in the process and at the same time, people played their own roles in determining what sort of urban landscape took shape. I have also stressed how the spaces of urban life reflected social values and norms prevalent in the Middle Ages, and how these were connected with ideas about political authority and Christian morality. Really, the life of medieval towns is all about the life that was going on *within* towns, and vice versa. The inter-relationships played out between medieval towns and townspeople were highly intimate and complex, for both were closely bound together.

Reflecting on my time preparing and writing this book, I have come to realise all the more how important and fundamental it is that we give the people of the Middle Ages their say, and engage in a dialogue with them. To immerse ourselves in the life of towns and cities in the Middle Ages is to engage with the thoughts of lords as they were seeking to establish new towns on their lands, or the thoughts of merchants moving from city to city, or artisans looking to make a tidy profit from their wares. These thoughts, I would argue, are not only written down in documents, but are inscribed in all the forms of material culture associated with urban life: the houses that people lived in, the objects they owned, and the townscapes they shaped. Only when these various 'texts' are assembled, put together and contemplated will we be able to gain a deeper understanding of what urban life was like in the Middle Ages.

NOTES

Preface

1. J. Le Goff, *Medieval Civilisation, 400–500* (Oxford, 1988); R. H. Hilton, *English and French Towns in Feudal Society* (Cambridge, 1992); C. Dyer, 'How urbanised was medieval England?', in J-M. Duvosquel and E. Thoen (eds), *Peasants and Townsmen in Medieval Europe: Studia in Honorem Adriaan Verhulst* (Gent, 1995), pp. 169–84.
2. D. Nicholas, *The Growth of the Medieval City* (London, 1997); D. Nicholas, *The Late Medieval City, 1300–1500* (London, 1997).
3. H. Pirenne, *Medieval Cities. Their Origins and the Revival of Trade* (New York, 1956); F. Rörig, *The Medieval Town* (London, 1967); E. Ennen, *The Medieval Town* (Amsterdam, 1979).
4. W. Braunfels, *Mittelalterliche Stadtbaukunst in der Toskana* (Berlin, 1953); E. Guidoni, *La Città dal Medioevo al Rinascimento* (Bari, 1981).
5. H. B. Clarke and A. Simms (eds), *The Comparative History of Urban Origins in Non-Roman Europe. Ireland, Wales, Denmark, Germany, Poland and Russia from the Ninth to the Thirteenth Century* (Oxford, 1985).
6. H. Swanson, *Medieval British Towns* (London, 1999); J. Schofield and A. Vince, *Medieval Towns* (London, 1994).
7. M. W. Beresford, *New Towns of the Middle Ages. Town Plantation in England, Wales and Gascony* (London, 1967).
8. Hilton, *English and French Towns.*
9. C. Dyer, *Standards of Living in the Later Middle Ages* (Cambridge, 1989).

Introduction

1. J. F. Benton (ed.), *Town Origins. The Evidence from Medieval England* (Boston, Mass., 1968), pp. ix–x.
2. E. Ennen, 'The variety of urban development', in Benton (ed.), *Town Origins*, p. 12.
3. Ibid.
4. See Clarke and Simms (eds), *Comparative History*.
5. H. Fleure, 'Some types of cities in temperate Europe', *The Geographical Review*, 10 (1920), pp. 357–74; Ennen, 'Urban development', p. 12.
6. Ibid.

7. Ibid.
8. Clarke and Simms (eds), *Comparative History*, pp. 670–2.
9. Ennen, 'Urban development'.
10. Clarke and Simms (eds), *Comparative History*, p. 674; D. M. Palliser, 'Introduction', in D. M. Palliser (ed.), *The Cambridge Urban History of Britain*, Volume I, *600–1540* (Cambridge, 2000), p. 5; S. Reynolds, 'The writing of medieval urban history in England', *Theoretische Geschiedenis*, 19 (1992), pp. 49–50.
11. R. Hodges, *Dark Age Economics. The Origins of Towns and Trade, AD600–1000* (London, 1982), p. 23.
12. Ennen, 'Urban development', p. 12.
13. B. Ward-Perkins, 'The towns of northern Italy: rebirth or renewal?', in R. Hodges and B. Hobley (eds), *The Rebirth of Towns in the West, AD700–1050* (London, 1988), pp. 16–27.
14. Nicholas, *Growth of the Medieval City*, pp. 18–19; see also C. Wickham, *Early Medieval Italy. Central Power and Local Society 400–1000* (London, 1981), pp. 80–1.
15. Ennen, 'Urban development', p. 12.
16. P. Csendes, 'Urban development and decline on the central Danube, 100–1600', in T. R. Slater (ed.), *Towns in Decline, AD100–1600* (Aldershot, 2000), p. 143.
17. Ibid.
18. A. Simms, 'The early origins and morphological inheritance of European towns', in J. W. R. Whitehand and P. J. Larkham (eds), *Urban Landscapes: International Perspectives* (London, 1992), p. 25.
19. Ibid.
20. S. T. Loseby, 'Urban failures in late-antique Gaul', in Slater (ed.), *Towns in Decline*, p. 73.
21. R. White, 'Wroxeter and the transformation of late-Roman urbanism', in Slater (ed.), *Towns in Decline*, pp. 114–15.
22. Ibid., p. 116.
23. T. Tatton-Brown, 'The Anglo-Saxon towns of Kent', in D. Hooke (ed.), *Anglo-Saxon Settlements* (Oxford, 1988), pp. 214–15.
24. D. Hill, 'Towns as structures and functioning communities through time: the development of central places from 600 to 1066', in Hooke (ed.), *Anglo-Saxon Settlements*, p. 198; P. Ottaway, *Archaeology in British Towns. From the Emperor Claudius to the Black Death* (London, 1992), p. 118; see also S. Esmonde Cleary, *The Ending of Roman Britain* (London, 1989).
25. Hodges, *Dark Age Economics*, pp. 50, 66–86; R. A. Hall, 'The decline of the *Wic*?', in Slater (ed.), *Towns in Decline*, pp. 120–1.
26. Ennen, 'Urban development', p. 15; A. Vince, *Saxon London. An Archaeological Investigation* (London, 1990), pp. 13–25.
27. Ennen, 'Urban development', p. 14.
28. Hodges, *Dark Age Economics*, pp. 51–2.
29. Ibid., p. 23.
30. Clarke and Simms (eds), *Comparative History*, pp. 678–87.
31. Ibid., p. 678.

32. Hodges, *Dark Age Economics*, p. 52.
33. Clarke and Simms (eds), *Comparative History*, pp. 681–4.
34. Ibid., p. 681.
35. A. Verhulst, 'The origins of towns in the Low Countries and the Pirenne Thesis', *Past and Present*, 122 (1989), pp. 4–5.
36. Ibid., p. 32; Pirenne, *Medieval Cities*.
37. Clarke and Simms (eds), *Comparative History*, pp. 684–6.
38. Ibid., p. 685.
39. Ibid., pp. 685–6.
40. L. A. S. Butler, '"The Monastic City" in Wales: myth or reality?', *Bulletin of the Board of Celtic Studies*, 28 (1979), pp. 458–67.
41. Clarke and Simms (eds), *Comparative History*, pp. 686–7.
42. Ennen, 'Urban development'.
43. Clarke and Simms (eds), *Comparative History*, p. 686.
44. Ibid., p. 671.
45. Benton (ed.), *Town Origins*, p. x.
46. Nicholas, *Growth of the Medieval City*, p. 84.
47. P. Geddes, *Cities in Evolution* (London, 1915).
48. M. Barber, *The Two Cities. Medieval Europe, 1050–1320* (London, 1992).
49. G. Duby, *The Three Orders. Feudal Society Imagined* (London, 1980), p. 103.
50. Ibid., p. 105.
51. Ibid., p. 93.
52. Barber, *Two Cities*, p. 43.
53. Duby, *Three Orders*, pp. 212–13; Barber, *Two Cities*, p. 48.
54. D. Austin and J. Thomas, 'The "proper study" of medieval archaeology: a case study', in D. Austin and L. Alcock (eds), *From the Baltic to the Black Sea. Studies in Medieval Archaeology* (London, 1990), p. 53, following A. Giddens, *A Contemporary Critique of Historical Materialism* (London, 1981).
55. Barber, *Two Cities*, pp. 6–7.
56. B. A. Hanawalt, *Growing Up in Medieval London. The Experience of Childhood in History* (Oxford, 1993).
57. Gerald of Wales, *The Journey Through Wales*, ed. L. Thorpe (London, 1978), p. 75.
58. P. Bourdieu, *Outline of a Theory of Practice* (Cambridge, 1977), p. 80.
59. C. Frayling, *Strange Landscape. A Journey Through the Middle Ages* (London, 1995), p. 30.

1 Urban Legacies

1. Giordano da Pisa, *Prediche Inedite Recitate in Firenze dal 1302 al 1305*, ed. E. Narducci (Bologna, 1867), p. 404.
2. K. D. Lilley, 'Modern visions of the medieval city: competing conceptions of urbanism in European civic design', *Environment and Planning B: Planning and Design*, 26 (1999), pp. 427–46.
3. Le Corbusier, *The City of To-morrow and its Planning* (Cambridge, Mass., 1971), pp. 12–13.

4. G. R. Collins and C. C. Collins, *Camillo Sitte: The Birth of Modern City Planning* (New York, 1986); R. Unwin, *Town Planning in Practice* (London, 1909).

5. Lilley, 'Modern visions', p. 444.

6. A. E. J. Morris, *History of Urban Form* (London, 1994), pp. 112–18.

7. R. Samuel, *Theatres of Memory: Past and Present in Contemporary Culture* (London, 1994).

8. T. F. Heffernan, *Wood Quay. The Clash over Dublin's Viking Past* (Austin, Tex., 1988).

9. H. Clarke and B. Ambrosiani, *Towns in the Viking Age* (London, 1991).

10. R. Bartlett, *The Making of Europe. Conquest, Colonisation and Cultural Change, 950–1350* (London, 1993).

11. G. H. Orpen, *Ireland under the Normans* (Oxford, 1911–20), 4 vols.

12. Bartlett, *Making of Europe*, p. 31.

13. J. Bradley, 'Recent archaeological research on the Irish town', in H. Jäger (ed.), *Stadtkernforschung*, 27 (1987), pp. 321–70.

14. Bartlett, *Making of Europe*, pp. 169–77.

15. For example, A. Höenig, *Deutscher Städtbau in Böhmen* (Prague, 1921); W. Geisler, *Die Deutscher Stadt: ein Beitrage zur Morphologie der Kulturlandschaft* (Stuttgart, 1924).

16. See B. Zientara, 'Socio-economic and spatial transformation of Polish towns during the period of location', *Acta Poloniae Historica*, 34 (1976), pp. 53–83; M. Koter and M. Kulesza, 'The plans of medieval Polish towns', *Urban Morphology*, 3 (1999), pp. 63–78.

17. T. R. Slater, 'Medieval and Renaissance urban morphogenesis in eastern Poland', *Journal of Historical Geography*, 15 (1989), pp. 239–59.

18. C. Frugoni, *A Distant City. Images of Urban Experience in the Medieval World* (Princeton, NJ, 1991), pp. 118–88.

19. D. C. Douglas and G. W. Greenway (eds), *English Historical Documents, 1140–1189* (Oxford, 1953), pp. 956–9.

20. Barber, *Two Cities*, pp. 431–2.

21. Le Goff, *Medieval Civilisation*, p. 165.

22. Bonvicinus de Rippa, *De magnalibus urbis Mediolani*, ed. F. Novati, *Bollettino dell' Istituto Storico Italiano*, 20 (1898), pp. 67–114. For a translation, see J. H. Mundy and P. Riesenberg, *The Medieval Town* (New York, 1958), pp. 100–1.

23. D. Waley, *The Italian City-Republics* (London, 1988), p. 104.

24. Frugoni, *Distant City*.

25. Ibid., pp. 24–7.

26. Bartlett, *Making of Europe*, pp. 198–211.

27. M. T. Clanchy, *From Memory to Written Record* (London, 1985).

28. A. Ballard (ed.), *British Borough Charters, 1042–1216* (Cambridge, 1913); C. Stephenson, *Borough and Town. A Study of Urban Origins in England* (Cambridge, Mass., 1933); J. Tait, *The Medieval English Borough. Studies on its Origins and Constitutional History* (Manchester, 1936).

29. F. Braudel, *Capitalism and Material Life* (New York, 1974); H. C. Darby, *Domesday England* (Cambridge, 1977); Beresford, *New Towns*.

30. H. E. Salter, *Medieval Oxford* (Oxford, 1936); W. Urry, *Canterbury under the Angevin Kings* (London, 1967); L. A. Burgess (ed.), *The Southampton Terrier of 1454*, Southampton Records Series, 15 (1976).
31. D. Keene, *Survey of Medieval Winchester* (Oxford, 1985), 2 vols; S. Kelly, E. Rutledge and M. Tillyard, *Men of Property. An Analysis of the Norwich Enrolled Deeds, 1285–1311* (Norwich, 1983); R. H. Leech, *The Topography of Medieval and Early Modern Bristol*, Bristol Records Society, 48 (1997).
32. See Le Goff, *Medieval Civilisation*; Duby, *Three Orders*.
33. For example, B. Geremek, *The Margins of Society in Late Medieval Paris* (Cambridge, 1987).
34. See M. Carver, *Underneath English Towns. Interpreting Urban Archaeology* (London, 1987).
35. To get an idea of this, compare excavation reports in early issues of *Medieval Archaeology* with those of more recent years.
36. For example, Austen and Alcock, *From the Baltic to the Black Sea*; Clarke and Ambrosiani, *Towns in the Viking Age*; Schofield and Vince, *Medieval Towns*.
37. In the case of Norwich, for example, see *East Anglian Archaeology*, 26 (1985).
38. M. Carver, 'Three Saxo-Norman tenements in Durham City', *Medieval Archaeology*, 23 (1979), pp. 1–20.
39. Schofield and Vince, *Medieval Towns*, pp. 178–203.
40. R. H. Jones, 'Industry and environment in medieval Bristol', in G. L. Good, R. H. Jones and M. W. Ponsford (eds), *Waterfront Archaeology*, Council for British Archaeology Research Report, 74 (1991), pp. 19–26.
41. Urry, *Canterbury*, p. 191.
42. See P. D. A. Harvey, 'Local and regional cartography in medieval Europe', in J. B. Harley and D. Woodward (eds), *Cartography in Prehistoric, Ancient and Medieval Europe and the Mediterranean* (Chicago, 1987), pp. 464–501.
43. D. Woodward, 'Reality, symbolism, time and space in medieval world maps', *Annals of the Association of American Geographers*, 75 (1985), pp. 510–21; Frugoni, *Distant City*, pp. 3–29.
44. P. D. A. Harvey and R. A. Skelton (eds), *Local Maps and Plans from Medieval England* (Oxford, 1986).
45. K. D. Lilley, 'Mapping the medieval city: plan analysis and urban history', *Urban History*, 27 (2000), pp. 5–30.
46. N. F. Cantor, *Inventing the Middle Ages. Lives, Works and Ideas of the Great Medievalists of the Twentieth Century* (London, 1992).

2 Institutional Urbanism

1. *Bristol Charters, 1155–1373*, ed. N. Dermott Harding, Bristol Records Society, 1 (Bristol, 1930), p. 3.
2. G. H. Martin, 'The English borough in the thirteenth century', in

Holt and Rosser (eds), *Medieval Town*, pp. 29–48; J. F. Benson (ed.), *Town Origins. The Evidence from Medieval England* (Boston, Mass., 1968).

3. S. Reynolds, *Kingdoms and Communities in Western Europe, 900–1300* (Oxford, 1984), pp. 155–218.

4. S. Reynolds, 'Towns in Domesday Book', in J. C. Holt (ed.), *Domesday Studies* (London, 1987), p. 306.

5. Beresford and Finberg, *English Medieval Boroughs*, p. 179.

6. F. W. Maitland, *Township and Borough* (Cambridge, 1898), p. 173.

7. Reynolds, 'Towns in Domesday Book'.

8. M. Gelling, *The West Midlands in the Early Middle Ages* (Leicester, 1992), pp. 153–5.

9. H. B. Clarke and A. Simms, 'Towards a comparative history of urban origins', in Clarke and Simms (eds), *Comparative History*, pp. 547, 676–7.

10. H. Quirin, 'The colonial town as seen in the documents of east German settlement', in Clarke and Simms (eds), *Comparative History*, p. 510.

11. Beresford and Finberg, *English Medieval Boroughs*, p. 120; S. Quail, *The Origins of Portsmouth and the First Charter* (Portsmouth, 1991), pp. 14–15.

12. Beresford and Finberg, *English Medieval Boroughs*, p. 26.

13. K. D. Lilley, *Norman Towns in Southern England. Urban Morphogenesis in Hampshire and the Isle of Wight*, Urban Morphology Research Monograph, 5 (Birmingham, 1999), pp. 56–70.

14. Ballard, *British Borough Charters*, p. xli.

15. Bartlett, *Making of Europe*, p. 169.

16. Clarke and Simms, 'Towards a comparative history', p. 692.

17. Ballard, *British Borough Charters*, pp. xxi–xxv.

18. Stephenson, *Borough and Town*, pp. 29–43.

19. Ballard, *British Borough Charters*, p. xciv.

20. Stephenson, *Borough and Town*, pp. 34–6.

21. Reynolds, *Kingdoms and Communities*.

22. Hilton, *English and French Towns*, p. 128.

23. Quirin, 'Colonial town', p. 509.

24. Ballard, *British Borough Charters*, p. cxxxiv.

25. Stephenson, *Borough and Town*, p. 123, note 2.

26. Ballard, *British Borough Charters*, p. cxxxiv.

27. Ibid., p. cxxxv.

28. Stephenson, *Borough and Town*, p. 30.

29. Ibid., pp. 30–1.

30. Ibid., p. 31.

31. Ibid., p. 32.

32. L. Musset, 'Peuplement en bourgages et bourgs ruraux en Normandie du Xe au XIIIe siècles', *Cahiers de Civilisation Médiévale*, 9 (1966), pp. 177–208.

33. G. Duby, *The Early Growth of the European Economy* (London, 1974), p. 238; Ennen, *Medieval Town*, p. 88.

34. Ballard, *British Borough Charters*, p. cvii.
35. Ibid., p. cviii.
36. Ibid., pp. cv–cvii.
37. Ibid., p. cviii.
38. Bartlett, *Making of Europe*, p. 173.
39. Stephenson, *Borough and Town*, p. 33.
40. Ibid.
41. Ballard, *British Borough Charters*, p. cxxii.
42. Ibid.
43. Ibid., pp. cxxxii–iv.
44. A. MacKay, *Spain in the Middle Ages. From Frontier to Empire, 1000–1500* (London, 1977), p. 55.
45. Ibid., pp. 52–3.
46. Ibid., p. 56.
47. Ballard, *British Borough Charters*, p. cxxxiii.
48. MacKay, *Spain*, p. 56.
49. M. Weinbaum, *The Incorporation of Boroughs* (Manchester, 1937); C. Petit Dutaillis, *The French Communes in the Middle Ages* (Amsterdam, 1978); Ennen, *Medieval Town*.
50. Stephenson, *Borough and Town*, but see Tait, *Medieval English Borough*.
51. Stephenson, *Borough and Town*, p. 46.
52. Hilton, *English and French Towns*, p. 127.
53. Ballard, *British Borough Charters*, p. cxviii.
54. Ibid., pp. cxviii–xix.
55. Stephenson, *Borough and Town*, p. 35.
56. Ibid., p. 41.
57. Ballard, *British Borough Charters*, p. cxix.
58. Ibid., p. cxx.
59. Petit Dutaillis, *French Communes*, p. 32.
60. N. M. Trenholme, *The English Monastic Borough. A Study in Medieval History* (New York, 1927), p. 80.
61. Stephenson, *Borough and Town*, p. 33, note 4.
62. Waley, *Italian City-Republics*, p. 36; J. H. Mundy, *Liberty and Political Power in Toulouse, 1050–1230* (New York, 1954), p. 54.
63. W. Hudson and J. C. Tingey, *Revised Catalogue of the Records of the City of Norwich* (Norwich, 1898), p. 9.
64. Waley, *Italian City-Republics*, p. 37.
65. Ibid.; also see J. M. Najemy, *Corporatism and Consensus in Florentine Electoral Politics, 1280–1400* (Chapel Hill, NC, 1982).
66. Stephenson, *Borough and Town*, pp. 174–5.
67. Waley, *Italian City-Republics*, pp. 36–7.
68. Clarke and Simms, 'Towards a comparative history', p. 690.
69. Hudson and Tingey, *Revised Catalogue*, p. 9; Waley, *Italian City-Republics*, p. 65.
70. Reynolds, *Kingdoms and Communities*, pp. 168–202.
71. J. Campbell, 'Norwich', in M. D. Lobel (ed.), *Historic Towns II* (Oxford, 1975), p. 3.
72. Reynolds, 'Towns in Domesday', p. 306.

73. Hudson and Tingey, *Revised Catalogue*, p. 8.
74. Ibid.
75. Campbell, 'Norwich', p. 9.
76. Hudson and Tingey, *Revised Catalogue*, p. 9.
77. Ibid.
78. Weinbaum, *Incorporation*, p. 2.
79. Beresford and Finberg, *English Medieval Boroughs*, pp. 111, 174.
80. Weinbaum, *Incorporation*, p. 3.
81. M. Grace, *Records of the Gild of St George in Norwich, 1389–1547*, Norfolk Record Society, 9 (Norwich, 1937), pp. 12–13.
82. Stephenson, *Borough and Town*, p. 42; see P. Strait, *Cologne in the Twelfth Century* (Gainesville, Fla., 1974).
83. Ibid., pp. 44–5, 138.
84. Ibid., pp. 11–12.
85. Ibid., p. 66.
86. Ibid., pp. 62, 139.
87. Ibid., pp. 12, 16, 66.
88. Ibid., pp. 61, 72.
89. Ibid., pp. 25–9.
90. Ibid., p. 31.
91. Ibid., pp. 20–3, 39.
92. Petit Dutaillis, *French Communes*, pp. 19–20.
93. Ibid., p. 19.
94. Strait, *Cologne*, p. 45.
95. Ibid., p. 46.
96. Ibid., pp. 51, 55.
97. Ibid., pp. 65–6.
98. Ibid., p. 62.
99. Ibid., p. 73.
100. Ibid., pp. 140–1.
101. Mundy, *Liberty and Political Power*.
102. Ibid., pp. xii–xiii.
103. Ibid., p. 24.
104. Ibid., p. 32.
105. Ibid., p. 38.
106. Ibid., pp. 55–63, 149.
107. Ibid., p. 67.
108. Ibid., pp. 105–9.
109. Ibid., p. 156.
110. Ibid.
111. Ibid., p. 158.
112. Ibid., pp. 151–2.
113. Ibid., pp. 58–60.
114. Ibid., p. 54.
115. Najemy, *Corporatism and Consensus*; C. Lansing, *The Florentine Magnates. Lineage and Faction in a Medieval Commune* (Princeton, NY, 1991).

116. Ibid., p. 9.
117. Ibid.
118. Ibid., p. 10.
119. Ibid.
120. Ibid., p. 11.
121. Ibid.
122. Waley, *Italian City-Republics*, p. 43.
123. Lansing, *Florentine Magnates*, p. 11.
124. Ibid., pp. 12, 193.
125. Waley, *Italian City-Republics*, p. 132.
126. Lansing, *Florentine Magnates*, p. 12.
127. Najemy, *Corporatism and Consensus*, p. 17.
128. Ibid., p. 19.
129. Ibid., pp. 9, 10.
130. Ibid., pp. 13, 18.
131. Ibid., p. 17.
132. Lansing, *Florentine Magnates*, p. 16.
133. Najemy, *Corporatism and Consensus*, p. 3.
134. Ibid., p. 7.
135. Reynolds, 'Towns in Domesday', p. 306.

3 Geographies of Urban Law

1. William of Malmesbury, *Gesta Regum Anglorum*, ed. R. A. B. Mynors (Oxford, 1998), p. 739.
2. Ballard, *British Borough Charters*, p. 137.
3. Bartlett, *Making of Europe*, p. 310.
4. Ibid., pp. 172–82.
5. Ballard, *British Borough Charters*, p. cviii, Stephenson, *Borough and Town*, pp. 120–1.
6. Ibid., p. 125.
7. M. Bateson, 'The Laws of Breteuil', *English Historical Review*, 15 (1900), pp. 73–8, 302–18, 496–523, 754–7; 16 (1901), pp. 92–110, 332–45.
8. Bateson, 'Laws of Breteuil', p. 74.
9. K. D. Lilley, '"*Non urbe, non vico, non castris*": territorial control and the colonisation and urbanisation of Wales and Ireland under Anglo-Norman lordship', *Journal of Historical Geography*, 26 (2000), pp. 518–20.
10. Gelling, *West Midlands*, p. 162.
11. K. D. Lilley, 'Urban landscapes and the cultural politics of territorial control in Anglo-Norman England', *Landscape Research*, 24 (1999), pp. 12–14.
12. Beresford, *New Towns*, p. 119, note 19.
13. Bateson, 'Laws of Breteuil'.
14. Ibid., pp. 754–7.
15. Ibid., pp. 311–14.
16. Beresford, *New Towns*, p. 199; J. Hillaby, 'The Norman new town of Hereford: its street pattern and European context', *Transactions of the Woolhope Naturalists' Field Club*, 44 (1982), pp. 181–95.

17. Beresford, *New Towns*, p. 199.
18. Lilley, '*Non urbe*', pp. 520–3.
19. Bateson, 'Laws of Breteuil', pp. 311–14.
20. Ibid., p. 74.
21. Ibid., p. 73.
22. Bartlett, *Making of Europe*, pp. 31–2.
23. G. Fehring, *The Archaeology of Medieval Germany* (London, 1992), pp. 189–99; G. Fehring, 'Origins and development of Slavic and German Lübeck', in Austin and Alcock (eds), *Baltic to the Black Sea*, pp. 251–66.
24. Quirin, 'Colonial town', pp. 508, 517–21; J. Schildhauer, *The Hansa. History and Culture* (Leipzig, 1988), p. 213.
25. Bartlett, *Making of Europe*, p. 174.
26. Ibid., pp. 121–3.
27. Quirin, 'Colonial town'.
28. Stephenson, *Borough and Town*, p. 25.
29. W. Schich, 'Slavic proto-towns and the German colonial town in Brandenburg', in Clarke and Simms (eds), *Comparative History*, pp. 539–40.
30. Bartlett, *Making of Europe*, pp. 121–3.
31. Quirin, 'Colonial town', pp. 506, 514, 516.
32. Ibid., p. 512.
33. Schich, 'Slavic proto-towns', p. 538.
34. Quirin, 'Colonial town', p. 512.
35. Schich, 'Slavic proto-towns', p. 538.
36. Zientara, 'Polish towns', p. 76.
37. W. Kalinowski, 'City development in Poland', in E. A. Gutkind (ed.), *Urban Development in East Central Europe* (New York, 1973), p. 36.
38. Zientara, 'Polish towns', p. 75.
39. Ibid., p. 76.
40. Bartlett, *Making of Europe*, p. 174.
41. W. Kuhn, 'German town foundations of the thirteenth century in western Pomerania', in Clarke and Simms (eds), *Comparative History*, p. 533.
42. Ibid., p. 554.
43. Ibid., p. 557.
44. Ibid., pp. 566, 570, 573.
45. Ibid., p. 570.
46. Quirin, 'Colonial town', p. 508.
47. Ibid.
48. Ibid., p. 509.
49. Schildhauer, *Hansa*, p. 214.
50. Ibid., p. 213; H. Birnbaum, 'Kiev, Novgorod, Moscow: three varieties of society in east Slavic territory', in B. Krekic (ed.), *Urban Society of Eastern Europe in Pre-Modern Times* (Los Angeles, 1987), pp. 44–5.
51. Campbell, 'Norwich', p. 9.
52. Bateson, 'Laws of Breteuil', p. 307.
53. *Domesday Book*, ed. A. Farley (London, 1783), I, f. 252.

54. My thanks to Dr Nigel Baker for sharing his knowledge of early Norman Shrewsbury with me.

55. A. Ballard, *The Domesday Boroughs* (Oxford, 1904), pp. 84, 86.

56. *Domesday Book*, I, f. 179a.

57. Bateson, 'Laws of Breteuil', p. 305.

58. Stephenson, *Borough and Town*.

59. *Domesday Book*, I, f. 280.

60. Stephenson, *Borough and Town*, pp. 197–8.

61. For Nottingham and Hereford, see M. D. Lobel (ed.), *Historic Towns. Maps and Plans of Towns and Cities in the British Isles, with Historical Commentaries, from Earliest Times to 1800* (Oxford, 1969).

62. D. Sibley, *Geographies of Exclusion: Society and Difference in the West* (London, 1995).

63. J. Riley Smith, *Atlas of the Crusades* (London, 1991).

64. J. Prawer, 'Crusader cities', in H. A. Miskimin, D. Herlihy and A. L. Udovitch (eds), *The Medieval City* (London, 1977), p. 180.

65. Ibid., p. 182, note 7.

66. J. Prawer, *Crusader Institutions* (Oxford, 1980), pp. 252–3.

67. Ibid., p. 222.

68. Ibid.

69. D. Jacoby, 'Crusader Acre in the thirteenth century: urban layout and topography', *Studi Medievali*, 20 (1979), pp. 19–30.

70. Ibid., pp. 230–7; Prawer, 'Crusader cities', p. 187.

71. Ibid., pp. 190–1.

72. Ibid., p. 194.

73. Ibid.

74. Ibid., p. 195.

75. Ibid., p. 194.

76. Lilley, '*Non urbe*', pp. 523–8.

77. Bateson, 'Laws of Breteuil', p. 74.

4 Lordship and Urbanisation

1. A. Ballard and J. Tait (eds), *British Borough Charters 1216–1307* (Cambridge, 1923), p. 2.

2. Ibid., p. 3.

3. Hilton, *English and French Towns*, p. 38.

4. Dyer, *Standards of Living*.

5. D. Crouch, *William Marshall. Court, Career and Chivalry in the Angevin Empire* (London, 1990), pp. 168–9.

6. Ibid., p. 101.

7. A. L. Poole, *From Domesday Book to Magna Carta, 1087–1216* (Oxford, 1955), pp. 16–17.

8. J-P. Poly and E. Bournazel, *The Feudal Transformation, 900–1200* (London, 1991), pp. 187–92.

9. Jean de Joinville, *Life of Saint Louis*, ed. M. R. B. Shaw (London, 1963), p. 250.

10. Bartlett, *Making of Europe*, p. 127; R. Hoffmann, *Land, Liberties and Lordship in a Late Medieval Countryside: Agrarian Structures and Change in the Duchy of Wrocław* (Philadelphia, 1989), pp. 61–92.
11. A. J. Forey, *The Templars in the Corona de Aragón* (London, 1973); B. J. Graham, 'Anglo-Norman colonisation and the size and spread of the colonial town in medieval Ireland', in Clarke and Simms (eds), *Comparative History*, pp. 355–73.
12. B. A. Lees, *Records of the Templars in England in the Twelfth Century* (London, 1935).
13. Bartlett, *Making of Europe*, p. 128.
14. Hilton, *English and French Towns*; Dyer, *Standards of Living*; R. H. Britnell, *The Commercialisation of English Society, 1000–1500* (Cambridge, 1991).
15. Beresford, *New Towns*.
16. R. A. Holt and G. Rosser, 'Introduction: the English town in the Middle Ages', in Holt and Rosser (eds), *Medieval Town*, p. 3.
17. R. A. Holt, *The Early History of the Town of Birmingham*, Dugdale Society Occasional Paper (Oxford, 1985), pp. 2–3.
18. Beresford and Finberg, *English Medieval Boroughs*; Britnell, *Commercialisation*.
19. Clanchy, *Memory to Written Record*.
20. See R. A. Griffiths (ed.), *Boroughs of Mediaeval Wales* (Cardiff, 1978); I. Soulsby, *The Towns of Medieval Wales* (Chichester, 1983).
21. Beresford, *New Towns*.
22. Ibid., p. 335.
23. Ibid., pp. 461, 473–4; J. Bilson, 'Wyke upon Hull in 1293', *Transactions of the East Riding Antiquarian Society*, 26 (1928), pp. 37–105.
24. Hill, 'Towns as structures', pp. 201–8.
25. See J. Haslam (ed.), *Anglo-Saxon Towns in Southern England* (Chichester, 1984).
26. D. Hall, 'The Five Boroughs of the Danelaw: a review of present knowledge', *Anglo-Saxon England*, 18 (Cambridge, 1989), pp. 149–206.
27. T. R. Slater, 'Benedictine town planning in medieval England: evidence from St Albans', in T. R. Slater and G. Rosser (eds), *The Church in the Medieval Town* (Aldershot, 1998), pp. 155–76.
28. Beresford, *New Towns*, pp. 261, 267.
29. Ibid., pp. 297, 301.
30. E. Searle, *Battle Abbey and its Banlieu* (Toronto, 1980); Slater, 'Benedictine town planning'; M. D. Lobel, *The Borough of Bury St Edmunds* (Oxford, 1935).
31. Peterborough and Coventry, for example.
32. C. J. Bond, 'The estates of Evesham abbey: a preliminary survey of their medieval topography', *Vale of Evesham Historical Society*, 4 (1973), pp. 44–50.
33. R. H. Hilton, *A Medieval Society. The West Midlands at the End of the Thirteenth Century* (Cambridge, 1983); C. C. Dyer, *Lords and Peasants in a Changing Society. The Estates of the Bishopric of Worcester, 680–1540* (Cambridge, 1981).

34. Royal Commission on the Historical Monuments of England, *Salisbury. The Houses of the Close* (London, 1993), pp. 1–6.
35. J. Haslam, *Wiltshire Towns. The Archaeological Potential* (Devizes, 1976), pp. 19–20; K. D. Lilley, *The Norman Town in Dyfed*, Urban Morphology Research Monograph, 1 (Birmingham, 1996), p. 42.
36. E. M. Carus Wilson, 'The first half century of the borough of Stratford upon Avon', in Holt and Rosser (eds), *Medieval Town*, pp. 49–70; M. W. Beresford, 'The six new towns of the bishops of Winchester, 1200–1255', *Medieval Archaeology*, 3 (1959), pp. 187–215.
37. Bilson, 'Wyke', p. 67.
38. Soulsby, *Towns of Medieval Wales*, pp. 110–15.
39. Bees, *Records of the Templars*, p. cli.
40. Ibid., p. cxxxxi.
41. M. W. Beresford and J. K. St Joseph, *Medieval England. An Aerial Survey* (Cambridge, 1958), p. 212.
42. J. Blair, 'Minster churches in the landscape', in Hooke (ed.), *Anglo-Saxon Settlement*, pp. 35–58.
43. R. H. Britnell, 'The proliferation of markets and fairs in England before 1349', *Economic History Review*, 34 (1981), pp. 209–21; Beresford and St Joseph, *Medieval England*, pp. 146–7.
44. C. C. Dyer, 'The hidden trade of the Middle Ages: evidence from the West Midlands of England', *Journal of Historical Geography*, 18 (1992), pp. 141–57.
45. Beresford, 'Six new towns'.
46. L. Butler, 'The origins of the Honour of Richmond and its castles', *Chateau Gaillard*, 16 (1994), pp. 69–77.
47. *Domesday Book*, I, f. 248b.
48. See M. Altschul, *A Baronial Family in Medieval England. The Clares, 1217–1314* (Baltimore, 1965); J. E. Wrightman, *The Lacy Family in England and Normandy, 1066–1194* (Oxford, 1966).
49. C. P. Lewis, 'The formation of the Honor of Chester', in A. T. Thacker (ed.), *The Earldom of Chester and its Charters* (Chester, 1991), pp. 37–68.
50. K. D. Lilley, 'Urban planning and the design of towns in the Middle Ages: the Earls of Devon and their new towns', *Planning Perspectives*, 16 (2001), pp. 1–24.
51. R. Bearman (ed.), *Charters of the de Redvers family and the Earldom of Devon, 1090–1217* (Exeter, 1994), p. 34.
52. Beresford, *New Towns*, pp. 499–500.
53. Kuhn, 'German town foundations', p. 569.
54. M. Prestwich, *Edward I* (London, 1997), p. 299; A. Lauret, R. Malebranche and G. Seraphin, *Bastides: Villes Nouvelles du Moyen Âge* (Toulouse, 1988), pp. 37–9.
55. J-P. Trabut Cussac, 'Bastides ou forteresses: les bastides de l'Aquitaine anglais et les intentions de leurs fondateurs, *Le Moyen Âge*, 60 (1954), pp. 81–135.
56. Beresford, *New Towns*, pp. 331, 363.
57. Lauret *et al.*, *Bastides*, p. 36.

58. Ibid., p. 293.
59. C. M. Higounet, 'Nouvelles réflections sur les bastides "Cisterciennes"', in C. M. Higounet, *Villes, Sociétés et Économies Médiévales* (Bordeaux, 1992), pp. 149–55.
60. See Prestwich, *Edward I*, p. 376.
61. Beresford, *New Towns*, pp. 30–1.
62. Hilton, *English and French Towns*, p. 36; Lauret *et al.*, *Bastides*, p. 282.
63. Beresford, *New Towns*, pp. 243–4.
64. Ibid., p. 355.
65. Ibid., p. 596.
66. Ibid., p. 619.
67. Ibid., pp. 132, 604.
68. Ibid., p. 355.
69. A. Randolph, 'The bastides of south-west France', *Art Bulletin*, 77 (1995), p. 300.
70. Beresford, *New Towns*, p. 608.
71. Ibid., p. 29.
72. Ibid., p. 579.
73. Ibid., pp. 3–28; W. Maclean Homan, 'The founding of New Winchelsea', *Sussex Archaeological Transactlons*, 88 (1949), pp. 22–41.
74. Ibid., pp. 22–3.
75. Beresford, *New Towns*, p. 6.
76. See Lilley, *Norman Towns*, pp. 61–3.
77. Zientara, 'Polish towns', pp. 62–3.
78. Quirin, 'Colonial town', p. 509.
79. Bartlett, *Making of Europe*, p. 122.
80. Ibid., p. 142.
81. Quirin, 'Colonial town', p. 509.
82. Ibid., p. 512.
83. Ibid., p. 523.
84. Ibid.
85. Bartlett, *Making of Europe*, pp. 142–3.
86. Quirin, 'Colonial town', pp. 510, 523.
87. Zientara, 'Polish towns'.
88. Ibid., pp. 65–6.
89. Ibid., p. 73.
90. Bartlett, *Making of Europe*, pp. 121–2.

5 Urban Landscapes

1. *Calendar of Patent Rolls*, 1281, p. 217.
2. Beresford, *New Towns*, pp. 472–8.
3. *The Ecclesiastical History of Orderic Vitalis*, ed. and trans. M. Chibnall (Oxford, 1969–80), Vol. 4, p. 238.
4. Lilley, 'Urban landscapes', pp. 12–14.
5. P. Hofer, *The Zähringer New Towns* (Thun, 1966).
6. Lilley, 'Urban landscapes', pp. 9–17.
7. Ibid., p. 13.

8. Lilley, *Norman Towns*, pp. 71–98; Lobel, *Historic Towns*.
9. Searle, *Battle Abbey*.
10. R. Cazelles, *Nouvelle Histoire de Paris, 1223–1380* (Paris, 1973).
11. B. Gauthiez, *Atlas Morphologique des Villes de Normandie* (Lyon, 1999).
12. See, for example, P. Laveden and J. Hugueney, *L'Urbanisme au Moyen Âge* (Geneva, 1974).
13. Beresford, *New Towns*, pp. 437–41; Beresford and St Joseph, *Medieval England*, pp. 167–8.
14. D. Friedman, *Florentine New Towns. Urban Design in the Late Middle Ages* (Cambridge, Mass., 1988), pp. 92–3; Lilley, 'Urban landscapes', p. 14.
15. Schich, 'Slavic proto-towns', pp. 532–42.
16. For an overview of the atlases see H. Stoob, 'The historic town atlas: problems and working methods', in Clarke and Simms (eds), *Comparative History*, pp. 583–616.
17. K. D. Lilley, 'Urban design in Medieval Coventry: the planning of Much and Little Park Streets within the Earl of Chester's fee', *Midland History*, 23 (1998), pp. 1–20.
18. Ibid., p. 14.
19. M. Carus Wilson, 'Bristol', in Lobel (ed.), *Historic Towns II*.
20. See Cazelles, *Nouvelle Histoire*; M. Rykhaert, *Historische Stedenatlas van Belgie. Brugge* (Brussels, 1991); V. Huml, 'Research in Prague – an historical and archaeological review of the development of Prague from the ninth century to the middle of the fourteenth century', in Austin and Alcock (eds), *Baltic to the Black Sea*, pp. 267–84.
21. Lilley, 'Urban design', p. 16.
22. Lilley, 'Urban landscape', pp. 14–17.
23. M. R. G. Conzen, 'The use of town plans in the study of urban history', in H. J. Dyos (ed.), *The Study of Urban History* (London, 1968), pp. 113–30; T. R. Slater, 'Ideal and reality in English episcopal medieval town planning', *Transactions of the Institute of British Geographers*, 2 (New Series) (1987), pp. 191–203.
24. Lilley, 'Urban landscape', pp. 17–19.
25. Conzen, 'Town plans'; T. R. Slater, 'English medieval new towns with composite plans', in T. R. Slater (ed.), *The Built Form of Western Cities* (Leicester, 1990), pp. 60–82.
26. See Lilley, 'Mapping the medieval city'.
27. M. Biddle, 'Early Norman Winchester', in J. C. Holt (ed.), *Domesday Studies* (Woodbridge, 1987), pp. 311–31; D. Keene, *Medieval Winchester*.
28. Biddle, 'Early Norman Winchester', pp. 316–17.
29. Ottaway, *Archaeology in British Towns*, pp. 133–7.
30. Biddle, 'Early Norman Winchester', p. 314; M. Biddle (ed.), *Object and Economy in Medieval Winchester* (Oxford, 1990), pp. 1174–9.
31. Ibid., Figure 382.
32. B. Ayers, *Excavations within the North-East Bailey of Norwich Castle*, East Anglian Archaeology Report, 28 (Norwich, 1985), pp. 63–6.
33. Ballard, *Domesday Boroughs*, pp. 84–6; Carus Wilson, 'Bristol', pp. 3–4.
34. Conzen, 'Town plans', p. 127; Slater, 'Ideal and reality'.

35. See B. Price, *Medieval Thought: an Introduction* (Oxford, 1992).
36. See C. Burnett (ed.), *Adelard of Bath. An English Scientist and Arabist of the Early Twelfth Century* (London, 1987).
37. C. H. Haskins, *The Renaissance of the Twelfth Century* (Cambridge, Mass., 1927).
38. F. Bucher, *Architector. The Lodge Books and Sketchbooks of Medieval Architects* (London, 1979). pp. 98–124.
39. Friedman, *Florentine New Towns*, p. 125.
40. Zientara, 'Polish towns', p. 734.
41. J. Schulz, 'Jacopo de' Barbari's View of Venice: map-making, city views, and moralised geography before the year 1500', *Art Bulletin*, 60 (1978), p. 432, note 20; Friedman, *Florentine New Towns*, p. 106, note 3.
42. Beresford, *New Towns*, pp. 3–5, 19; Friedman, *Florentine New Towns*, p. 149; Beresford and St Joseph, *Medieval England*, pp. 221–6.
43. Friedman, *Florentine New Towns*, p. 149.
44. F. Bucher, 'Medieval architectural design methods, 800–1560', *Gesta*, 11 (1972), p. 43; K. D. Lilley, 'Taking measures across the medieval landscape: aspects of urban design before the Renaissance', *Urban Morphology*, 2 (1998), pp. 82–92.
45. J. Gimpel, *The Cathedral Builders* (London, 1983), pp. 101–5.
46. U. T. Holmes, *Daily Living in the Twelfth Century. Based on the Observations of Alexander Neckam in London and Paris* (London, 1952), p. 275, note 33; Harvey, 'Local and regional cartography', pp. 491–2.
47. See G. Lesser, *Gothic Cathedrals and Sacred Geometry* (London, 1957); see also H. Hiscock, *The Wise Master Builder. Platonic Geometry in Plans of Medieval Abbeys and Cathedrals* (Aldershot, 1999).
48. Friedman, *Florentine New Towns*, pp. 117–48.
49. Ibid., p. 121.
50. Ibid., pp. 121–9, 162–3.
51. Ibid., p. 153.
52. Ibid., pp. 155–6.
53. Ibid., p. 162.
54. Frayling, *Strange Landscape*, p. 64.
55. See Lesser, *Gothic Cathedrals*; also E. Panofsky, *Gothic Architecture and Scholasticism* (Latrobe, Pa, 1951).
56. Frayling, *Strange Landscape*, p. 39.
57. U. Eco, *Art and Beauty in the Middle Ages* (London, 1986), p. 23.
58. Ibid., p. 58.
59. Ibid., p. 70.
60. Today, in an age when we are used to seeing aerial photographs of towns, it is easy to forget that in the Middle Ages there was no way of looking vertically down on a town from above.
61. 'A ceremony performed at the founding of a bastide confirms the ritual importance of the market place as the symbolic, if not always the physical, centre of the town'; Randolph, 'Bastides', p. 300.
62. J. K. Hyde, 'Medieval descriptions of cities', *Bulletin of the John Rylands Library*, 48 (1966), pp. 308–40.

63. D. Palliser, *Chester. Contemporary Descriptions by Residents and Visitors* (Chester, 1980), p. 10.
64. For example, Giordano da Pisa, see Frugoni, *Distant City*, pp. 97–100.
65. See Harvey, 'Local and regional cartography', pp. 494–5.
66. For example, both by Beresford, *New Towns*; Morris, *History of Urban Form*.
67. W. M. Bowsky, *A Medieval Italian Commune. Siena Under the Nine, 1387–1355* (Berkeley, 1981), pp. xx, 260–98.
68. Ibid., p. 286.
69. Waley, *Italian City Republics*, pp. 12–13.
70. Bowsky, *Medieval Italian Commune*, p. 286; Waley, *Italian City Republics*, p. 13.
71. Bowsky, *Medieval Italian Commune*, p. 295; D. Friedman, 'Palaces and the street in late-medieval and Renaissance Italy', in J. W. R. Whitehand and P. J. Larkham (eds), *Urban Landscapes: International Perspectives* (London, 1992), p. 107, note 4.
72. Bowsky, *Medieval Italian Commune*, p. 295; Friedman, 'Palaces and the street', p. 94.
73. Bowsky, *Medieval Italian Commune*, p. 296.
74. Waley, *Italian City Republics*, p. 13.
75. Ibid.
76. F. Sznura, 'Civic urbanism in medieval Florence', in A. Molho, K. Raaflaub and J. Emden (eds), *City States in Classical Antiquity and Medieval Italy* (Michigan, 1991), pp. 407, 409.
77. Ibid., p. 407.
78. Ibid.
79. Ibid., p. 408.
80. Ibid., p. 410.
81. Friedman, *Florentine New Towns*, p. 207.
82. Ibid., p. 209.
83. Ibid., p. 207.
84. Sznura, 'Civic urbanism', p. 410.
85. Friedman, *Florentine New Towns*, p. 207.
86. Ibid., p. 205.
87. Mundy, *Liberty and Political Power*, pp. 105, 195.
88. Strait, *Cologne in the Twelfth Century*, pp. 34–5.
89. Carus Wilson, 'Bristol', p. 7; K. D. Lilley, *Modernising the Medieval City: Urban Design and Civic Improvement in the Middle Ages*, Department of Geography Research Paper, Royal Holloway, University of London (1999), pp. 11–19.
90. S. Seyer, *Memoirs, Historical and Topographical of Bristol and its Neighbourhood*, Vol. 2 (Bristol, 1823), p. 15.
91. J. C. Tingey (ed.), *The Records of the City of Norwich*, Vol. 2 (Norwich, 1910), pp. 32–7.
92. Ibid., p. 52.
93. Ibid.
94. Lilley, *Modernising the Medieval City*, p. 24.

95. R. Fitch, *Views of the Gates of Norwich* (Norwich, 1861), pp. xv–xviii; H. Harrod, 'Queen Elizabeth Woodville's visit to Norwich in 1469 from the Chamberlain's accounts for the ninth and tenth years of King Edward IV', *Norfolk Archaeology*, 5 (1859), pp. 32–7.

6 Urban Property and Landholding

1. *Calendar of Charter Rolls*, II, p. 337.
2. Ballard, *Domesday Boroughs*, p. 50.
3. Hilton, *English and French Towns*, pp. 25–52.
4. P. R. Coss (ed.), *Early Records of Medieval Coventry* (London, 1986), p. 33.
5. A. Gooder and E. Gooder, 'Coventry before 1355: unity or division', *Midland History*, 6 (1981), pp. 1–38.
6. K. D. Lilley, 'Trading places: monastic initiative and the development of high-medieval Coventry', in Slater and Rosser (eds), *Church in the Medieval Town*, pp. 198–200.
7. N. Tanner, 'The cathedral and the city', in I. Atherton, E. Fernie, C. Harper-Bill and H. Smith (eds), *Norwich Cathedral: Church, City and Diocese, 1096–1996* (London, 1996), pp. 255–80.
8. Hilton, *English and French Towns*, p. 45.
9. Ibid., p. 46; Cazelles, *Nouvelle Histoire*.
10. Hilton, *English and French Towns*, p. 46.
11. Holmes, *Daily Living*, p. 276, note 47.
12. Musset, 'Peuplement en bourgage', p. 569.
13. Beresford, *New Towns*, p. 332; Musset, 'Peuplement en bourgage', p. 570.
14. D. Bates, *Normandy Before 1066* (London, 1982), p. 131.
15. Ibid.
16. Musset, 'Peuplement en bourgage', p. 573.
17. Bates, *Normandy*, p. 2.
18. Ibid., p. 129.
19. Beresford and Finberg, *English Medieval Boroughs*, pp. 106–7.
20. Ballard, *Domesday Boroughs*, p. 91.
21. G. Rosser, 'The essence of medieval urban communities: the vill of Westminster, 1200–1540', in Holt and Rosser (eds), *Medieval Town*, pp. 218–9.
22. Hilton, *English and French Towns*, p. 48.
23. Ibid., pp. 218–19, 221.
24. Ibid., p. 237.
25. Ballard, *Domesday Boroughs*, p. 5.
26. Ibid., p. 28.
27. Hilton, *English and French Towns*, pp. 42–3.
28. Ibid.
29. Ballard, *Domesday Boroughs*, p. 6, my emphasis.
30. Ibid., pp. 29, 31.
31. Vince, *Saxon London*, p. 20.

32. T. Dyson, 'Two Saxon landgrants at Queenhithe', in J. Bird, H. Chapman and J. Clark (eds), *Collectanea Londiniensa: Studies in London Archaeology and History Presented to R. Merrifield* (London, 1978), pp. 200–15.
33. Ballard, *Domesday Boroughs*, pp. 11–13.
34. Hilton, *English and French Towns*.
35. Lansing, *Florentine Magnates*, p. 5.
36. Ibid.
37. Ibid.
38. Waley, *Italian City Republics*, pp. 69–87.
39. Lansing, *Florentine Magnates*, pp. 48–9.
40. Waley, *Italian City Republics*, pp. 124–6.
41. Lansing, *Florentine Magnates*, p. 53.
42. Ibid., pp. 64–5.
43. Ibid., pp. 12–17.
44. Ibid., p. 95.
45. J. Grenville, *Medieval Housing* (London, 1997), pp. 181–9.
46. Lansing, *Florentine Magnates*, p. 92.
47. Holmes, *Daily Living*, p. 62.
48. For examples, see Coss, *Early Records*; Keene, *Survey of Medieval Winchester*.
49. Holmes, *Daily Living*, pp. 81–2.
50. For examples, see Keene, *Survey of Medieval Winchester*.
51. Douglas and Greenway (eds), *English Historical Documents*, p. 957.
52. G. Rosser, 'London and Westminster: the suburb in the urban economy in the later Middle Ages', in J. A. F. Thompson (ed.), *Towns and Townspeople in the Fifteenth Century* (Gloucester, 1988), p. 52.
53. Ottaway, *Archaeology in British Towns*, p. 173.
54. Schulz, 'Jacapo de' Barbari', p. 432, note 20.
55. Fehring, 'Slavic and German Lübeck', pp. 200–1.
56. F. Löbbecke, 'Traufenhaus und Kemenate. Wohnbauten des 12. und 13. Jahrhunderts in Freiburg im Breisgau', in G. De Boe and F. Verhaeghe (eds), *Urbanism in Medieval Europe* (Zellik, 1997), pp. 271–6; M. Bures, V. Kaspar and P. Vareka, 'The formation of the high medieval tenements along the Old Town Square in Prague', in De Boe and Verhaeghe (eds), *Urbanism in Medieval Europe*, pp. 205–10.
57. F. Redi, 'Pisa medievale: una lettura alternativa delle strutture esistenti. Architecturra, cultura materiale, storia urbana, archeologia e topografia', in J-M. Vigueur (ed.), *D'Une Ville à l'Autre: Structures Matérielles et Organisation de l'Espace dans les Villes Européennes (XIII–XVI Siècle)* (Rome, 1989), pp. 591–607.
58. C. Platt, *Medieval Southampton* (London, 1973).
59. Redi, 'Pisa medievale', pp. 598–9.
60. Schofield and Vince, *Medieval Town*, p. 135.
61. D. M. Goodburn, 'London's early medieval timber buildings. Little known traditions of construction', in De Boe and Verhaeghe (eds), *Urbanism in Medieval Europe*, pp. 249–57.

62. O. M. Ioannisyan, 'Archaeological evidence for the development and urbanisation of Kiev from the eighth to the fourteenth centuries', in Austin and Alcock (eds), *Baltic to the Black Sea*, pp. 300–3.
63. A. V. Tsoonya, *Dwellings in Riga, 12ᵗʰ to the 14ᵗʰ Century. Based on Data from Archaeological Excavations* (Riga, 1984), p. 79.
64. N. W. Alcock, 'The Catesbys in Coventry: a medieval estate and its archives', *Midland History*, 15 (1990), pp. 1–36.
65. D. Keene, 'The property market in English towns', in Vigueur (ed.), *D'Une Ville à L'Autre*, p. 204.
66. Alcock, 'Catesbys in Coventry'.
67. The following is derived from Keene, 'Property market', pp. 207–9.
68. Ibid.
69. Ibid.
70. Ibid., p. 207.
71. Ibid.
72. Hanawalt, *Growing Up in Medieval London*, p. 29.
73. Keene, 'Property market', p. 207.
74. Biddle, 'Early Norman Winchester'.
75. G. Rosser, *Medieval Westminster, 1200–1540* (Oxford, 1989), pp. 45–6.
76. Löbbecke, 'Traufenhaus und Kemenate', pp. 272–3.
77. Ibid.
78. Schofield and Vince, *Medieval Towns*, pp. 76–9.
79. Ibid.
80. J. Schofield, P. Allen and C. Taylor, 'Medieval buildings and property development in the area of Cheapside', *Transactions of the London and Middlesex Archaeological Society*, 41 (1990), pp. 186–9.
81. See K. D. Lilley, 'Decline or decay?' Urban landscapes in late-medieval England', in Slater (ed.), *Towns in Decline*, p. 245; also Lilley, 'Urban design', p. 10.
82. For example, see Coss, *Early Records*, pp. 140–1.
83. F. B. Bickley, *A Calendar of Deeds (Chiefly Relating to Bristol)* (Edinburgh, 1899), pp. 88, 123.
84. Coss, *Early Records*, pp. 317–18.
85. Keene, 'Property market', pp. 221–2.
86. Grenville, *Medieval Housing*, p. 190.
87. Keene, 'Property market', pp. 232–3.
88. F. W. B. Charles, 'Timber-framed houses in Spon Street, Coventry', *Transactions of the Birmingham and Warwickshire Archaeological Society*, 89 (1978–79), pp. 91–122.
89. Hilton, *English and French Towns*.

7 Townspeople and Townscapes

1. *Ancrene Riwle*, ed. J. Morton (London, 1853), pp. 152–3.
2. Ibid., pp. 88–91.
3. Dyer, *Standards of Living*; Hanawalt, *Growing Up in Medieval London*.
4. Hilton, *English and French Towns*.

5. Dyer, *Standards of Living*, p. 20.
6. Ibid., p. 24.
7. Hanawalt, *Growing Up in Medieval London*, pp. 129–72.
8. Ibid., pp. 173–98.
9. Ibid., p. 174.
10. Swanson, *Medieval Artisans*, pp. 96–7.
11. Hanawalt, *Growing Up in Medieval London*, pp. 175–8.
12. Dyer, *Standards of Living*, p. 238.
13. Ibid.
14. Ibid., pp. 235–7.
15. R. Gilchrist, 'Christian bodies and souls: the archaeology of life and death in later medieval households', in S. Bassett (ed.), *Death in Towns. Urban Responses to the Dying and the Dead, 100–1600* (London, 1992), p. 116.
16. Dyer, *Standards of Living*, p. 242.
17. Gilchrist, 'Christian bodies and souls', p. 103; Dyer, *Standards of Living*, pp. 242–6.
18. Dyer, *Standards of Living*, p. 228.
19. Swanson, *Medieval Artisans*, pp. 156–9.
20. J. Schofield, *The Building of London from the Conquest to the Great Fire* (London, 1984), p. 89.
21. Hanawalt, *Growing Up in Medieval London*, pp. 25–6.
22. See Holmes, *Daily Living*.
23. Ibid., pp. 82–3.
24. Ibid., p. 87.
25. Ibid., p. 91.
26. Ibid., p. 93.
27. Schofield and Vince, *Medieval Towns*, p. 142.
28. D. Keene, 'Medieval London and its region', *London Journal*, 14 (1989), pp. 99–111.
29. J-L. Abbé, 'Le parcellaire rural des bastides du sud-ouest de la France: l'apport des sources écrits et planimétriques', in G. De Boe and F. Verhaeghe (eds), *Rural Settlements in Medieval Europe* (Zellik, 1997), pp. 309–19.
30. Maitland, *Township and Borough*, p. 65.
31. Coss, *Early Records*, pp. 214, 236, 238.
32. Dyer, *Standards of Living*, p. 197.
33. Ibid., p. 199.
34. Gilchrist, 'Christian bodies and souls', pp. 107–8.
35. Schofield and Vince, *Medieval Towns*, p. 198.
36. Ibid., p. 197.
37. Ibid.
38. Ibid., p. 198.
39. S. Shahar, *Childhood in the Middle Ages* (London, 1990), p. 35. On the other hand, Hanawalt points out that the large number of widows recorded in medieval urban records shows that many married women were outliving their husbands! See Hanawalt, *Growing Up in Medieval London*, p. 43.

40. Hanawalt, *Growing Up in Medieval London*, p. 57.
41. Shahar, *Childhood in the Middle Ages*, p. 146; C. Platt, *King Death. The Black Death and its Aftermath in Late-Medieval England* (London, 1996); J. Henderson, 'The Black Death in Florence: medical and communal responses', in Bassett (ed.), *Death in Towns*, pp. 136–50.
42. Gilchrist, 'Christian bodies and souls', p. 109; Holmes, *Daily Living*, p. 136.
43. K. I. Sandred and B. Lindstöm, *The Place-Names of the City of Norwich* (Nottingham, 1989), pp. 71–82, Figure 3.
44. Dyer, 'Hidden trade'; Hilton, *English and French Towns*, p. 45.
45. Nicholas, *Growth of the Medieval City*, pp. 113–14; Britnell, 'Markets and fairs in England'.
46. Keene, *Survey of Medieval Winchester*, p. 1092, Figure 144.
47. See M. Kowaleski, *Local Markets and Regional Trade in Medieval Exeter* (Cambridge, 1995).
48. E. T. Jones, 'River navigation in medieval England', *Journal of Historical Geography*, 26 (2000), p. 60.
49. G. Milne and D. Goodburn, 'The early medieval port of London, 700–1200', *Antiquity*, 64 (1990), pp. 629–36; Jones, 'Industry and environment in medieval Bristol', in Good *et al.* (eds), *Waterfront Archaeology*, pp. 19–26.
50. B. S. Ayers, 'From cloth to creel – riverside industries in Norwich', in Good *et al.* (eds), *Waterfront Archaeology*, pp. 1–8.
51. Ottoway, *Archaeology in British Towns*, p. 191.
52. H. Bush, *Bristol Town Duties* (Bristol, 1828), p. 17.
53. A. E. Herteig, *The Buildings at Bryggen: their Topographical and Chronological Development* (Bergen, 1991).
54. R. H. Jones, *Excavations in Redcliffe, 1983–5* (Bristol, 1986), pp. 5–6.
55. Schofield and Vince, *Medieval Towns*, pp. 91–2; Platt, *English Medieval Town*, pp. 57–8.
56. Ryckhaert, *Brugge*, pp. 62–3.
57. Ibid., pp. 104–5.
58. Zientara, 'Polish towns', p. 80.
59. Prawer, 'Crusader cities', pp. 186, 188–9; Jacoby, 'Crusader Acre', p. 43.
60. Lilley, *Norman Towns*, pp. 90–1.
61. Lilley, 'Trading places', p. 193.
62. Sandred and Lindstöm, *Place-Names of the City of Norwich*, pp. 71–82, Figure 3.
63. Lilley, 'Trading places', p. 187.
64. Aston and Bond, *Landscape of Towns*, p. 96.
65. Grenville, *Medieval Houses*.
66. Hilton, *English and French Towns*, p. 79.
67. Ibid., p. 78.
68. Lauret *et al.*, *Bastides*, pp. 204–6.
69. Sandred and Lindstöm, *Place-Names of the City of Norwich*, pp. 71–82, Figure 3; Ryckhaert, *Brugge*, pp. 160–1.
70. Hilton, *English and French Towns*, pp. 63–4.
71. Swanson, *Medieval Artisans*, p. 2.
72. Ibid., p. 161.

73. Hilton, *English and French Towns*, pp. 63–4.
74. Swanson, *Medieval Artisans*, p. 2.
75. Ibid., p. 5.
76. Hilton, *English and French Towns*, p. 75.
77. Waley, *Italian City-Republics*, pp. 134, 145.
78. Ibid., p. 60.
79. Hilton, *English and French Towns*, p. 72.
80. Ibid., p. 66.
81. M. Atkin, 'Excavations on Alms Lane', in M. Atkin, A. Carter and D. H. Evans, 'Excavations in Norwich 1971–78, Part II', *East Anglian Archaeology*, 26 (1985), pp. 144–260.
82. Ioannisyan, 'Development and urbanisation of Kiev', p. 302.
83. Lilley, 'Urban design', p. 9.
84. Schofield and Vince, *Medieval Towns*, pp. 93–4.
85. Swanson, *Medieval Artisans*, pp. 30–1.
86. Ibid., pp. 32–3.
87. Ibid., pp. 40–2.
88. R. A. Holt, *The Mills of Medieval England* (Oxford, 1988).
89. H. S. A. Fox, 'Exeter, Devonshire, c.1420', in Skelton and Harvey (eds), *Local Maps*, pp. 163–9.
90. Swanson, *Medieval Artisans*, p. 42.
91. Schofield and Vince, *Medieval Towns*, p. 119.
92. See E. M. Veale, 'Craftsmen and the economy of London in the fourteenth century', in Holt and Rosser (eds), *Medieval Town*, pp. 120–40.
93. A. R. Bridbury, *Economic Growth. England in the Later Middle Ages* (London, 1962).
94. J. C. Lancaster, 'Coventry', in Lobel (ed.), *Historic Towns II*, p. 7.
95. Swanson, *Medieval Artisans*, p. 16.
96. K. G. T. McDonnell, *Medieval London Suburbs* (Chichester, 1978), p. 60.
97. Rosser, 'Medieval urban communities', in Holt and Rosser (eds), *Medieval Town*, pp. 225–6.
98. Schofield and Vince, *Medieval Towns*, pp. 109–11.
99. Ibid., pp. 99–100.
100. Keene, 'Suburban growth', in Holt and Rosser (eds), *Medieval Town*, p. 116.
101. Swanson, *Medieval Artisans*, p. 54.
102. Schofield and Vince, *Medieval Towns*, p. 119.
103. Swanson, *Medieval Artisans*, pp. 55–62.
104. Schofield and Vince, *Medieval Towns*, pp. 99–127.
105. See Carus Wilson, 'Borough of Stratford upon Avon'; Veale, 'Economy of London'.
106. Swanson, *Medieval Artisans*, p. 2.
107. Hilton, *English and French Towns*, p. 78.
108. Ibid., pp. 80–1.
109. Ibid., p. 79.
110. Ibid., p. 83.
111. Lilley, 'Trading places', p. 187; Swanson, *Medieval Artisans*, p. 18.

112. Schofield and Vince, *Medieval Towns*, p. 119.
113. See Atkin, 'Excavations at Alms Lane'.
114. J. Bennett, *Ale, Beer and Brewsters in Medieval England. Women's Work in a Changing World, 1300–1600* (Oxford, 1996).
115. See Dyer, 'Hidden trade'.
116. L. F. Salzman, *Building in England down to 1540* (Oxford, 1965), pp. 432–4; *The Pittancer's Rental, 1410–11*, ed. A. Gooder, E. Gooder, J. Hunt, J. Shulman, C. Steele and C. Walker (Birmingham, 1973), p. 7.
117. Salzman, *Building in England*, pp. 432–4.
118. Ibid.
119. Hilton, *English and French Towns*, p. 81.
120. Geremek, *Margins of Society*.
121. R. M. Karras, *Common Women: Prostitution and Sexuality in Medieval England* (Oxford, 1996).
122. Geremek, *Margins of Society*.
123. L. L. Otis, *Prostitution in Medieval Society: the History of an Urban Institution in Languedoc* (Chicago, 1985).
124. See A. McKall, *The Medieval Underworld* (London, 1979).
125. J. Rykwert, *The Idea of a Town. The Anthropology of Urban Form in Rome, Italy and the Ancient World* (London, 1988); see also V. Burgin, *In/different Spaces* (Berkeley, 1996).
126. See Woodward, 'Medieval world maps'.
127. Frugoni, *Distant City*.
128. Bowsky, *Medieval Italian Commune*, p. 276.
129. Ibid.
130. A. Hanawalt and K. L. Reyerson (eds), *City and Spectacle in Medieval Europe* (Minneapolis, 1994), p. xviii.
131. Harrod, 'Visit to Norwich'.
132. L. Atreed, 'The politics of welcome: ceremonies and constitutional development in later medieval English towns', in Hanawalt and Reyerson (eds), *City and Spectacle*, p. 209.
133. *The Little Red Book of Bristol*, ed. F. W. Bickley (Bristol, 1900), p. 33.
134. Geremek, *Margins of Society*, p. 222 note 65.
135. Ibid.; Otis, *Prostitution in Medieval Society*; M. Carlin, *Medieval Southwark* (London, 1996).
136. Geremek, *Margins of Society*, p. 217.
137. Ibid., pp. 93–4, 219–20.
138. Carus Wilson, 'Bristol'.
139. P. H. Culham, 'Leperhouses and borough status in the thirteenth century', *Thirteenth Century England*, 3 (1991), p. 44.
140. R. Gilchrist, *Contemplation and Action. The Other Monasticism* (London, 1995).
141. V. D. Lipman, *The Jews of Medieval Norwich* (London, 1967), pp. 113–41.
142. Ibid., p. 141.
143. N. Golb, *The Jews in Medieval Normandy* (Cambridge, 1998), pp. 33–6.
144. R. Chazen, *Medieval Jewry in Northern France. A Political and Social History* (London, 1973), p. 50.

145. M. Adler, *Jews of Medieval England* (London, 1939); Chazen, *Medieval Jewry*.
146. G. Kisch, *The Jews in Medieval Germany: a Study of their Legal and Social Status* (Chicago, 1949), p. 293.
147. See R. Sennett, *Flesh and Stone. The Body and the City in Western Civilisation* (London, 1994).

Conclusion

1. See T. Unwin, *The Place of Geography* (London, 1992).
2. A. Giddens, *The Consequences of Modernity* (London, 1990); D. Harvey, *The Condition of Post-Modernity* (Oxford, 1989).
3. G. Sjoberg, *The Pre-Industrial City* (London, 1960); P. Burke, 'Some reflections on the pre-industrial city', *Urban History Yearbook* 1975 (Leicester, 1975), pp. 13–21.
4. M. Johnson, *An Archaeology of Capitalism* (Oxford, 1996); R. Gilchrist, *Gender and Material Culture: the Archaeology of Religious Women* (London, 1994).
5. S. Satoh, 'The morphological transformation of Japanese castle-town cities', *Urban Morphology*, 1 (1997), pp. 11–18.
6. H-J. Nitz, 'Planned temple-towns and Brahmu villages as spatial expressions of the ritual polities of medieval kingdoms in south India', in A. Baker and G. Biger (eds), *Ideology and Landscape in Historical Perspective* (Cambridge, 1992), pp. 107–24.
7. See Friedman, *Florentine New Towns*; Frugoni, *Distant City*; W. Boerefijn, 'Geometry and medieval town planning: a contribution to the discussion', *Urban Morphology*, 4 (2000), pp. 25–7.
8. P. Wheatley, *The Pivot of the Four Quarters: a Preliminary Enquiry into the Origins and Character of the Ancient Chinese City* (Edinburgh, 1971).

Index

CPSIA information can be obtained
at www.ICGtesting.com
Printed in the USA
LVOW13s0019190118
563149LV00016B/311/P

9 780333 712498